IMAGES
of Rail

NORTH BEACH PENINSULA'S IR&N

I0806380

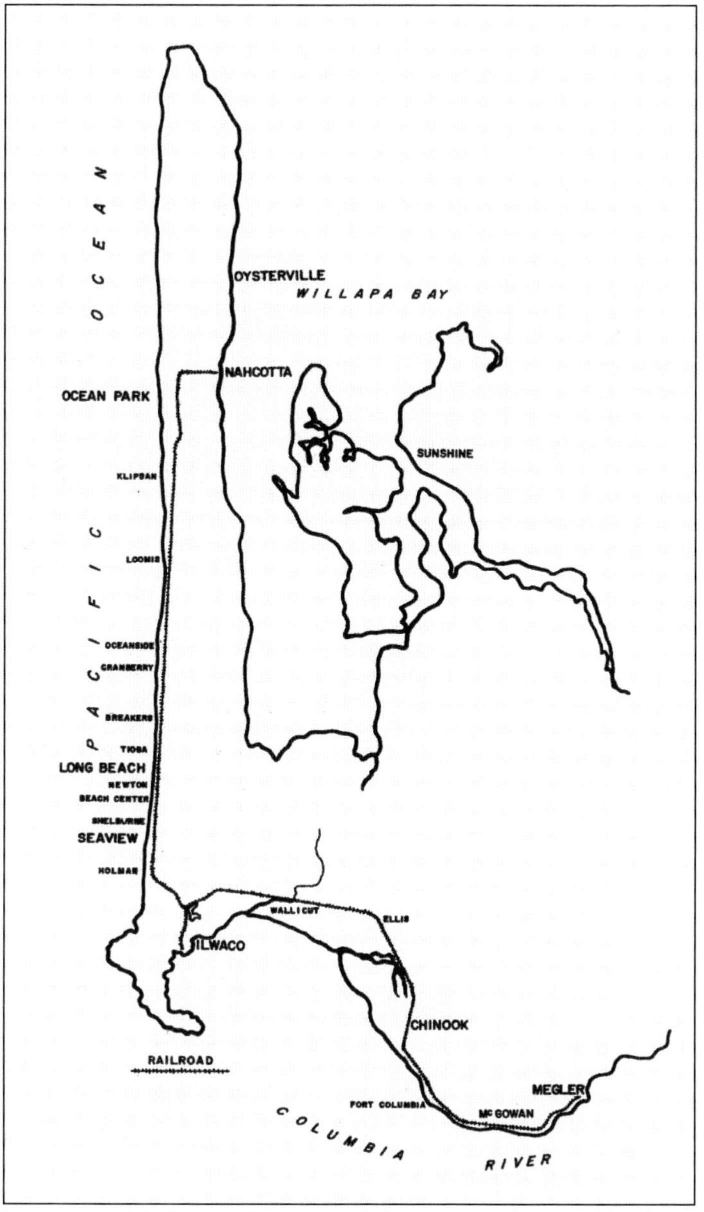

NORTH BEACH PENINSULA. Early travelers named the narrow finger of land jutting north from the Columbia River's mouth the "North Beach Peninsula" to differentiate it from Oregon beaches to the south. For centuries, the long, flat sand spit and surrounding waterways had been part of Native Americans' north-south transportation route—a route soon utilized by the first white settlers to the area. (Pacific Printing, Ilwaco.)

ON THE COVER: Purchased for $5,700 in July 1908 by the Ilwaco Railroad, this Baldwin 10-Wheeler, locomotive No. 6, was the heaviest locomotive ever used on the Ilwaco line. Although most of the 27 miles of track had been upgraded with 56-pound rails by the time it was purchased, the remaining 35-pound rails at the north end of the peninsula took a beating when No. 6 rolled over them. (Charles Mulvey.)

IMAGES *of Rail*

NORTH BEACH PENINSULA'S IR&N

Sydney Stevens and
the Columbia Pacific Heritage Museum

ARCADIA
PUBLISHING

ISBN 978-0-7385-7020-4

Published by Arcadia Publishing
Charleston, South Carolina

Printed in the United States of America

Library of Congress Control Number: 2009922889

For all general information contact Arcadia Publishing at:
Telephone 843-853-2070
Fax 843-853-0044
E-mail sales@arcadiapublishing.com
For customer service and orders:
Toll-Free 1-888-313-2665

Visit us on the Internet at www.arcadiapublishing.com

This book is dedicated to all those who have helped preserve the story of the North Beach Peninsula's "Irregular, Ramblin' and Never-Get-There-Railroad."

Contents

Acknowledgments

This book is a collaborative effort. It could not have happened without the generosity of dozens of people—people who have researched and gathered railroad memorabilia over the years; people who have generously donated railroad photographs and information; and people who have lent their expertise concerning the history of the North Beach Peninsula and its narrow-gauge railroad.

In particular, we would like to thank the following:

Researchers: Joan Mann Alkins, Harry Bell, Mark Clemmens, Nancy Gorshe, Glenn Guerra, Deborah Halliburton, Donella Lucero, Karla Nelson, Eileen Parsons, Liisa Penner, Steve Rogers, Jon Schmidt, Jeff Smith, Sydney Stevens, and Sandra Tellvik.

Technical assistants: Harry Bell, Nyel Stevens, David Tellvik, and Mark Tyler.

Resource material contributors: Kenneth Carlson, Dale Espy Little, Martha Murfin, Sydney Stevens, Sandra Tellvik, and the Les Wilson family.

Photograph contributors: Al's Saw Shop, Patricia Aslin, Adelle Beechey, C. V. Bell, Norma Clark, Charlotte Herrold Davis, Charles Doupé, Myra Elliott, Marjorie Fichter, Betty Forsberg, Lucille Freshley, Gertrude Goode, Charlotte Guerrant, William Haavisto, Brenda Hill, Ripley Hoffman, King Family Archive, Lucille Kozowski, Arlene Lindstrom, Whipple Manning family, Dan'l Markham, Louis Meyers, Doris Miller, Charles Mulvey, Adrian Munnick, Martha Murfin, Richard Murfin, Susan Murfin, Emery Neale, Richard Olsen, Nancy Olson, Edna Pearson, Henry Pitkanen, Dale Plumb, Ann Posey, Marion Rauch, Roselyn Slade, Sydney Stevens, Victoria Stoppiello, Martha Swan, Sandra Tellvik, Polly Vann, Eileen Weidner, Kenneth Wells, Dobby Wiegardt, Dorothy Trondsen Williams, Les Wilson family, Matt Winters, Edwin Wright, Marjorie Wright, and Beret Zweig.

Of those listed above, we would like to especially acknowledge Sandra Tellvik for her dedication and perseverance in tracking down images and information, Mark Clemmens for his knowledgeable and discerning eye with regard to all things "railroad," and Elizabeth Millard and Barbara Minard for managing to keep all of us on track throughout.

The images in this volume appear through the courtesy of the Columbia Pacific Heritage Museum unless otherwise noted or unless listed as follows: California State Railroad Museum (CSRM), Clatsop County Historical Society (CCHS), Columbia River Maritime Museum (CRMM), Fort Columbia Research Collection Washington State Parks (WSPRC), Illinois Railway Museum (IRM), National Museum of American History (NMAH), Oregon Historical Society (OHS), and Pacific County Historical Society (PCHS).

INTRODUCTION

The quirky little narrow-gauge railroad that once ran along the North Beach Peninsula in southwestern Washington is remembered by many names—"The Clamshell Line," "The Papa Train," "The Irregular, Rambling, and Never-Get-There Railroad," "The Delay, Linger, and Wait Railroad." The line, running from Ilwaco in the south to Nahcotta in the north, was completed in 1889, the same year Washington achieved statehood.

The driving force behind the railroad was Lewis Alfred Loomis. He had entered the transportation business in the 1870s by building a wharf at Ilwaco, acquiring a stage line, and establishing two navigation companies to handle the water transportation at each end of the peninsula. He soon secured the mail contract for the run from Astoria, Oregon, to Olympia, Washington's capital. Three steamers and three stage lines were required to make the journey, which followed the age-old Native American trail from the mouth of the Columbia River to Puget Sound by way of Shoalwater (now Willapa) Bay and Grays Harbor.

The most time-consuming part of the journey was the stage run along the hard-packed sand of the ocean beach on the North Beach (now called Long Beach) Peninsula. Also, an increasing number of families from the Portland area were seeking the cool coastal climate for their summer vacations—too many for the Loomis stagecoaches to accommodate. It was not long before he began to explore the possibility of using steam power for that part of the route, and in the early 1880s, Loomis began to seek support for a railroad line that would run from Ilwaco northward.

Loomis called his project the Ilwaco, Shoalwater Bay, and Grays Harbor Railroad and secured the help of Jacob Kamm of Portland. Kamm's background as a marine engineer, banker, and promoter enabled him to take an active part as vice president of Loomis's operation.

Rolling stock was purchased, and locomotive facilities, water towers, depots, warehouses, wharves, and 27 miles of track were constructed. Beginning in May 1889, under the management of the Ilwaco Railway and Navigation Company (IR&N), the fully equipped narrow-gauge railroad offered regularly scheduled passenger and freight service and the only land access to fledgling peninsula settlements. From its onset, the railroad provided employment as well as a unifying influence to the communities of the North Beach Peninsula.

Soon hotels sprang up all along the route, furnishing a variety of amenities to eager visitors. Miles of oceanfront vacation property became accessible, giving the North Beach Peninsula an edge over the isolated beaches of Oregon to the south. The peninsula's character as a tourist destination was established.

At first, a tide table, not a timetable, governed the railroad's schedule. Steamers transporting freight and passengers across the Columbia could reach the train dock at Ilwaco only after the tide was at mid-flood. Therefore, every few days, train departures were moved forward a half hour, and once a week the schedule was moved back two or three hours.

Old-timers of the area still talk about the train's unorthodox schedule and its informal and accommodating service. In autumn, when the geese were flying south, crew and passengers often carried their shotguns on the chance of bagging dinner along the route. Sometimes stops were made so passengers could see a whale that had washed ashore on the ocean beach.

Despite its relaxed attitude, the railroad prospered. By the mid-1890s, it looked likely that the IR&N could finally connect with the "outside" rail line to be constructed along the north bank of the Columbia by the Oregon Railway and Navigation Company (OR&N). The IR&N planned to extend its line 17 miles upriver from Ilwaco, where it would meet the OR&N's railway at Knappton. Loomis traveled to Washington D.C., where he acquired the necessary permits to build a railroad tunnel under the U.S. government reservation at Fort Columbia.

However, before the construction could begin, a number of financial issues developed, culminating in Kamm's sale of his IR&N holdings to the OR&N Company. In 1900, Loomis also sold out to the OR&N for $142,000 and, at age 70, retired.

In August of that year, the OR&N Company assumed active control of the Ilwaco line and immediately began to apply more orderly rules to its management. Train crews were now required to wear uniforms; air brakes and knuckle couplers became standard equipment; regular depots were built at Seaview and Long Beach to take the place of the former shed-like buildings; and a logging dock was added at Nahcotta. Finally, in November 1906, the long-awaited extension from Ilwaco was begun.

The slowest and most difficult part of the construction was the 800-foot tunnel through Scarborough Hill at Fort Columbia. Other problems also thwarted progress, including the announcement that the Ilwaco extension would not connect with an outside rail line after all. However, it would end at Megler with a dock extending directly into the deep water of the river. No longer would trains need to wait until the tide was right for steamers to dock; boats could meet the trains rather than the other way around.

But even with all the improvements, the little "Ilwaco Railroad," as it was still called, kept some of its free-and-easy customs. When the fall salmon run was on, the train crew often stopped along the Columbia to net a few fish before heading home, and one Christmas, in the spirit of the season, the locomotive was decorated with evergreens and holly. It was not unusual for the engineer to stop along the route so the fireman could pick a bouquet of wildflowers for his sweetheart in Ocean Park. And there was still some laxity about collecting fares in the wintertime when just local passengers were riding the train.

For almost 42 years, the train was the major transportation link from one end of the North Beach Peninsula to the other. During most of that period, it was the only north-south route available except for the occasional footpath through the woods, a few disconnected and deeply rutted wagon roads, or the ocean beach at low tide. In addition to providing access between communities, the train supplied a reliable route to "outside markets" for the area's major industries—oystering, logging, cranberry farming, and cannery products.

In the end, it was the automobile that led to the railroad's final decline. As soon as the first road was built from Long Beach to Ocean Park in 1911, those who could afford "machines" began to bring them to the peninsula. Patronage of the railroad diminished as year-round and summer residents discovered the increased independence provided by automobiles. Nor could the railroad compete with the lower rates and door-to-door delivery service of the emerging trucking companies.

The train's last run was on September 9, 1930. A sign on the last car said, "Gone but Not Forgotten"—an apt epitaph, as it turned out. Over the years, memorabilia from the railroad has become a treasured and well-guarded commodity. The best publicly accessible collection, including the only renovated train car that was in use on the line, can be found at the Columbia Pacific Heritage Museum in Ilwaco. Like train passengers of a century ago, visitors are still drawn to the peninsula by the train.

One

Beginnings

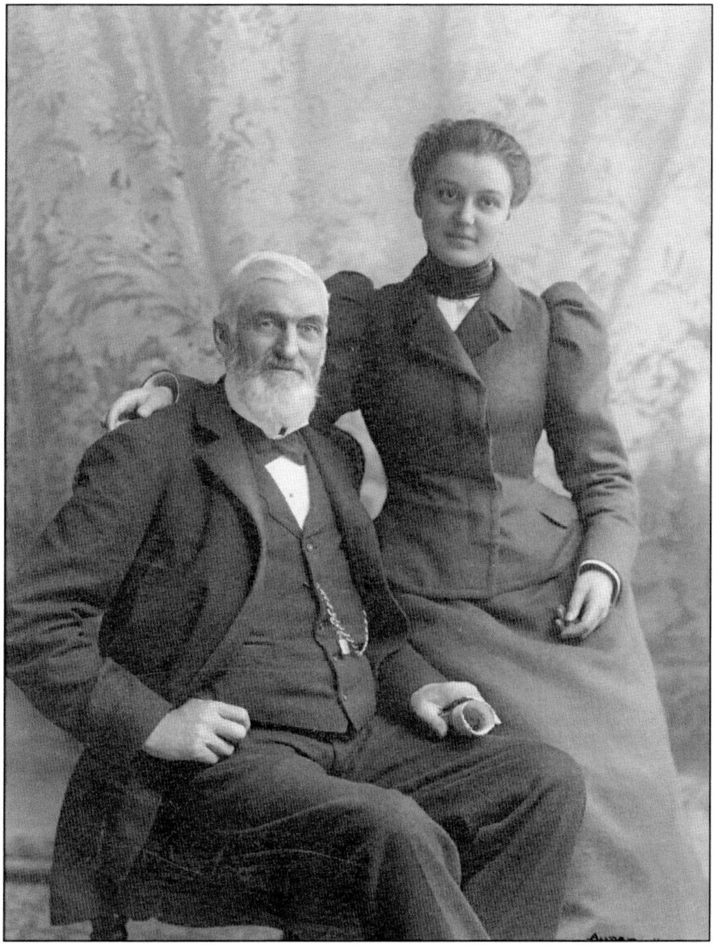

Lewis Alfred Loomis, 1830–1913. Transportation mogul Lewis Alfred Loomis is pictured here about 1895 with daughter Amelia. He first arrived on the North Beach Peninsula from his native New York in the mid-1850s, but before settling there permanently, he returned to the East, where he was employed building and repairing railroads for the army during the Civil War. (OHS-983D058.)

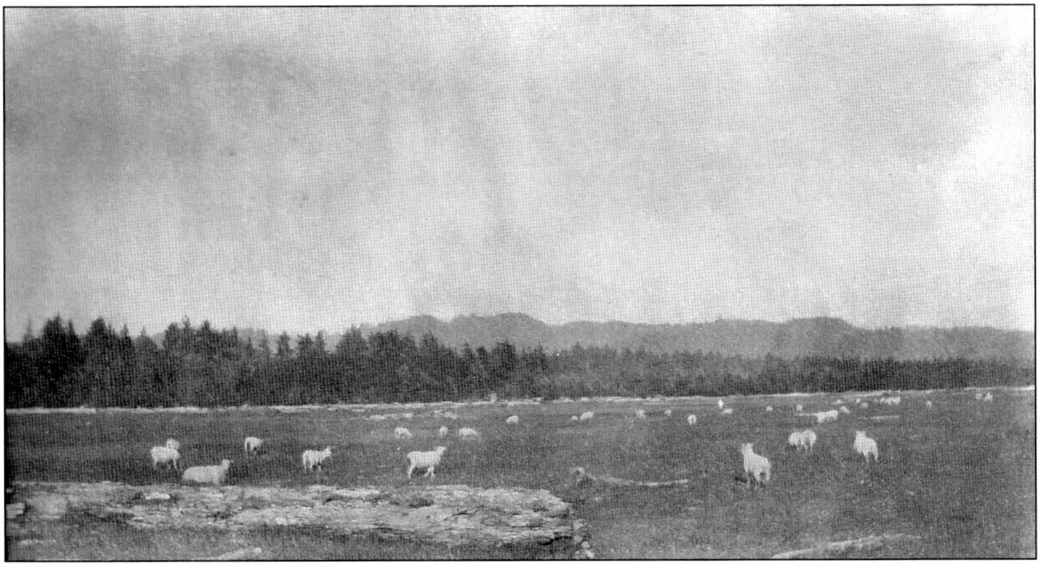

SHEEP FARMERS. In 1872, Loomis returned to the Pacific Coast, joining his brother, Edwin, who was living in Oysterville. The two men soon bought a tract of grassland east of the primary dune in the Klipsan area of the peninsula and began raising sheep. They produced a fine quality of wool, and their business prospered.

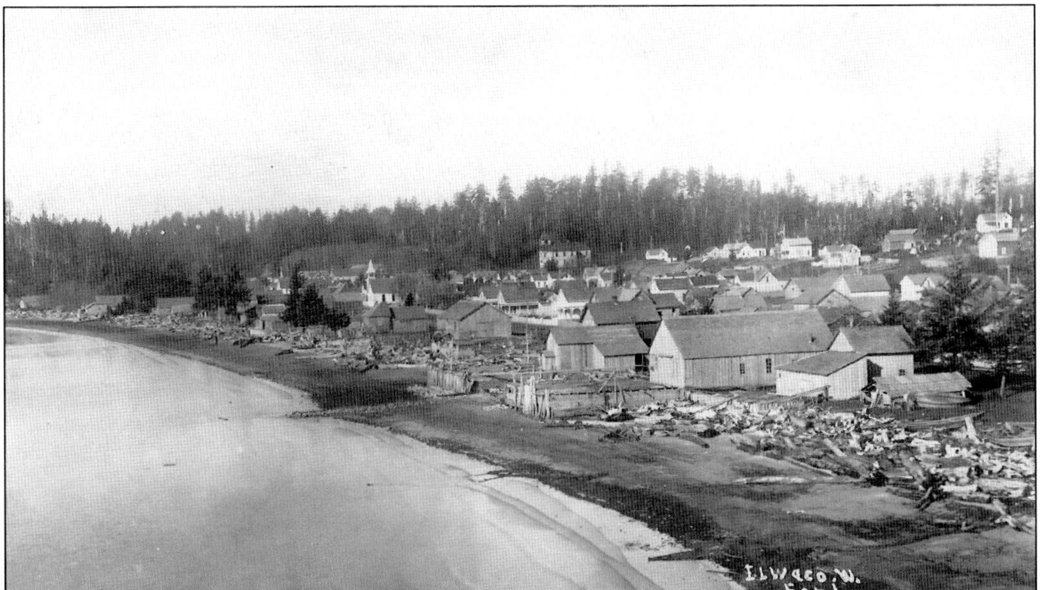

NORTH BEACH ARRIVALS AND DEPARTURES. In order to send their wool to market in San Francisco, the Loomis brothers, like all other North Beach businessmen, needed to first transport their product across the Columbia River to Astoria. The Columbia crossing began at Ilwaco, where buggies and wagons backed into the water, meeting rowboats dispatched from steamers anchored offshore.

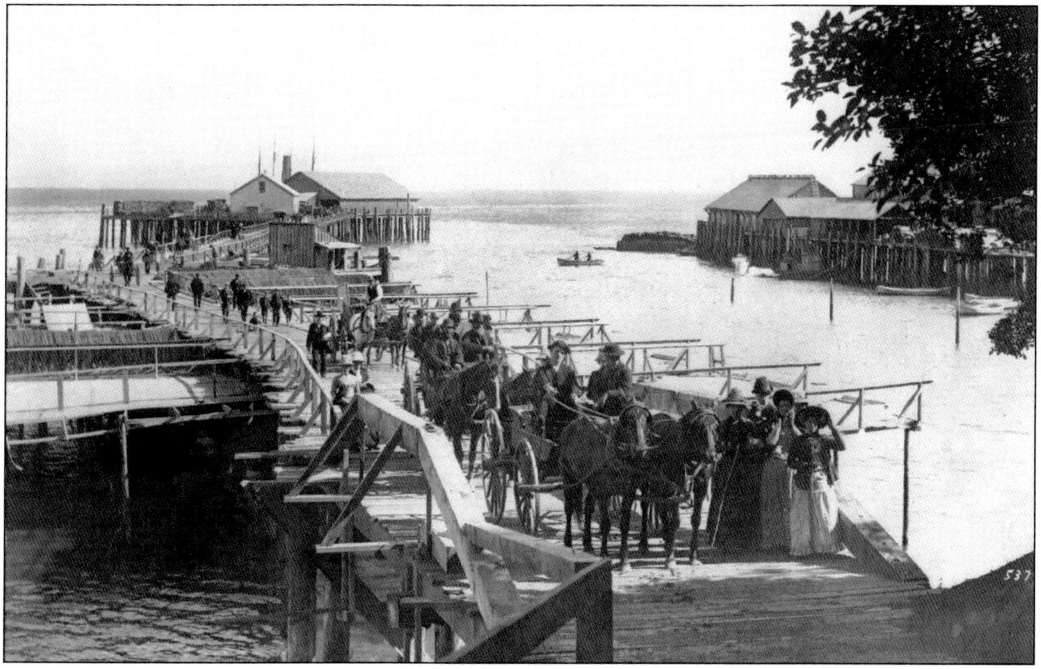

Ilwaco Wharf. Presumably, Lewis Loomis had an unfortunate experience "wetting a load of wool" between shore and steamer. This inspired step one in his transportation career—building a dock from which freight and passengers could be transferred directly to a launch. In 1874, he founded the Ilwaco Wharf Company, selling 50 shares and raising $2,500 to construct a long wharf and a freight warehouse on Bakers Bay at Ilwaco. (OHS-59269.)

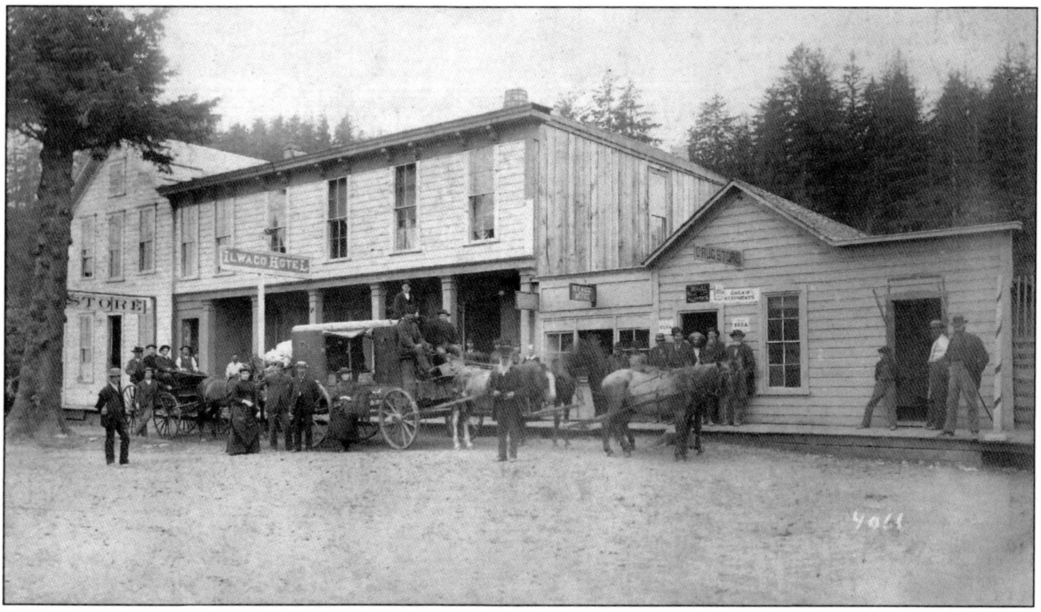

Ilwaco-to-Oysterville Stagecoach 1870–1889. With the wharf giving assurance of a convenient and reliable steamer connection, Loomis next acquired the stage line that ran between Ilwaco and Oysterville. Service was increased from three times a week to a daily schedule, and before long, Loomis was operating one coach and two freight wagons at a good profit.

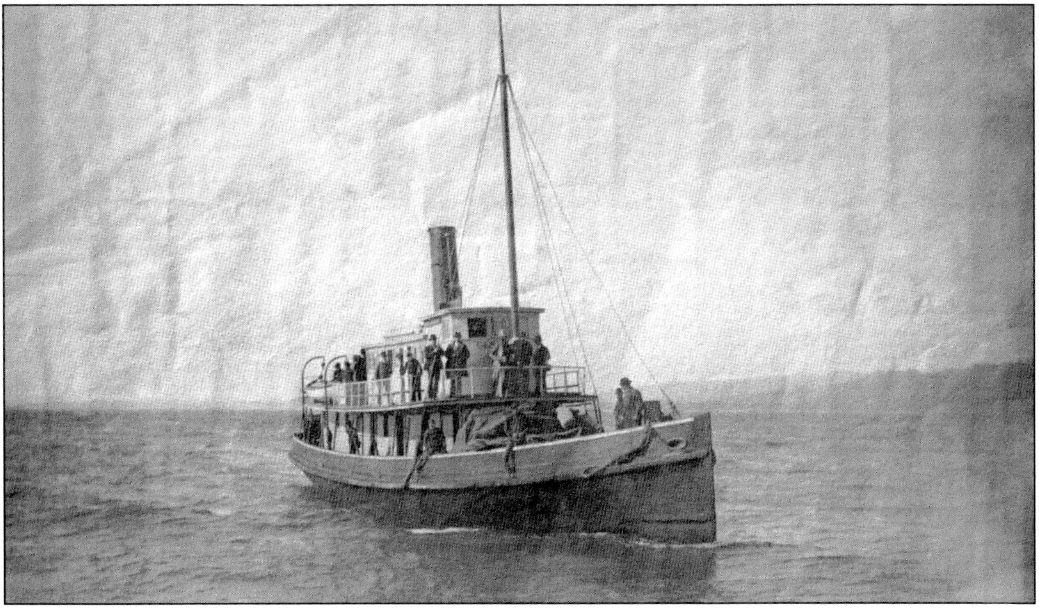

The Columbia Crossing. In 1875, Loomis organized the Ilwaco Steam Navigation Company and for $22,000 purchased the secondhand, but never used, *General Canby* for crossing the Columbia from Astoria to Ilwaco. The 110-foot-long seagoing passenger tug had been built for the South Bend Mill Company and was the first steamer constructed in the Shoalwater Bay region. Now the run from Astoria to Oysterville was controlled completely by Loomis. (CRMM.)

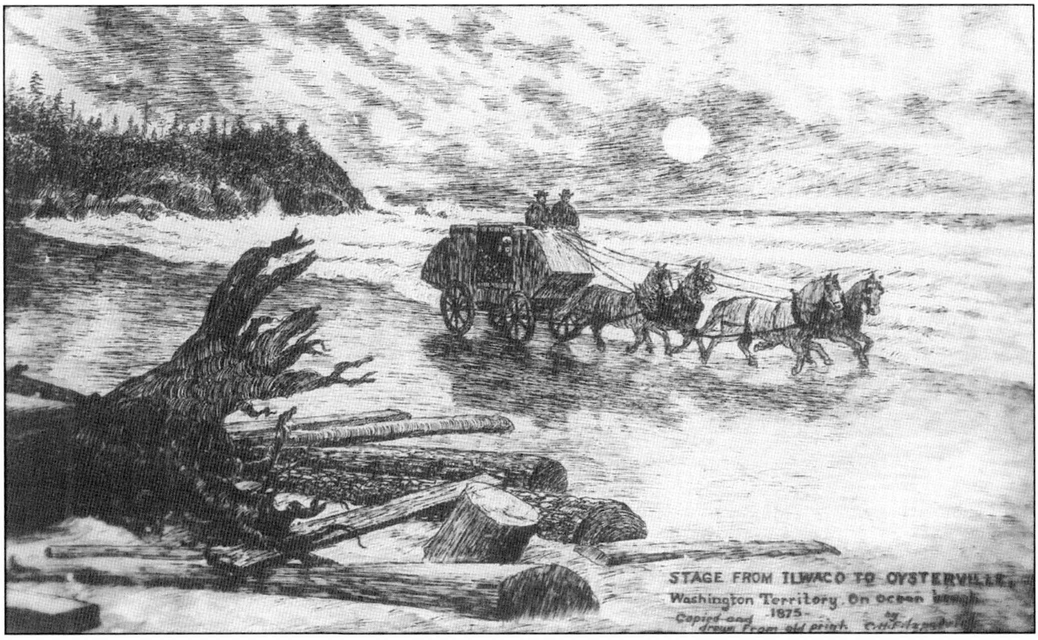

Scheduling by the Tide. Since steamers could reach the wharf in Ilwaco only at the tide's mid-flood, stage connections were adjusted according to the tide table. Every few days, departures were moved forward a half hour and, once a week, the schedule was moved back two or three hours. This unusual scheduling was easily accepted by the local population, who were used to organizing their activities according to the tide.

SECURING THE MAIL CONTRACT. With boat, dock, and stage line in place, Loomis was ready to procure the contract for carrying the mail between Astoria, Oregon, and Olympia, the capital of Washington Territory. Critics, feeling that he would lose money on the venture, were unwilling to put up the $50,000 required for the bond. However, Loomis appealed to old Oysterville friends John (right) and Thomas Crellin of the Morgan Oyster Company. The Crellins, after making a fortune in oysters, had moved to San Francisco but had kept their North Beach Peninsula connections. Tom Crellin signed the necessary paperwork without hesitation, and Loomis's mail contract was secured. (Right, the Whipple Manning family; below, Sydney Stevens.)

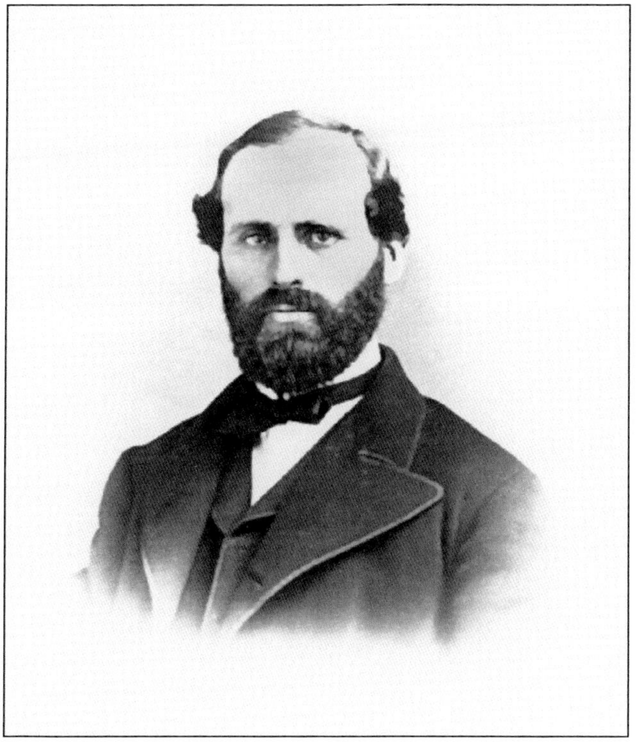

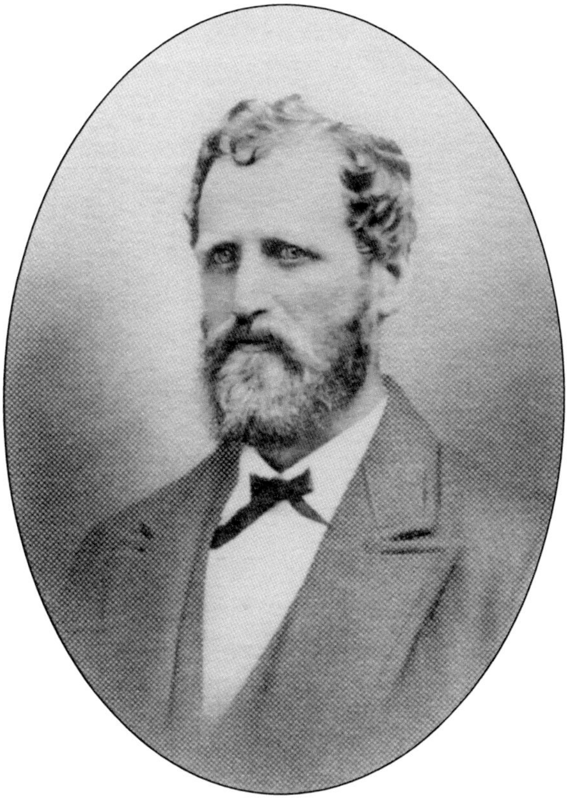

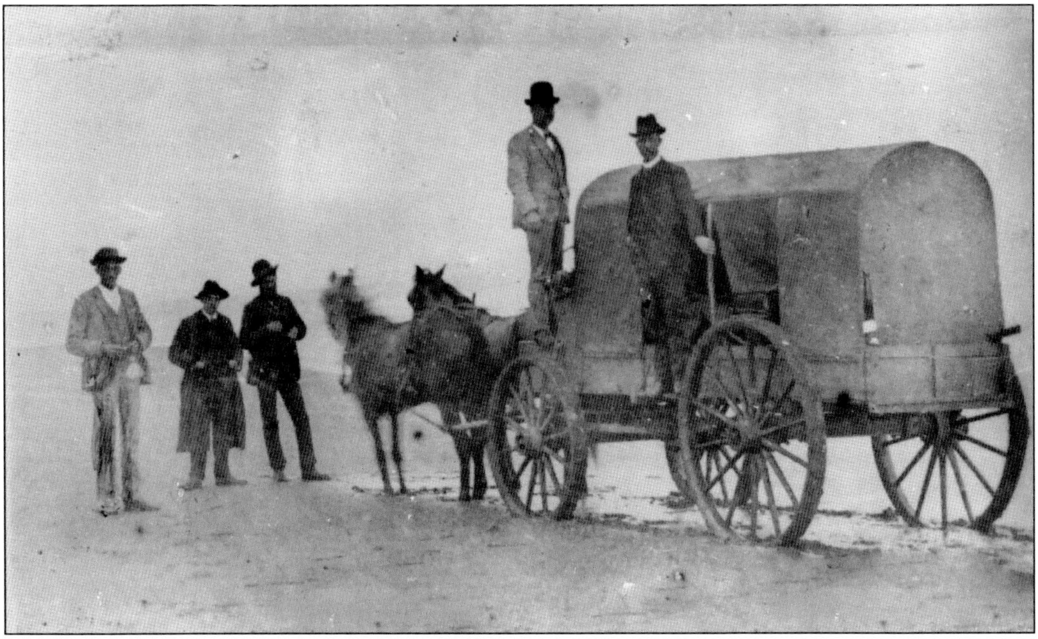

Stage Run along the Weatherbeach. Three steamers and three stage lines were required to make the mail run, which followed the old Native American trail from the Columbia River to Puget Sound. The most time-consuming portion of the trip was the 17-mile stretch between Ilwaco and Oysterville. The hard-packed sand of the ocean beach made "an ideal road when the tide was out, but a very unsatisfactory one when the tide was high," according to early stagecoach driver John Morehead. Also, increasing numbers of families from the Portland area were seeking the cool coastal climate for their summer vacations—too many folks for the stagecoaches to accommodate. By the early 1880s, Loomis began to look for support for a railroad that would replace the stage line from Ilwaco northward. (Above, Sydney Stevens; below, the Les Wilson family.)

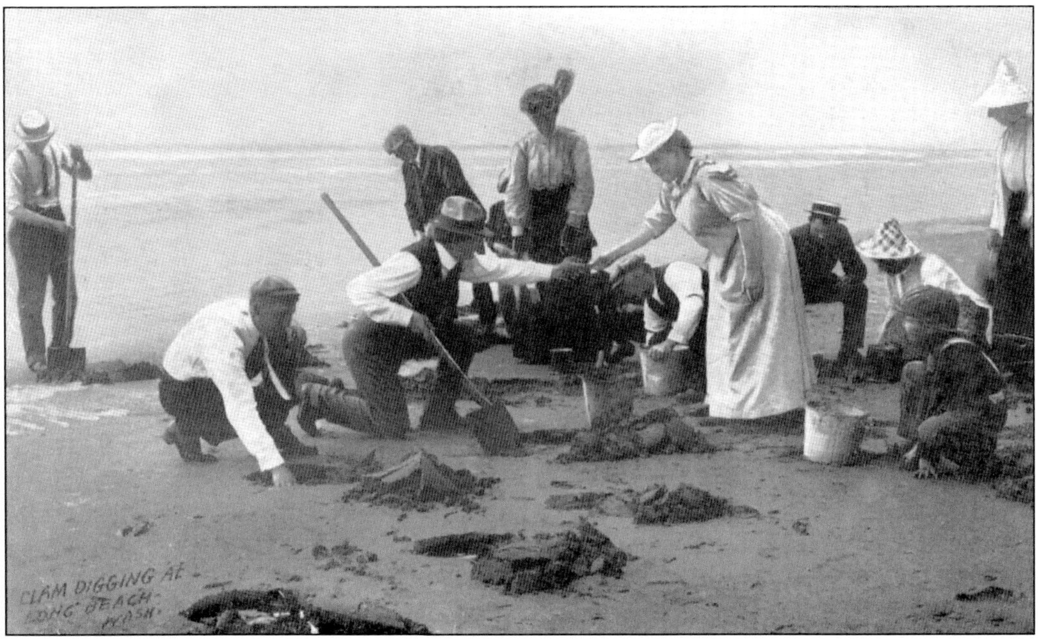

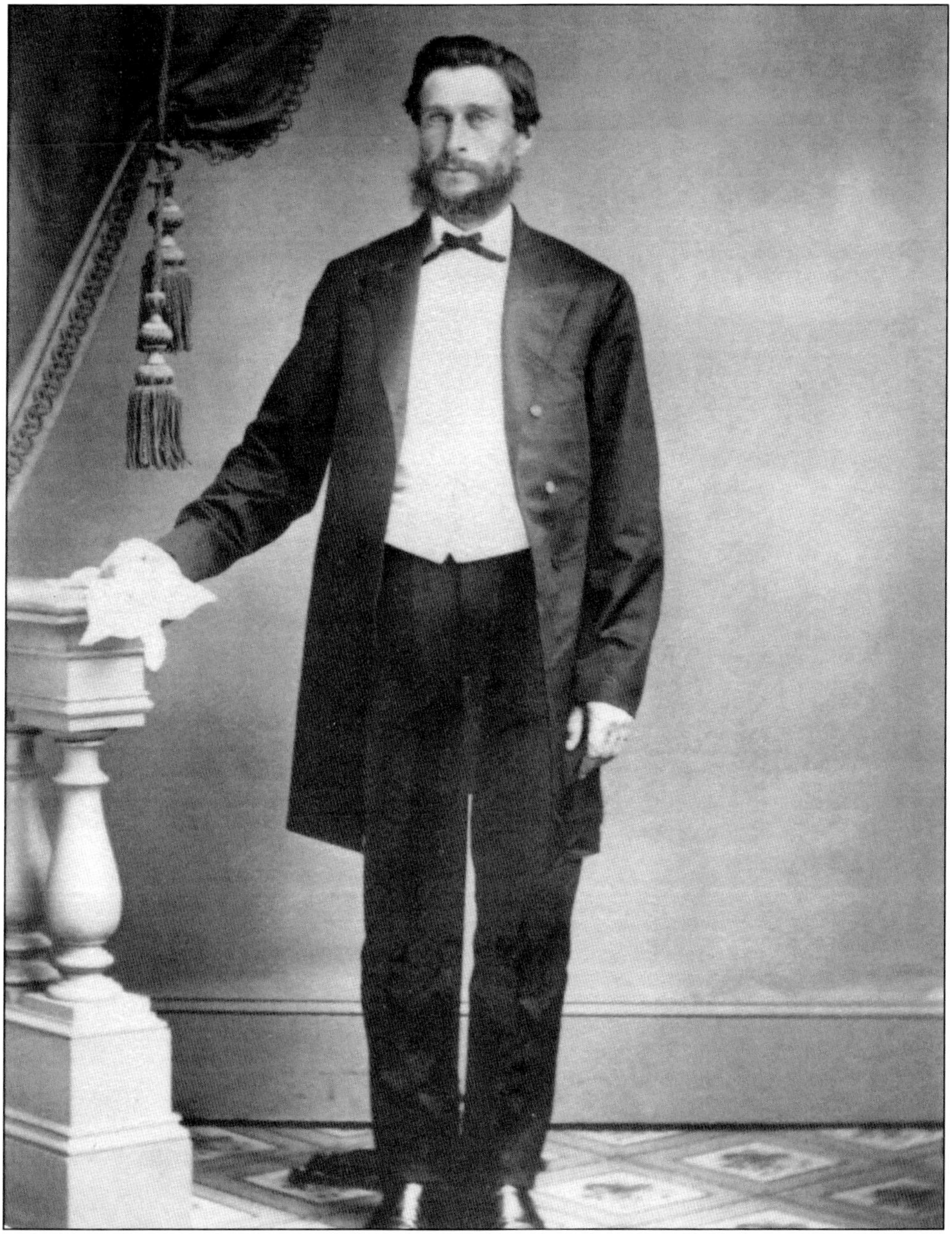

Preliminary Survey. In 1884, a preliminary survey indicated that a fully equipped line could be built from Ilwaco to Oysterville for $5,000 per mile. Since there would be no outside connection to a standard-gauge railroad, the figure was based upon construction costs for a less expensive narrow-gauge line. Among enthusiastic backers was R. H. Espy, cofounder of Oysterville, who purchased $10,000 in stock. He was convinced that the arrival of the railroad in Oysterville, or even to the proposed terminus of New Saratoga one-half mile to the south, would be the saving grace for "his" town. The little native oyster, upon which the town's prosperity and development depended, had slipped into a sharp decline. The railroad's proximity, with its promise of bringing Oysterville's isolation to an end, was a necessity as Espy saw it. Like his good friends the Crellin brothers, he invested heavily and without reservation. (Sydney Stevens.)

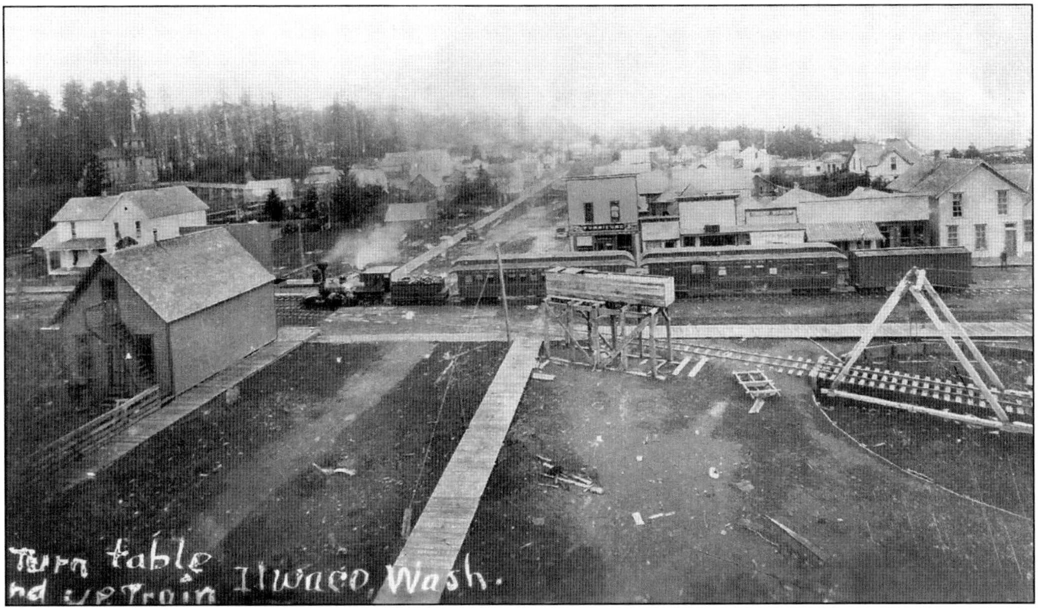

Building Begins. In the spring of 1888, the Ilwaco Steam Navigation Company was rechartered, becoming simply the Ilwaco Railroad. Land was cleared on the upper end of First Street in Ilwaco, and work began on the roadbed. An engine house, shops, turntable, water tank, and other facilities were built. Conveniently for cost-conscious Loomis, he was able to buy some obsolete narrow-gauge equipment, including rails and flatcars, at bargain prices. The locomotive, a 2-6-0 type built by Baldwin, cost $2,500. When the equipment arrived in June, tracklaying began. Crossties, cut from the plentiful stands of timber along the way, were laid as the roadbed advanced. Tracklayers followed, their supply of 35-pound rails on the flatcars behind them pushed by the locomotive, which was soon dubbed "the little engine that could." (Below, PCHS.)

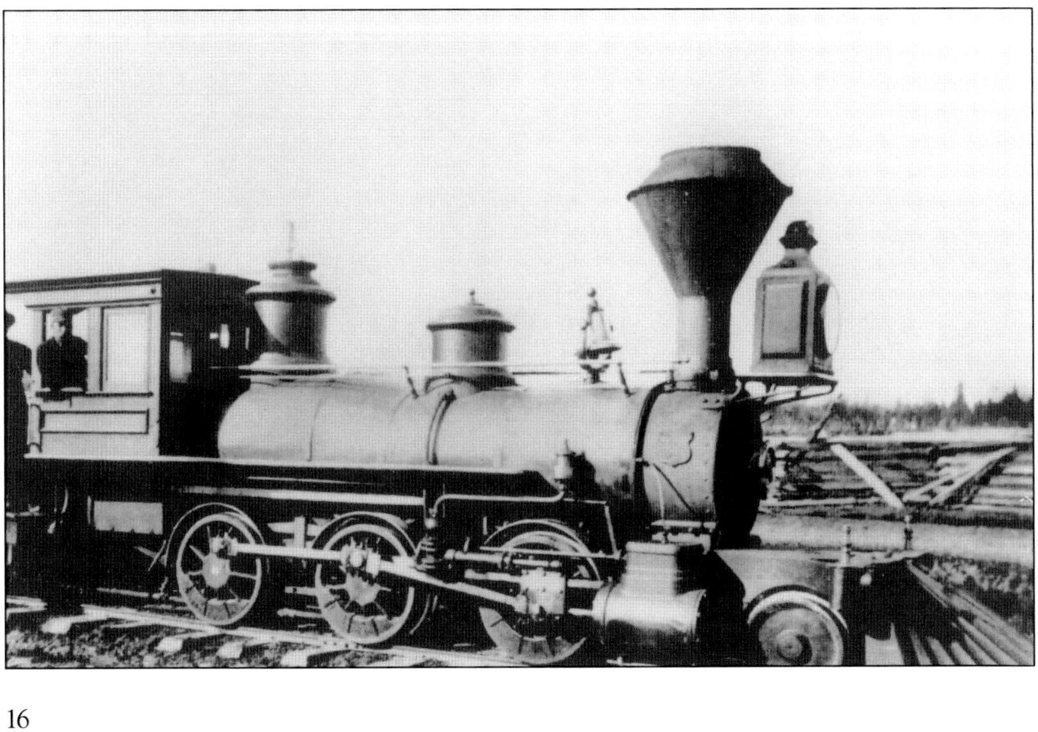

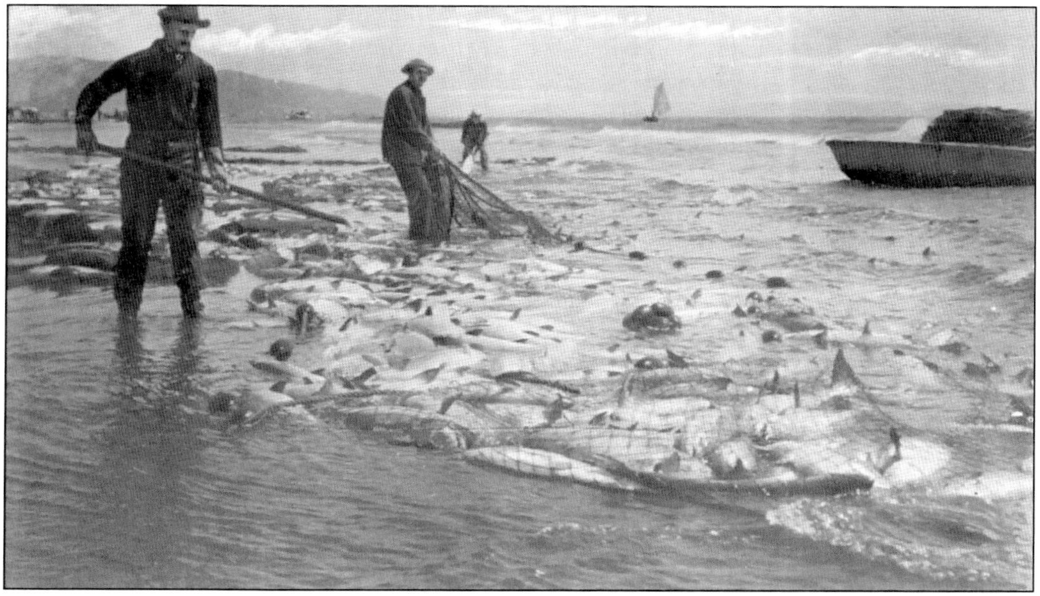

Business as Usual. Even as the train progressed northward, life on the peninsula went on pretty much as usual. Most residents were dependent upon fishing, farming, oystering, or logging, and work was done by hand or with the help of oxen or horses. The great mechanical beast that Loomis had put to work building the railroad was at once a curiosity and a sign of change. Although there was a sense of pride that progress was coming to the peninsula, the promise of a train had little impact on most people and their plans for the future. Only a handful of up-and-coming businessmen saw the potential the railroad held in connecting the isolated peninsula to growing markets in more populated areas.

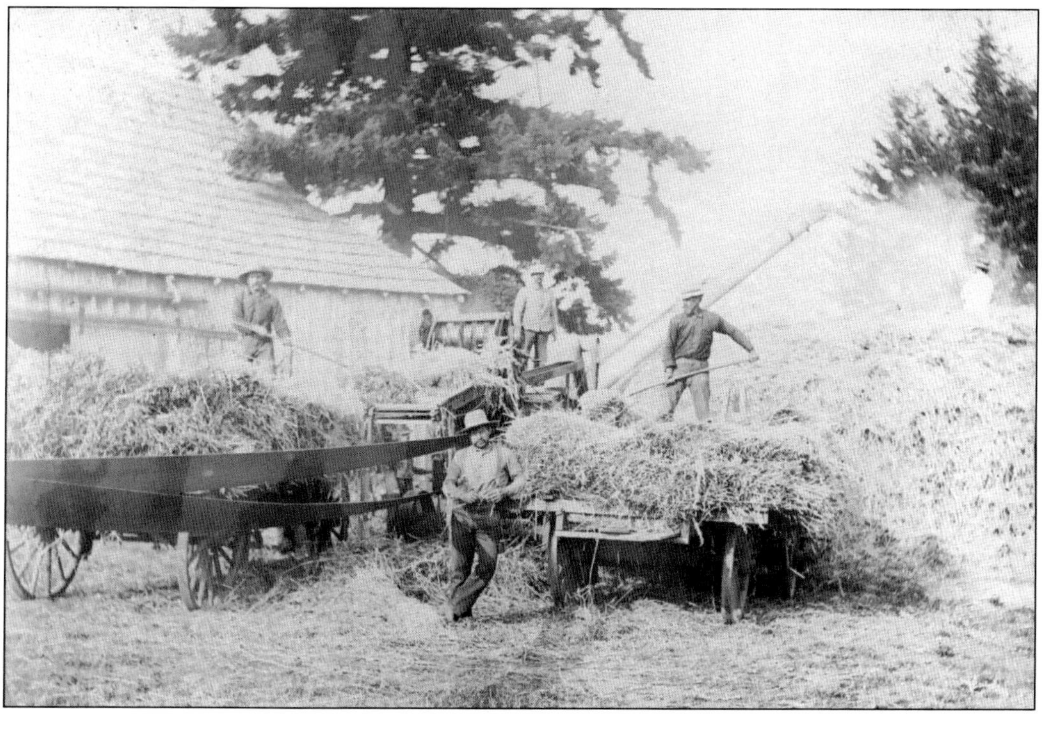

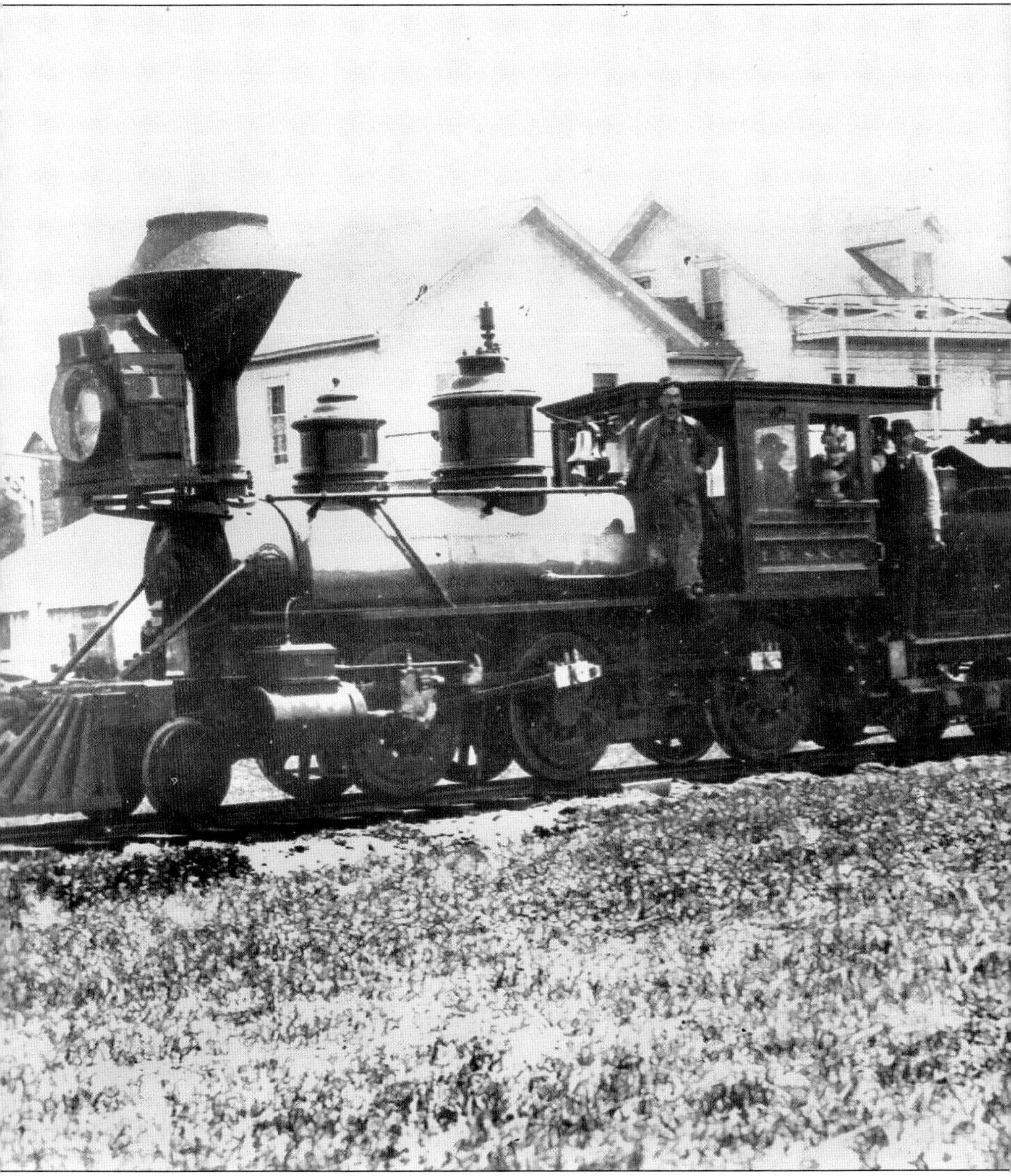

The First Celebration. On July 19, 1888, the Ilwaco Railroad held a grand celebration commemorating the completion of the line from Ilwaco to Long Beach. Locomotive No. 1, the Baldwin Mogul (2-6-0), pulled the four flatcars, which were outfitted with plank seats, side railings, and cloth canopies to ward off the summer sun. The engineer was George Jennings, and the

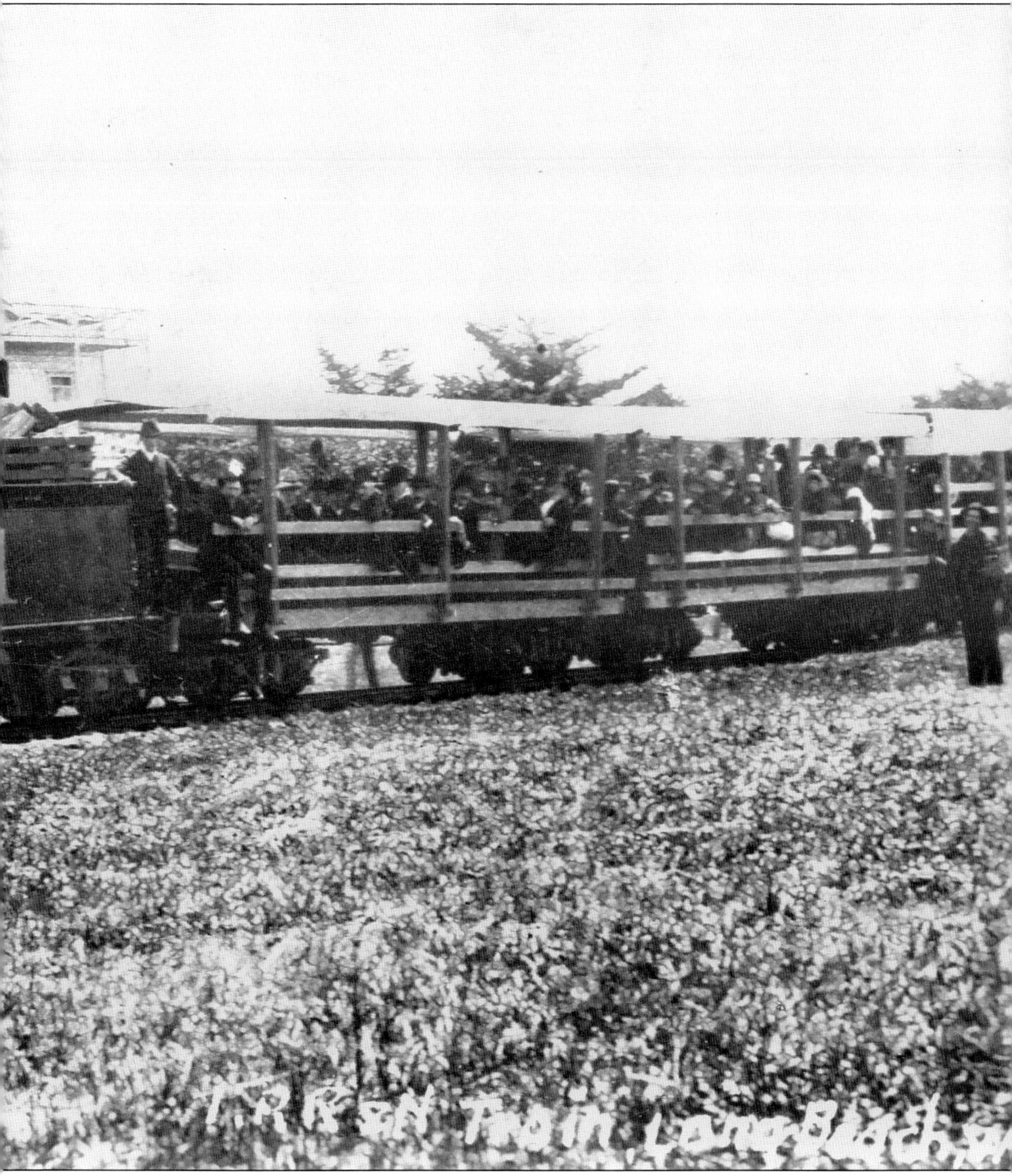

conductor was a man named Mr. Robinson. Every available space was occupied for the exciting 2.4-mile journey. At each end of the line, a big banquet was held, preceded by the "speechifying" of local dignitaries who predicted that this was but the first link in a series of rail lines that would run clear to San Francisco.

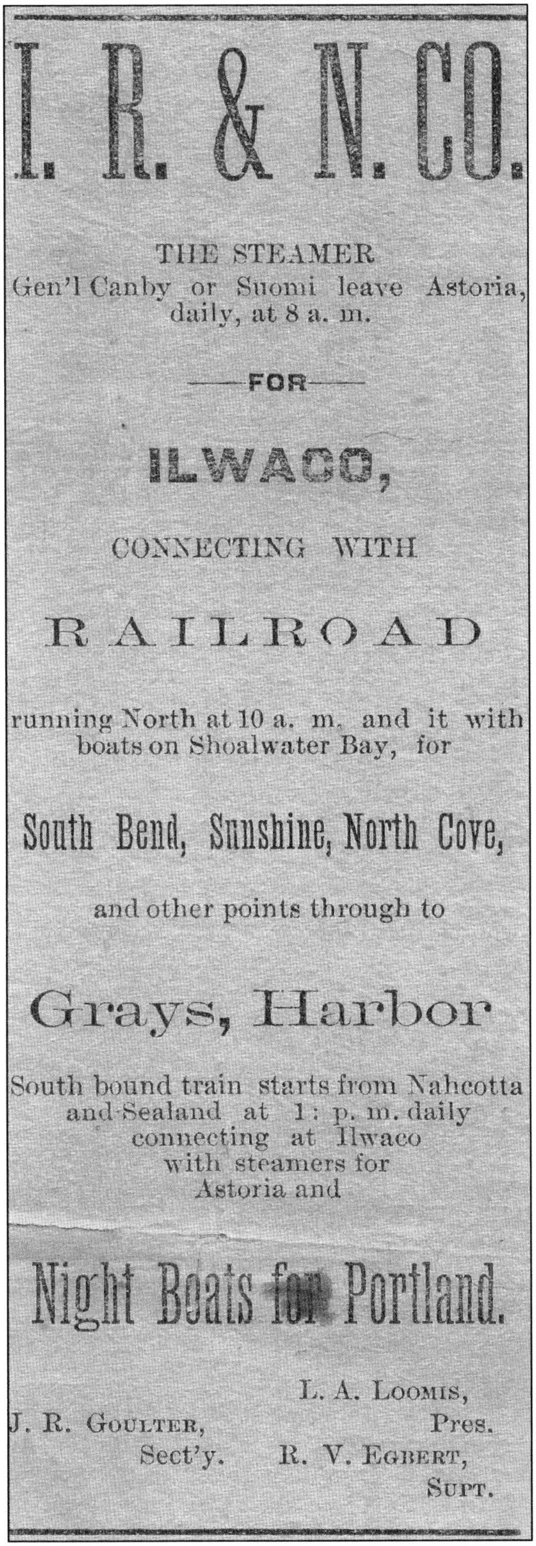

The IR&N. Less than a month after the initial celebration, another change in the railroad's corporate structure occurred and it was renamed Ilwaco Railway and Navigation Company, better known as the IR&N. Eight years later, those initials in combination with the line's unorthodox methods prompted the editor of the *Pacific Journal* to christen it the "Irregular, Rambling & Never-get-there Railroad," one of several nicknames that have endured. The moniker was introduced in the form of an advertisement, which said, "Makes all points on the peninsula between Ilwaco and Nahcotta sometime during the day unless unavoidably detained by running off the track. Train leaves Ilwaco dock when it gets ready, arriving at Nahcotta when it gets there. Notice—A spotter is employed on every train to prevent beach visitors from being robbed by the Ilwaco Councilmen and attorney, while en route through the city. Keep on the train and no danger need be apprehended from that source. Passengers persisting in alighting in Ilwaco do so at their own risk."

Two

North to Nahcotta

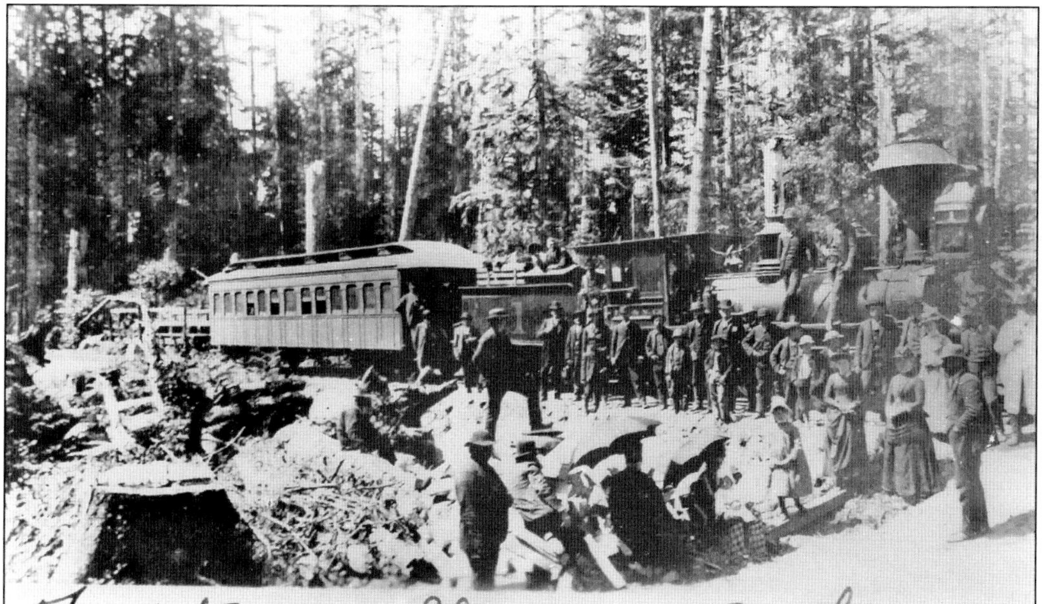

End of the Line. Money problems continued to plague the little rail line, and it was not until May 29, 1889, that the first train arrived in Nahcotta on Shoalwater Bay, 13 miles north of Ilwaco. Instead of the predicted $5,000 per mile, costs had soared to twice that amount. Nahcotta, the directors decided, would be the northern terminus of the railroad.

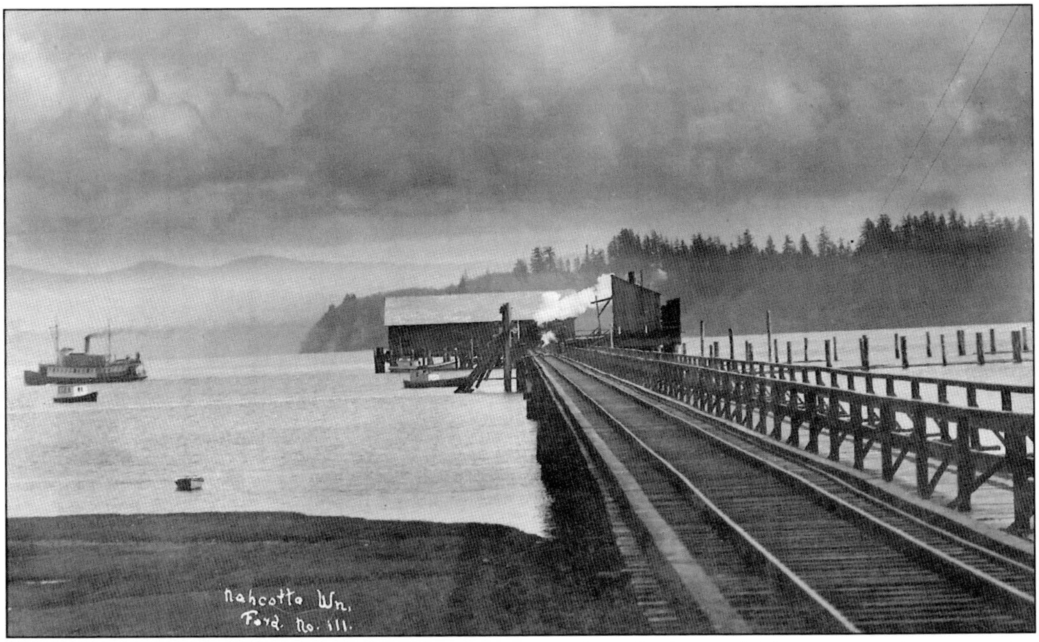

Deep Water Accessibility. Another advantage to ending the line at Nahcotta was the proximity to shore of a deep-water channel. A much shorter dock, only 1,700 feet, was needed in comparison to the mile-long wharf that would have been required at Oysterville. Train and boat connections at the Nahcotta end of the line would not be dependent upon the tide schedule. (PCHS.)

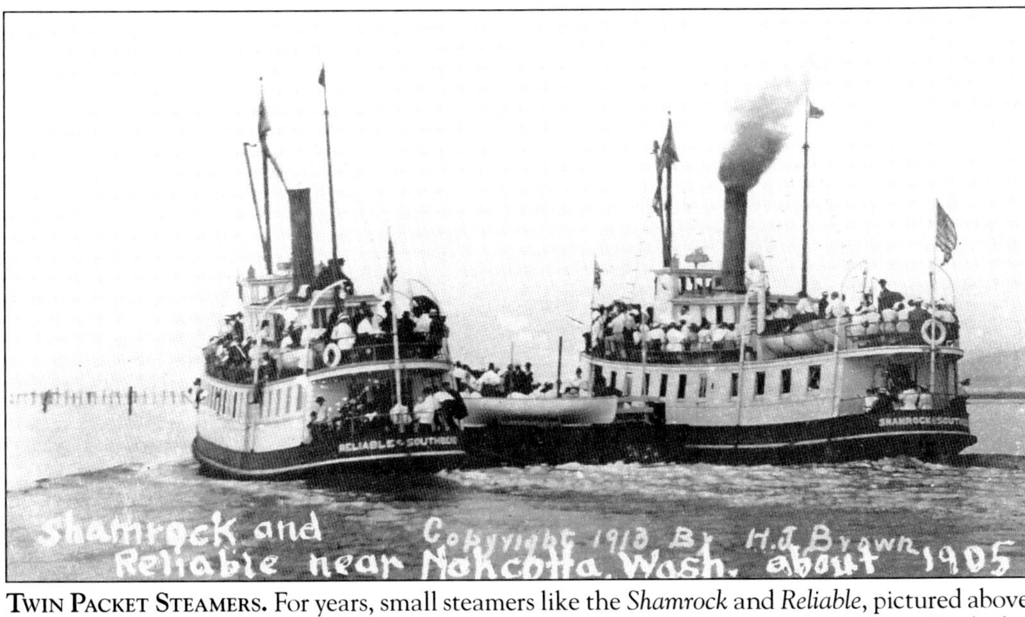

Twin Packet Steamers. For years, small steamers like the *Shamrock* and *Reliable*, pictured above, provided mail and passenger service between communities around Shoalwater Bay. Each day, one of the steamers made the morning and afternoon connections with the train at Nahcotta. Eventually, this bay crossing would link the Northern Pacific at South Bend with the Ilwaco Railroad, making it possible to travel by train and boat from Seattle to Portland.

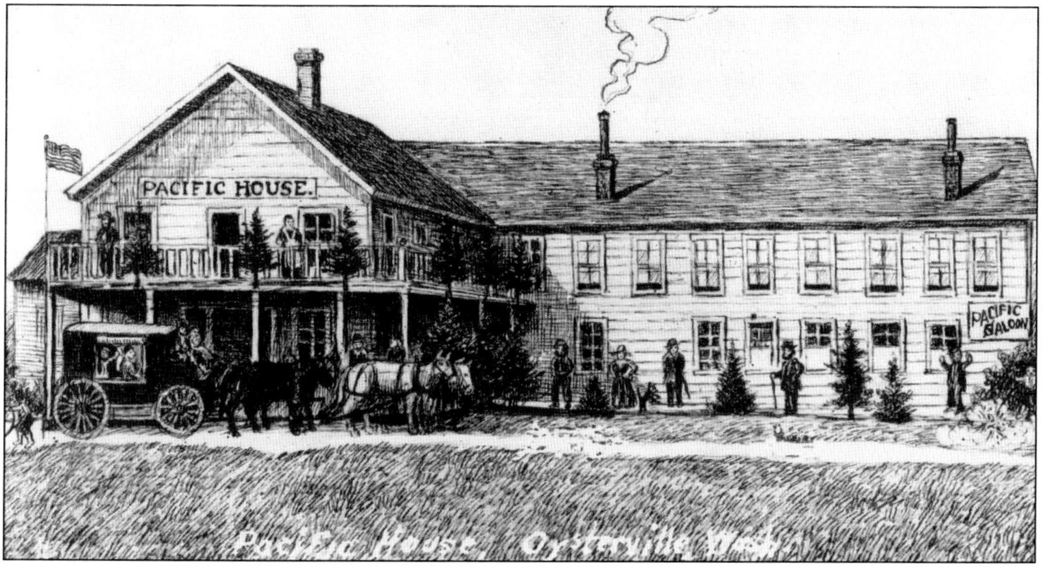

BOOMTOWN NO MORE. Since its founding in 1854, Oysterville had been the center of activity at the peninsula's north end. Then, as the supply of native oysters dwindled, Oysterville's boomtown status began to diminish. When Nahcotta was selected as the northern terminus for the IR&N, Oysterville businesses closed their doors and moved 4 miles south to the newly created town at the end of the line. (Sydney Stevens.)

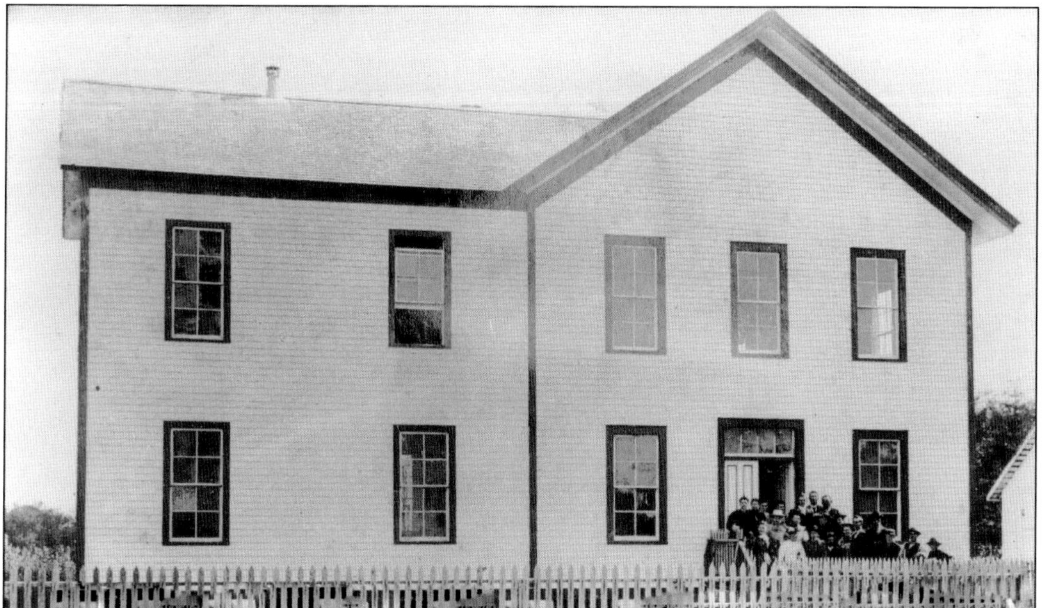

THE FINAL BLOW. In 1892, Pacific County voters elected to move the county seat from Oysterville to South Bend. Without train service, oyster industry, or courthouse, Oysterville's population declined and the town slowly sank into obscurity. A century after its founding, it was known only as one of Washington's obscure ghost towns. (Sydney Stevens.)

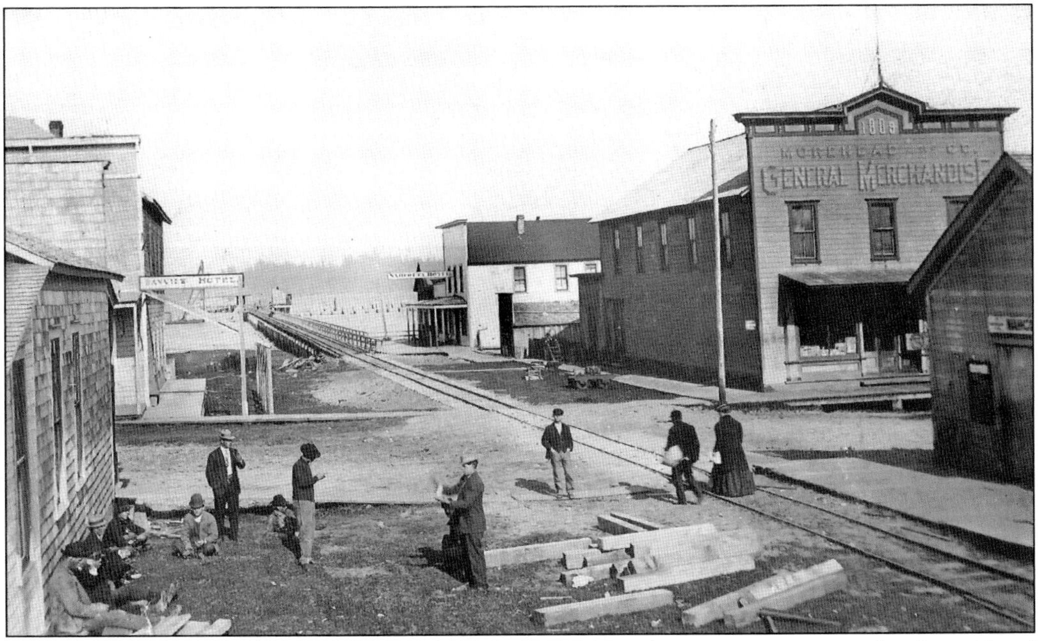

RIVAL TOWNS. Meanwhile, at the northern terminus, rival town sites occupied either side of the track. To the north was Sealand, platted on land owned by Sen. B. A. Seaborg, an IR&N stockholder hoping to profit by selling to the railroad. When pioneer cranberry grower John Peter Paul proposed donating part of his plat south of the track, Loomis accepted his offer and Nahcotta was established. (Dorothy Trondsen Williams.)

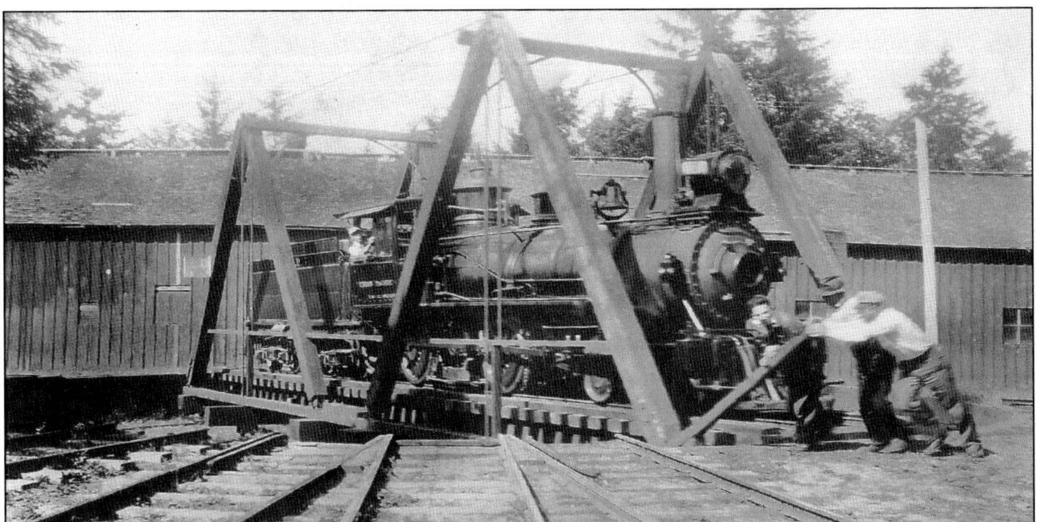

NAHCOTTA, THE WORKING END. In addition to freight and passenger depots, locomotive barn, wharf, and turntable, the railroad's shops were located at Nahcotta. Equipment not in use was stored there, and most of the crew lived nearby. Although the business headquarters of the IR&N remained at Ilwaco, local residents knew that the "real work" of the railroad took place at the north end of the line. (Edna Pearson.)

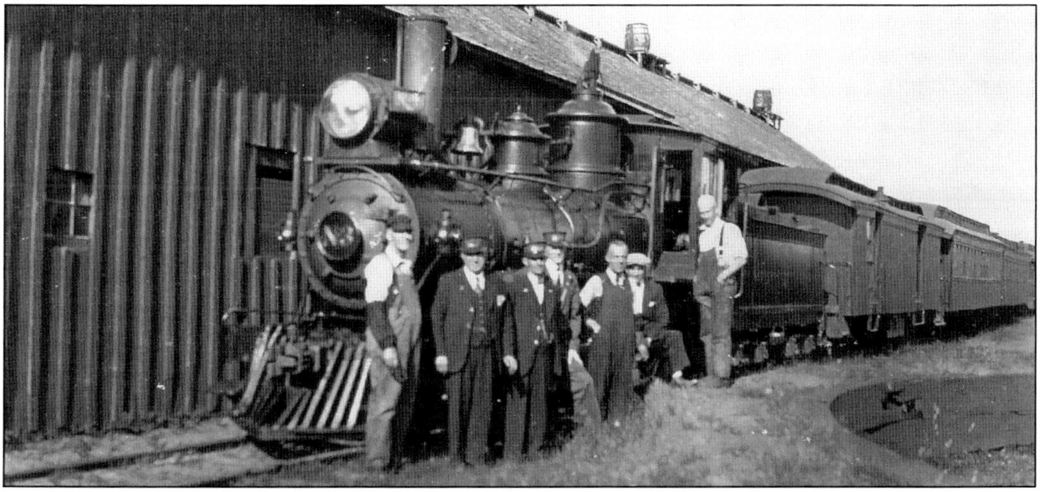

PROUD IR&N WORKERS. Crew members of both the trains and the steamers took pride in their work and became attached to the company and to the area. Many worked on the line for a lifetime. The September 12, 1930, issue of the *North Beach Tribune* listed the then-current employees with the dates they had gone to work for the line; many had been with the railroad for more than 15 years. Although Edward Budd retired three years before the last train ran, he was also listed in the article for having worked for the railway from 1905 to 1927. Employees had established themselves on the peninsula and had raised their families there, and their descendants are still among the residents of peninsula communities. (Below, CRMM.)

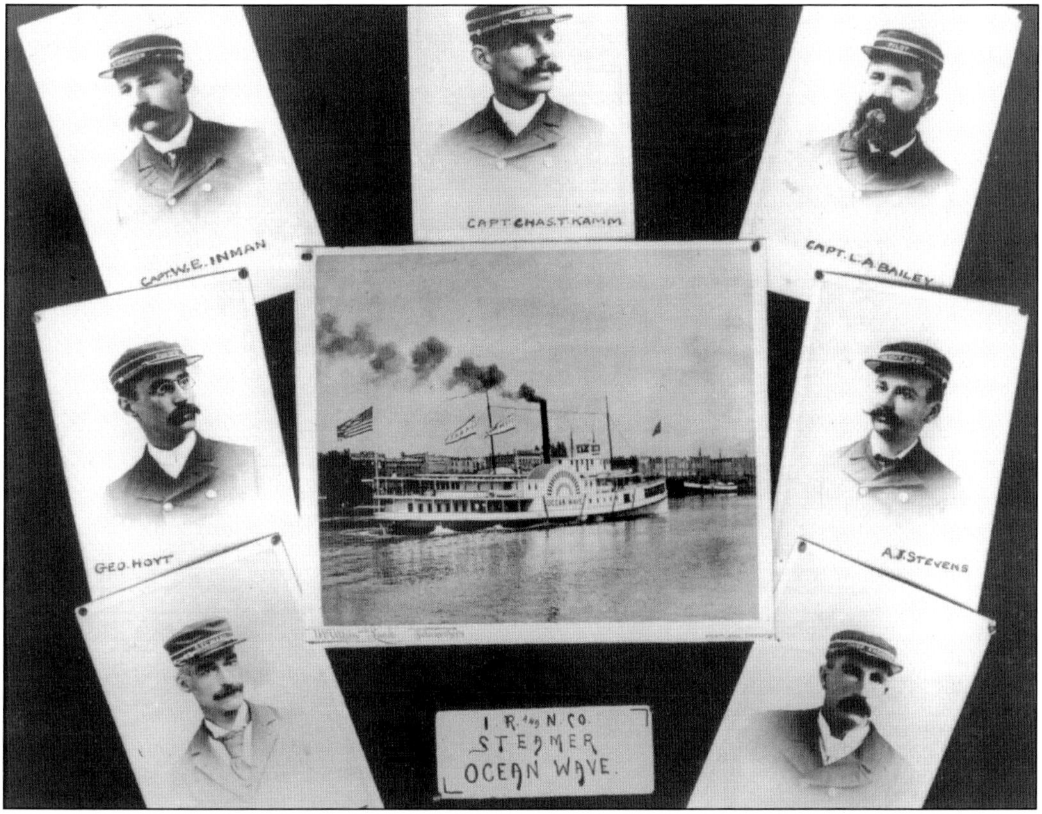

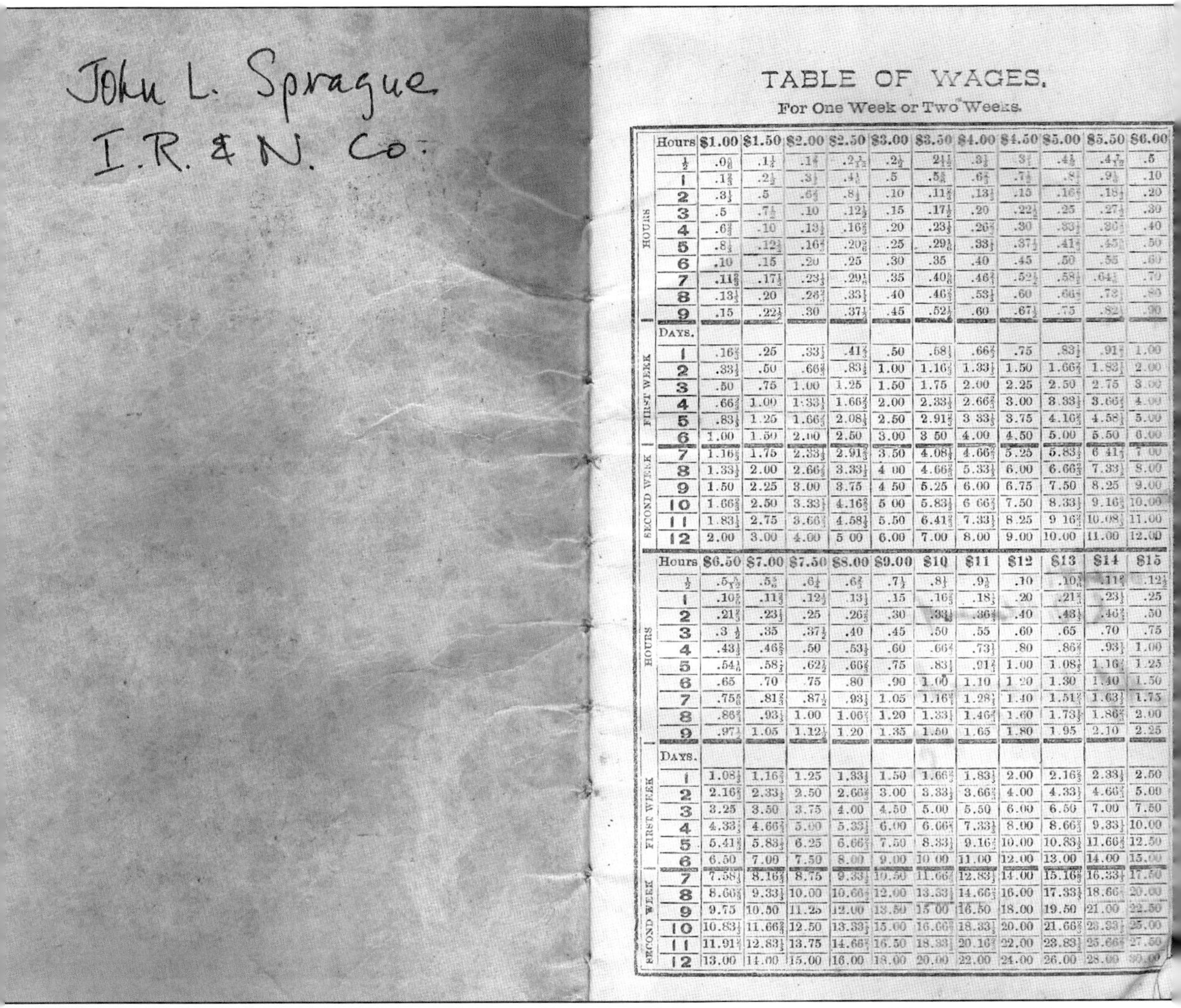

TABLE OF WAGES.

For One Week or Two Weeks.

	Hours	$1.00	$1.50	$2.00	$2.50	$3.00	$3.50	$4.00	$4.50	$5.00	$5.50	$6.00
HOURS	½	.0⅚	.1¼	.1⅔	.2 1/12	.2½	2 11/12	.3⅓	.3¾	.4⅙	.4 7/12	.5
	1	.1⅔	.2½	.3⅓	.4⅙	.5	.5⅚	.6⅔	.7½	.8⅓	.9⅙	.10
	2	.3⅓	.5	.6⅔	.8⅓	.10	.11⅔	.13⅓	.15	.16⅔	.18⅓	.20
	3	.5	.7½	.10	.12½	.15	.17½	.20	.22½	.25	.27½	.30
	4	.6⅔	.10	.13⅓	.16⅔	.20	.23⅓	.26⅔	.30	.33⅓	.36⅔	.40
	5	.8⅓	.12½	.16⅔	.20⅚	.25	.29⅙	.33⅓	.37½	.41⅔	.45⅚	.50
	6	.10	.15	.20	.25	.30	.35	.40	.45	.50	.55	.60
	7	.11⅔	.17½	.23⅓	.29⅙	.35	.40⅚	.46⅔	.52½	.58⅓	.64⅙	.70
	8	.13⅓	.20	.26⅔	.33⅓	.40	.46⅔	.53⅓	.60	.66⅔	.73⅓	.80
	9	.15	.22½	.30	.37½	.45	.52½	.60	.67½	.75	.82½	.90
	DAYS.											
FIRST WEEK	1	.16⅔	.25	.33⅓	.41⅔	.50	.58⅓	.66⅔	.75	.83⅓	.91⅔	1.00
	2	.33⅓	.50	.66⅔	.83⅓	1.00	1.16⅔	1.33⅓	1.50	1.66⅔	1.83⅓	2.00
	3	.50	.75	1.00	1.25	1.50	1.75	2.00	2.25	2.50	2.75	3.00
	4	.66⅔	1.00	1.33⅓	1.66⅔	2.00	2.33⅓	2.66⅔	3.00	3.33⅓	3.66⅔	4.00
	5	.83⅓	1.25	1.66⅔	2.08⅓	2.50	2.91⅔	3 33⅓	3.75	4.16⅔	4.58⅓	5.00
	6	1.00	1.50	2.00	2.50	3.00	3 50	4.00	4.50	5.00	5.50	6.00
SECOND WEEK	7	1.16⅔	1.75	2.33⅓	2.91⅔	3.50	4.08⅓	4.66⅔	5.25	5.83⅓	6 41⅔	7 00
	8	1.33⅓	2.00	2.66⅔	3.33⅓	4 00	4.66⅔	5.33⅓	6.00	6.66⅔	7.33⅓	8.00
	9	1.50	2.25	3.00	3.75	4 50	5.25	6.00	6.75	7.50	8.25	9.00
	10	1.66⅔	2.50	3.33⅓	4.16⅔	5 00	5.83⅓	6 66⅔	7.50	8.33⅓	9.16⅔	10.00
	11	1.83⅓	2.75	3.66⅔	4.58⅓	5.50	6.41⅔	7.33⅓	8.25	9 16⅔	10.08⅓	11.00
	12	2.00	3.00	4.00	5 00	6.00	7.00	8.00	9.00	10.00	11.00	12.00

	Hours	$6.50	$7.00	$7.50	$8.00	$9.00	$10	$11	$12	$13	$14	$15
HOURS	½	.5 5/12	.5⅚	.6¼	.6⅔	.7½	.8⅓	.9⅙	.10	.10⅚	.11⅔	.12½
	1	.10⅚	.11⅔	.12½	.13⅓	.15	.16⅔	.18⅓	.20	.21⅔	.23⅓	.25
	2	.21⅔	.23⅓	.25	.26⅔	.30	.33⅓	.36⅔	.40	.43⅓	.46⅔	.50
	3	.3 ½	.35	.37½	.40	.45	.50	.55	.60	.65	.70	.75
	4	.43⅓	.46⅔	.50	.53⅓	.60	.66⅔	.73⅓	.80	.86⅔	.93⅓	1.00
	5	.54⅙	.58⅓	.62½	.66⅔	.75	.83⅓	.91⅔	1.00	1.08⅓	1.16⅔	1.25
	6	.65	.70	.75	.80	.90	1.00	1.10	1 20	1.30	1.40	1.50
	7	.75⅚	.81⅔	.87½	.93⅓	1.05	1.16⅔	1.28⅓	1.40	1.51⅔	1.63⅓	1.75
	8	.86⅔	.93⅓	1.00	1.06⅔	1.20	1.33⅓	1.46⅔	1.60	1.73⅓	1.86⅔	2.00
	9	.97½	1.05	1.12½	1.20	1.35	1.50	1.65	1.80	1.95	2.10	2.25
	DAYS.											
FIRST WEEK	1	1.08⅓	1.16⅔	1.25	1.33⅓	1.50	1.66⅔	1.83⅓	2.00	2.16⅔	2.33⅓	2.50
	2	2.16⅔	2.33⅓	2.50	2.66⅔	3.00	3.33⅓	3.66⅔	4.00	4.33⅓	4.66⅔	5.00
	3	3.25	3.50	3.75	4.00	4.50	5.00	5.50	6.00	6.50	7.00	7.50
	4	4.33⅓	4.66⅔	5.00	5.33⅓	6.00	6.66⅔	7.33⅓	8.00	8.66⅔	9.33⅓	10.00
	5	5.41⅔	5.83⅓	6.25	6.66⅔	7.50	8.33⅓	9.16⅔	10.00	10.83⅓	11.66⅔	12.50
	6	6.50	7.00	7.50	8.00	9.00	10 00	11.00	12.00	13.00	14.00	15.00
SECOND WEEK	7	7.58⅓	8.16⅔	8.75	9.33⅓	10.50	11.66⅔	12.83⅓	14.00	15.16⅔	16.33⅓	17.50
	8	8.66⅔	9.33⅓	10.00	10.66⅔	12.00	13.33⅓	14.66⅔	16.00	17.33⅓	18.66⅔	20.00
	9	9.75	10.50	11.25	12.00	13.50	15 00	16.50	18.00	19.50	21.00	22.50
	10	10.83⅓	11.66⅔	12.50	13.33⅓	15.00	16.66⅔	18.33⅓	20.00	21.66⅔	23.33⅓	25.00
	11	11.91⅔	12.83⅓	13.75	14.66⅔	16.50	18.33⅓	20.16⅔	22.00	23.83⅓	25.66⅔	27.50
	12	13.00	14.00	15.00	16.00	18.00	20.00	22.00	24.00	26.00	28.00	30.00

A Working Wage. On the North Beach Peninsula, a popular adage was, "When the tide's out, the table's set." Even so, the economy was often marginal and jobs were scarce. Full-time residents earned $2 a cord for cutting firewood and stacking it beside the tracks to be picked up as needed for the wood-burning locomotives. Steady employment with the railway was a coveted occupation. Les Wilson (1911–2002) was 18 when he went to work for the railroad in 1929. "I worked on the trains for the last two years they were running," he said in 1999. "I started out at 38¢ an hour. I was acting fireman on the train's final run. By then I was making 42¢ an hour. The regular fireman was not able to work that day—incapacitated you might say. Well, he was drunk."

Three

THE IR&N FINDS ITS WAY

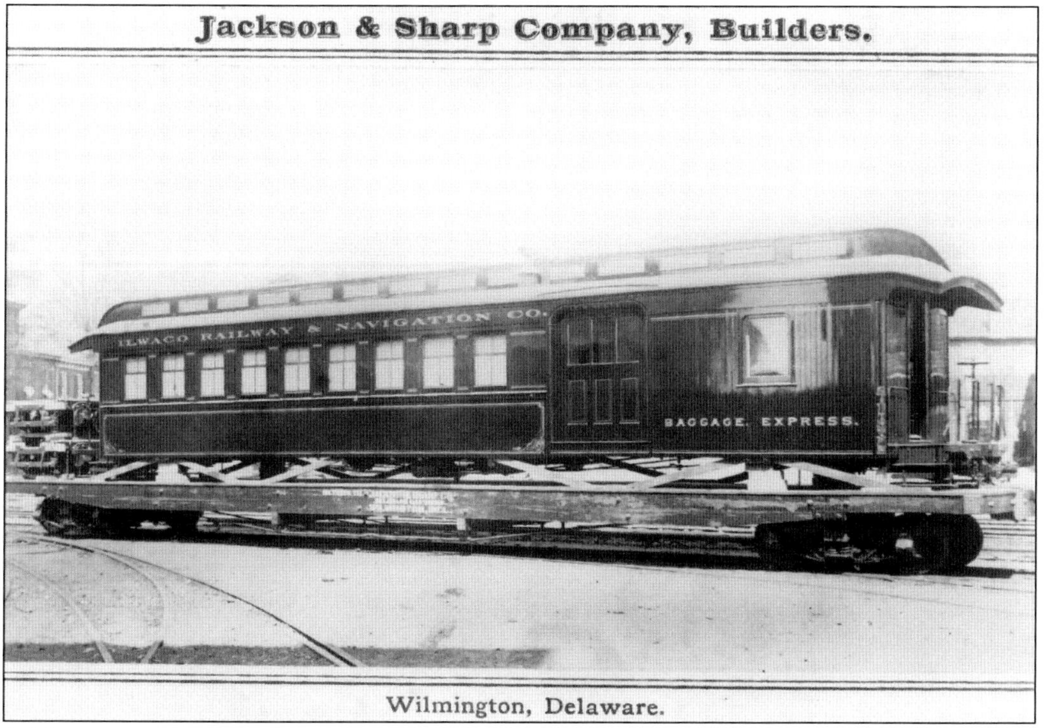

A NEED FOR NEW EQUIPMENT. Now that the railroad had become established and business was increasing, Jacob Kamm convinced Loomis that additional locomotives and rolling stock were needed to augment the line's meager secondhand equipment. Kamm traveled east to Pittsburgh and Wilmington, where he placed orders and oversaw construction. By early July 1890, a light Mogul locomotive, three coaches, and a combination passenger-baggage car were put into service. (CSRM.)

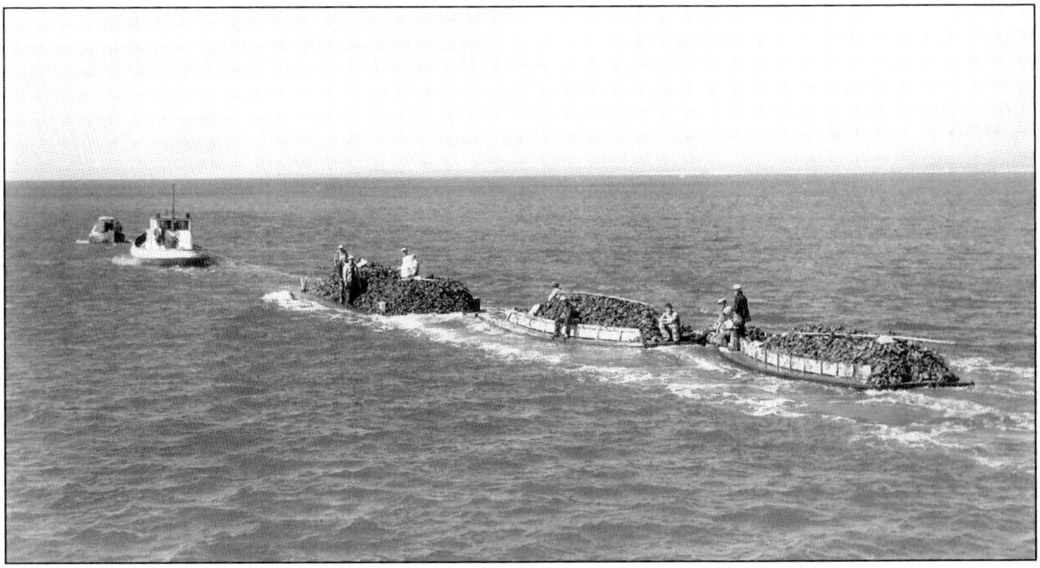

BIG BUSINESS IN OYSTERS. As native oysters became scarce, oystermen found that a somewhat larger oyster imported from the East Coast could be grown in Shoalwater Bay. When ready for market, "Easterns" were barged to Nahcotta for shipment by train to Ilwaco. There they were taken by steamer to Astoria, where they were sent on to San Francisco and Portland markets. Nearly 1,000 eighty-pound sacks of fresh oysters were loaded onto the train each week at Nahcotta at a freight charge, Nahcotta to Astoria, of 75¢ per sack. One day a week was the designated "oyster day," and as transfer from freight cars to steamer took a long time, local passengers planning a trip to Astoria usually avoided going on that particular day. Oyster shipments were a big factor in the initial prosperity of the IR&N. (Below, Sydney Stevens.)

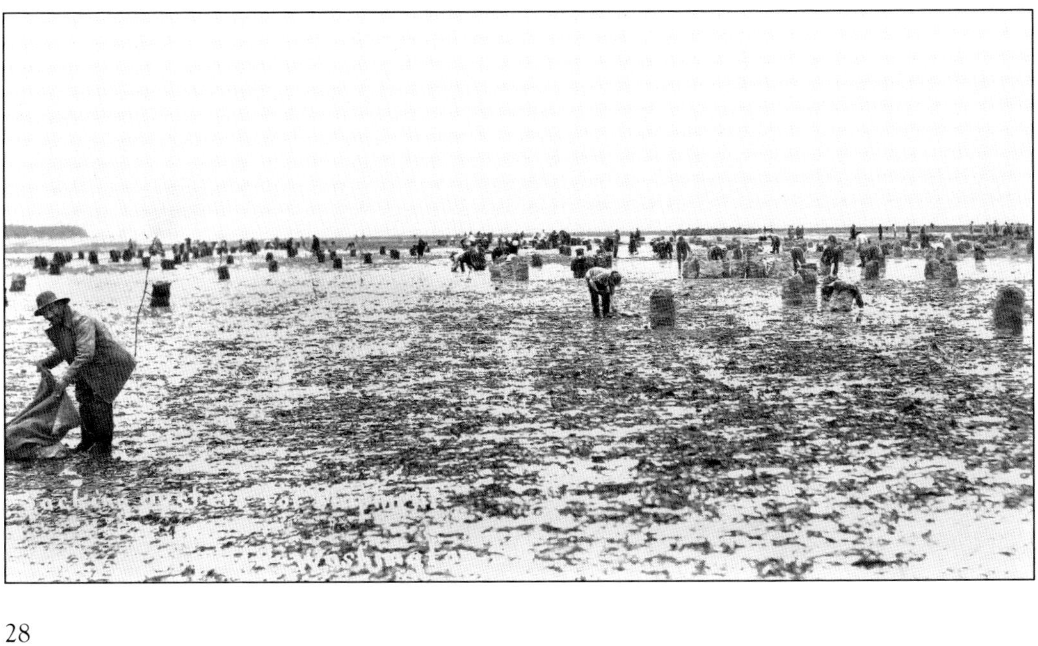

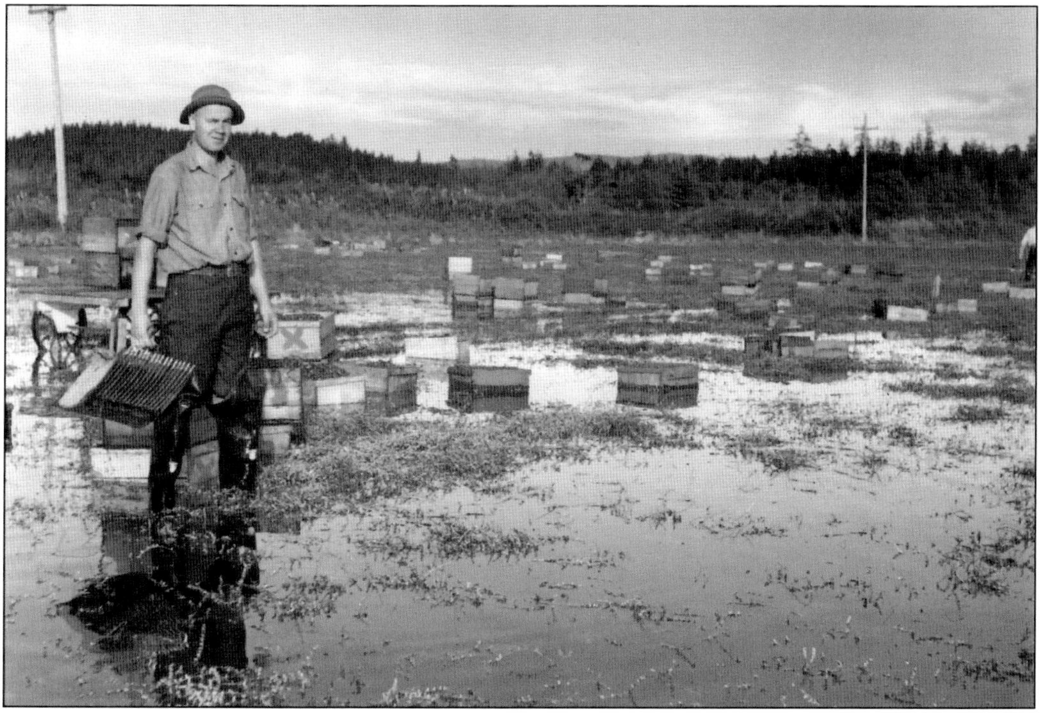

GROWTH IN CRANBERRIES. Though a more seasonal product than oysters, cranberries from local bogs were also a big freight item for the railroad. Since ancient times, native cranberry vines had thrived in the marshy areas of the peninsula, tended and harvested by indigenous peoples. Early white settlers also grew the native cranberries, sometimes on hand-prepared bogs. In 1881, pioneer Anthony Chabot planted 35 acres with vines imported from Cape Cod and hand harvested them several years later—the first domestic cranberries on the North Beach Peninsula. His success inspired others to cultivate cranberries, and soon the railroad was doing a big business shipping fresh cranberries after each autumn harvest. Eventually, the rail line built a large cranberry warehouse near the Ilwaco junction for storage of cranberries from the Black Lake region. (Below, Charlotte Herrold Davis.)

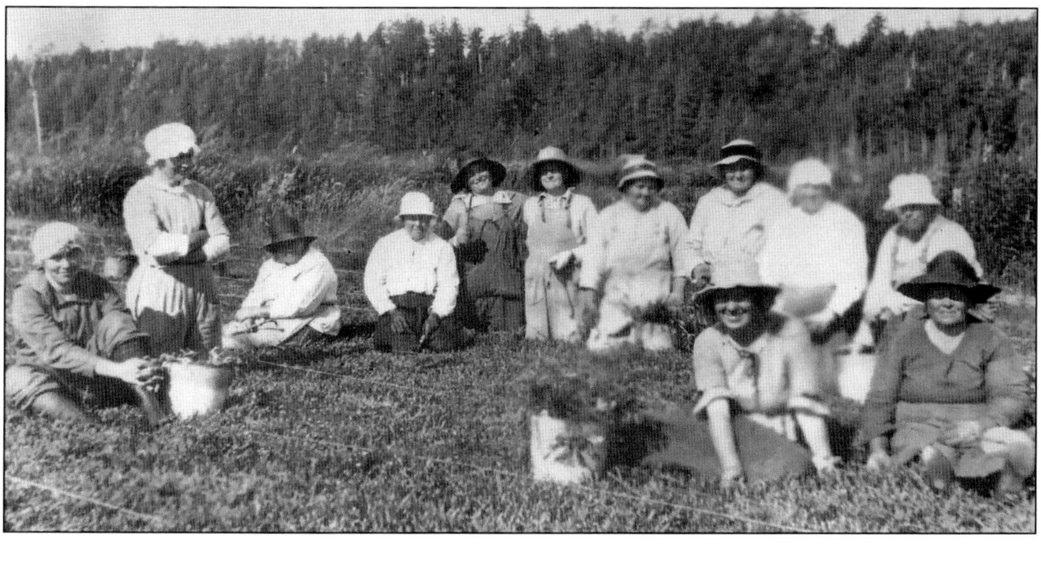

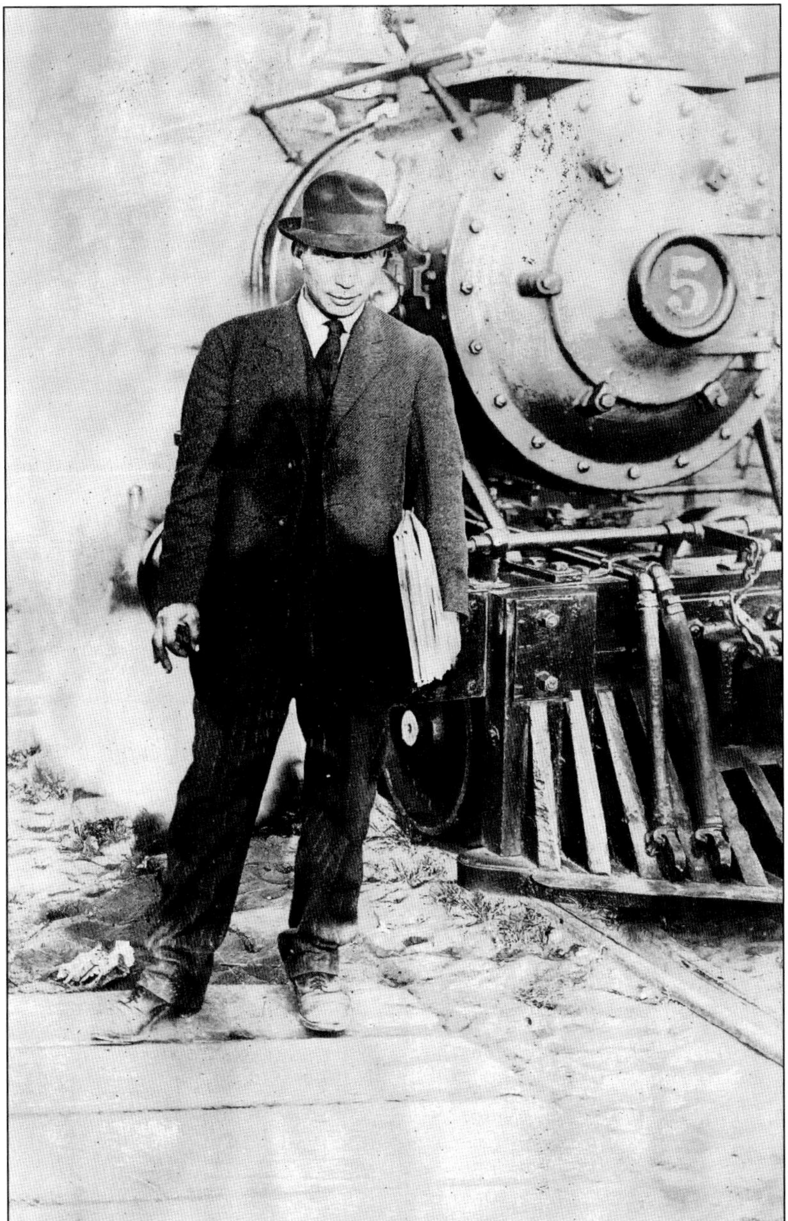

The Mail Must Go! The IR&N continued to bid successfully for the mail contract, which, after all, had been the impetus for the train in the first place. Though pickup and delivery to the train was still by horse and wagon, the schedule was maintained without fail. Helen Espy of Oysterville later remarked that she could write to her daughter in Portland on a Monday and could count on the response in Wednesday's mail, if Medora answered promptly. In addition to the mail, the train brought news in form of the weekly newspapers—the *South Bend Journal*, the *Raymond Herald*, and South Bend's *Willapa Harbor Pilot* from across the bay; the local weeklies, the *Chinook Observer* and the *Ilwaco Tribune*; and each day from Oregon, the *Daily Astorian* and Portland's *Oregonian*. Peninsula residents considered the train their most important link with the outside world. (The Les Wilson family.)

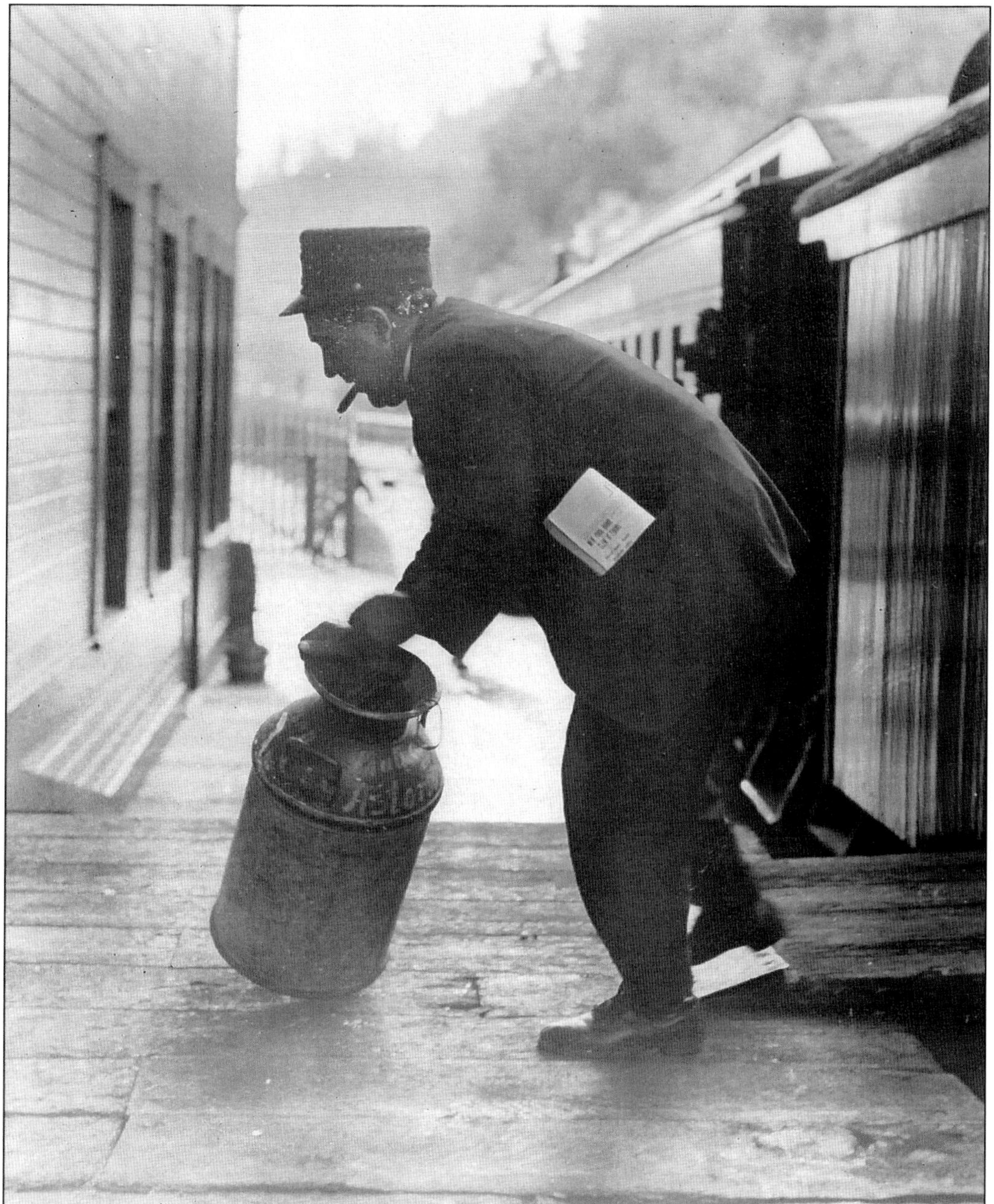

Miscellaneous Freight. Store supplies, household freight, farm produce, breeding stock for dairy farmers—anything and everything needed for daily life on the peninsula now arrived by train. In 2007, ninety-five-year-old Verna Smith Oller, who grew up near Cranberry Station, remembered that 5-gallon cans of cream and whole milk in 10-gallon cans were shipped to the Lower Columbia Dairy in Astoria: "They shipped out cranberries, mostly in half-barrel boxes. Alfalfa, hay, and feed was shipped to Cranberry and part of it stored in the depot. My father kept the key." In an article in the January 21, 1992, *Chinook Observer*, Edith Slingerland Olson (1904–1995) wrote, "Passengers, baggage, food, all things had to be hauled by the train. . . . It's hard to realize that there was not a road of consequence on the whole peninsula."

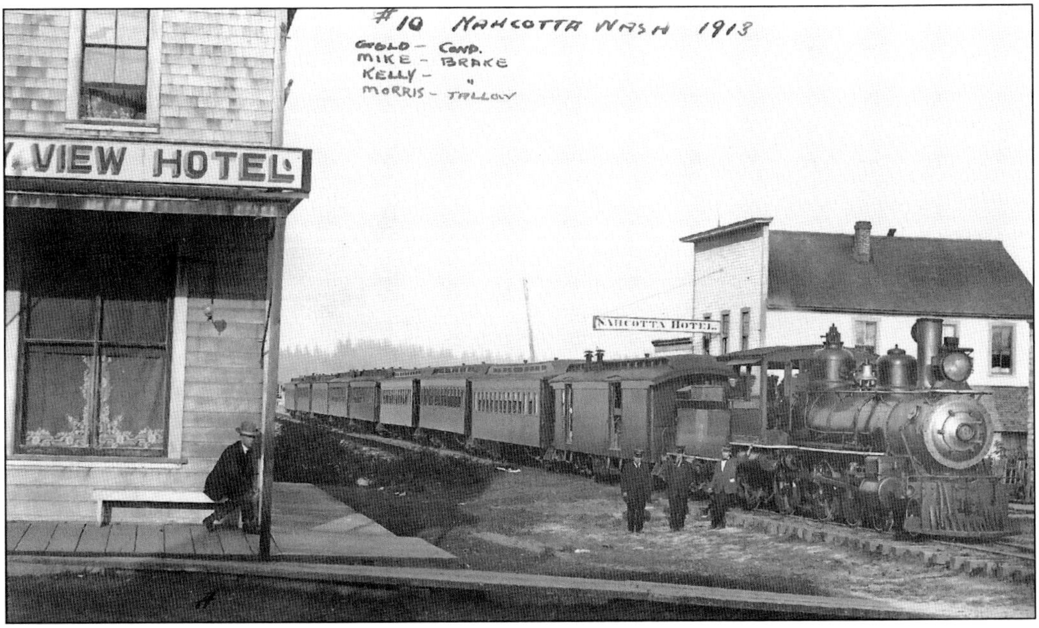

Bone-Bruising Proximity. Though passenger service on the train was a great improvement over the stagecoach, the new line did not offer much in the way of comfort to riders. The 35-pound rails, besides being secondhand, were too light for the equipment, resulting in a rough ride. One passenger was said to have quipped when the ride became a bit smoother, "We must be off the track now." Still, according to Frank Turner in his *Pacific Tribune* "Auld Lang Syne" column, "Many ocean beach affairs had their inception in coaches with seats so narrow that a girl of necessity sat mighty close to her boyfriend. It seemed hard to get away from a man under those circumstances." (Above, Edna Pearson; below, IRM.)

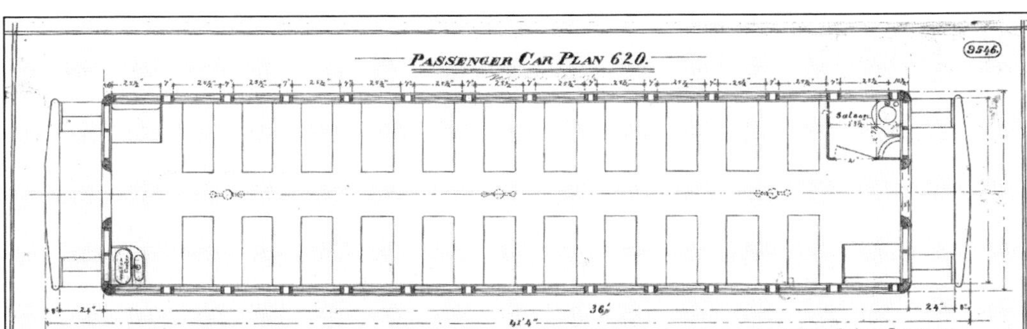

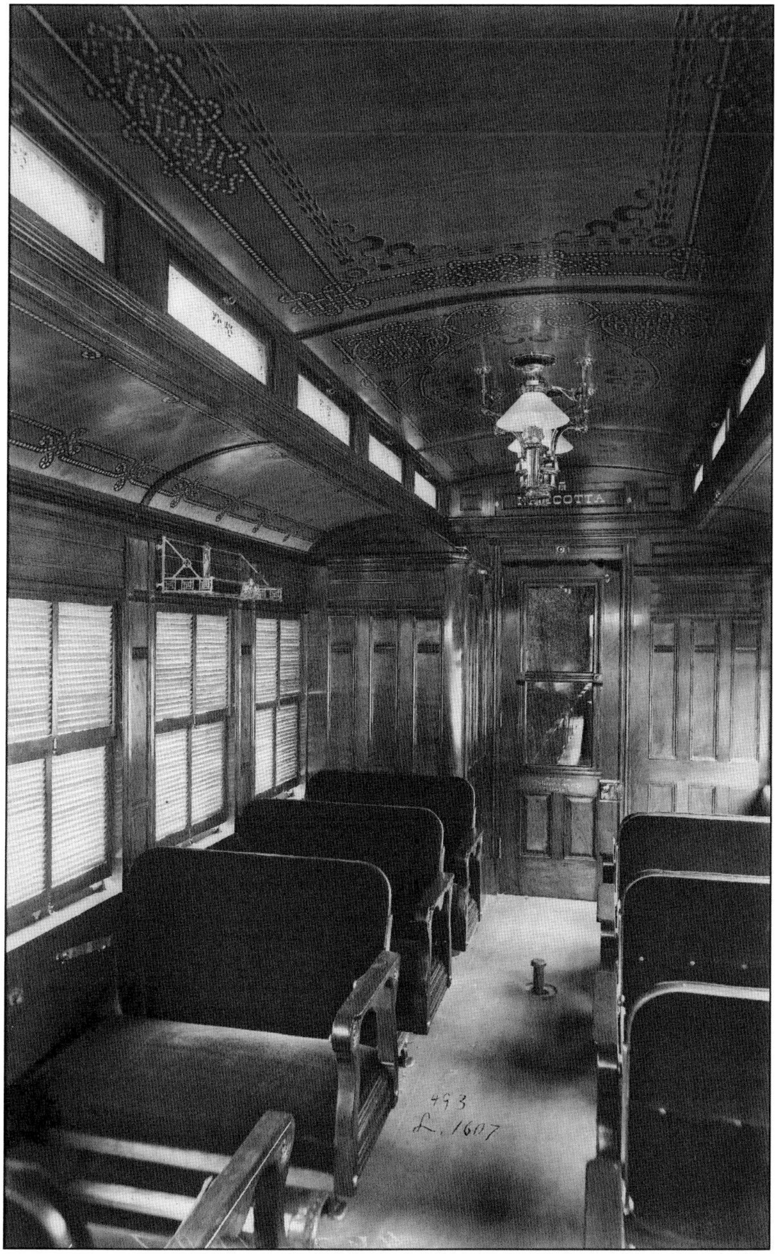

PASSENGER COACHES. North Beach's old-timers have vivid memories of the IR&N passenger coaches. According to Verna Smith Oller, "They had coal burning stoves at one end and a privy at the other end. The toilets only had a seat to sit on and a bottomless bucket that funneled out on to the tracks. It could only be used where the population was sparse. They would come lock the door as we approached populated places and unlock it again after it became appropriate." Charlotte Herrold Davis, who made a once-yearly round-trip on the train, also remembers the train coaches. Her father was manager of the Tokeland Oyster Company's oyster station east of Nahcotta in Willapa Bay. She said, "As soon as school was out for the summer we'd get on the train for Nahcotta on our way to the oyster station. How clean the train cars were! The material on the seats was bright red mohair. They looked like they'd be prickly, but they weren't." (NMAH.)

TRANSPORTATION

THE ILWACO RAILWAY & NAVIGATION CO.

Steamer Nahcotta and Rail Schedule

JUNE, 1905

JUNE	Str. Nahcotta: Astoria A. M.—Lv.	Str. Nahcotta: Ar. Ilwaco Dock	TRAIN LEAVES North Bound: Lv. Ilwaco	Seaview	Long Beach	Breakers	Loomis	Ocean Park	Ar. Nahcotta	TRAIN LEAVES South Bound: Nahcotta Lv	Ocean Park	Loomis	Breakers	Long Beach	Seaview	Ilwaco Ar	Str. Nahcotta: Ilwaco Dock Lv	Str. Nahcotta: Astoria Ar—P. M.	JUNE
M	...	.0	0.8	2.6	4.2	6.1	9.8	13.8	15.3	.0	1.5	5.5	9.2	11.1	12.7	14.5	15.3	......	M
1	7 00	9 00	9 30	9 37	9 50	9 55	10 05	10 20	10 30	1 00	1 03	1 20	1 30	1 35	1 45	2 00	2 30	4 30	1
2	7 30	9 30	10 00	10 07	10 20	10 25	10 35	10 50	11 00	1 00	1 03	1 20	1 30	1 35	1 45	2 00	2 30	4 30	2
3	8 30	10 30	11 00	11 07	11 20	11 25	11 35	11 50	12 00	1 00	1 03	1 20	1 30	1 35	1 45	2 00	2 30	4 30	3
4	9 00	11 00	11 15	11 22	11 35	11 40	11 50	12 05	12 15	1 15	1 18	1 35	1 45	1 50	2 00	2 15	2 30	4 30	4
5	9 30	11 30	11 45	11 52	12 05	12 10	12 20	12 35	12 45	1 30	1 33	1 50	2 00	2 05	2 15	2 30	3 00	5 00	5
6	10 00	12 00	12 15	12 22	12 35	12 40	12 50	1 05	1 15	1 30	1 33	1 50	2 00	2 05	2 15	2 30	3 00	5 00	6
7	4 50	6 50	8 00	8 07	8 20	8 25	8 35	8 50	9 00	1 00	1 03	1 20	1 30	1 35	1 45	2 00	2 30	4 30	7
8	5 40	7 30	8 00	8 07	8 20	8 25	8 35	8 50	9 00	1 00	1 03	1 20	1 30	1 35	1 45	2 00	2 30	4 30	8
9	6 40	8 30	9 00	9 07	9 20	9 25	9 35	9 50	10 00	1 00	1 03	1 20	1 30	1 35	1 45	2 00	2 30	4 30	9
10	7 00	9 10	9 40	9 47	10 00	10 05	10 15	10 30	10 40	1 00	1 03	1 20	1 30	1 35	1 45	2 00	2 30	4 30	10
11	7 30	9 30	9 45	9 52	10 05	10 10	10 20	10 35	10 45	1 00	1 03	1 20	1 30	1 35	1 45	2 00	2 30	4 30	11
12	7 00	9 00	9 30	9 37	9 50	9 55	10 05	10 20	10 30	1 00	1 03	1 20	1 30	1 35	1 45	2 00	2 30	4 30	12
13	7 00	9 00	9 30	9 37	9 50	9 55	10 05	10 20	10 30	1 00	1 03	1 20	1 30	1 35	1 45	2 00	3 00	5 00	13
14	6 30	8 30	9 00	9 07	9 20	9 25	9 35	9 50	10 00	11 30	11 33	11 50	12 00	12 05	12 15	12 30	1 00	3 00	14
15	7 00	9 00	9 30	9 37	9 50	9 55	10 05	10 20	10 30	12 33	12 50	1 20	1 00	1 05	1 15	1 30	2 00	4 00	15
16	7 15	9 15	9 45	9 52	10 05	10 10	10 20	10 35	10 45	1 00	1 03	1 20	1 30	1 35	1 45	2 00	2 30	4 30	16
17	8 00	10 00	10 30	10 37	10 50	10 55	11 05	11 20	11 30	1 00	1 03	1 20	1 30	1 35	1 45	2 00	2 30	4 30	17
18	9 00	11 00	11 30	11 37	11 50	11 55	12 05	12 20	12 30	1 00	1 03	1 20	1 30	1 35	1 45	2 00	2 30	4 30	18
19	9 30	11 30	11 45	11 52	12 05	12 10	12 20	12 35	12 45	1 00	1 03	1 20	1 30	1 35	1 45	2 00	2 30	4 30	19
20	5 00	6 45	8 00	8 07	8 20	8 25	8 35	8 50	9 00	1 00	1 03	1 20	1 30	1 35	1 45	2 00	2 30	4 30	20
21	5 30	7 20	8 00	8 07	8 20	8 25	8 35	8 50	9 00	1 00	1 03	1 20	1 30	1 35	1 45	2 00	2 30	4 30	21
22	6 15	8 10	8 40	8 47	9 00	9 05	9 15	9 30	9 40	1 00	1 03	1 20	1 30	1 35	1 45	2 00	2 30	4 30	22
23	7 00	9 00	9 30	9 37	9 50	9 55	10 05	10 20	10 30	1 00	1 03	1 20	1 30	1 35	1 45	2 00	2 30	4 30	23
24	7 00	9 00	9 30	9 37	9 50	9 55	10 05	10 20	10 30	1 00	1 03	1 20	1 30	1 35	1 45	2 00	2 30	4 30	24
25	7 30	9 30	9 45	9 52	10 05	10 10	10 20	10 35	10 45	1 00	1 03	1 20	1 30	1 35	1 45	2 00	2 30	4 30	25
26	7 00	9 00	9 30	9 37	9 50	9 55	10 05	10 20	10 30	1 00	1 03	1 20	1 30	1 35	1 45	2 00	2 30	4 30	26
27	7 00	9 00	9 30	9 37	9 50	9 55	10 05	10 20	10 30	1 00	1 03	1 20	1 30	1 35	1 45	2 00	2 30	4 30	27
28	7 00	9 00	9 30	9 37	9 50	9 55	10 05	10 20	10 30	1 00	1 03	1 20	1 30	1 35	1 45	2 00	2 30	4 30	28
29	7 00	9 00	9 30	9 37	9 50	9 55	10 05	10 20	10 30	1 00	1 03	1 20	1 30	1 35	1 45	2 00	2 30	4 30	29
30	7 00	9 00	9 30	9 37	9 50	9 55	10 05	10 20	10 30	1 00	1 03	1 20	1 30	1 35	1 45	2 00	2 30	4 30	30

Trains make direct connections at Nahcotta with steamer Reliable to and from South Bend; leaves South Bend 7:30 A. M.; returning, leaves Nahcotta on arrival of train.

DORSEY B. SMITH,
Superintendent.

A. L. CRAIG,
General Passenger Agent.

FAIR AND UNFAIR FARES. Like the quality of service, the rates charged by the railroad were a source of constant discussion and disagreement. At first, inexplicably, northbound passengers had to pay 50¢ more than southbound customers. Rates were finally adjusted to 75¢ for the rail journey from Nahcotta to Ilwaco, and 50¢ for the Columbia River crossing. The Nahcotta agent always referred to the fare to Portland as "four and six," meaning four dollars and six bits, or $4.75. Local fares were kept low. In winter, when there was not enough business to keep a ticket agent at each depot, fares were collected on the train . . . usually. The 10¢ fare from Ocean Park to Nahcotta was often completely disregarded by the conductor since most passengers were neighbors, friends, or even family. (Below, CSRM.)

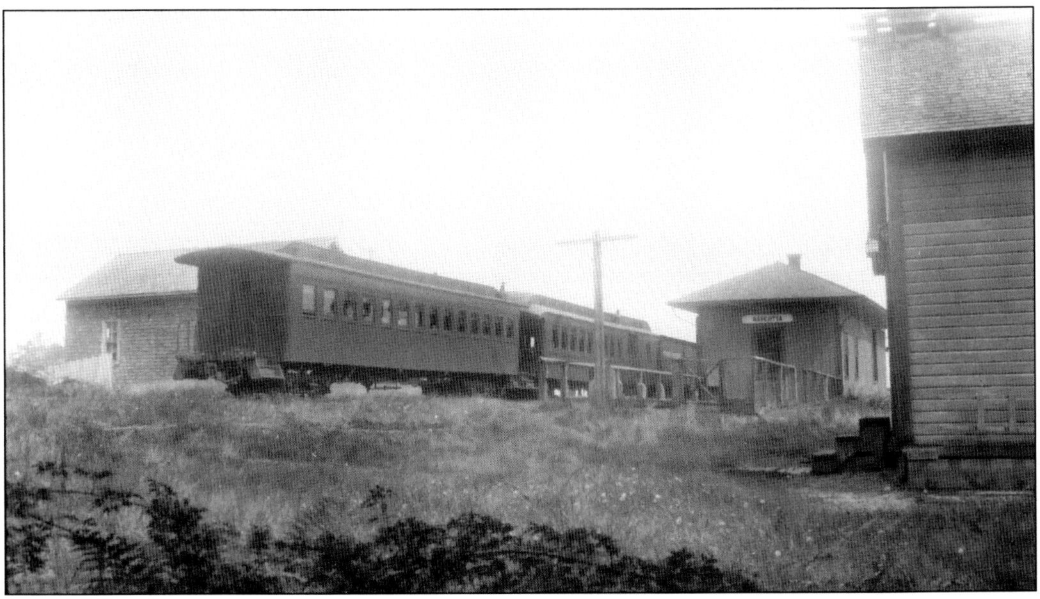

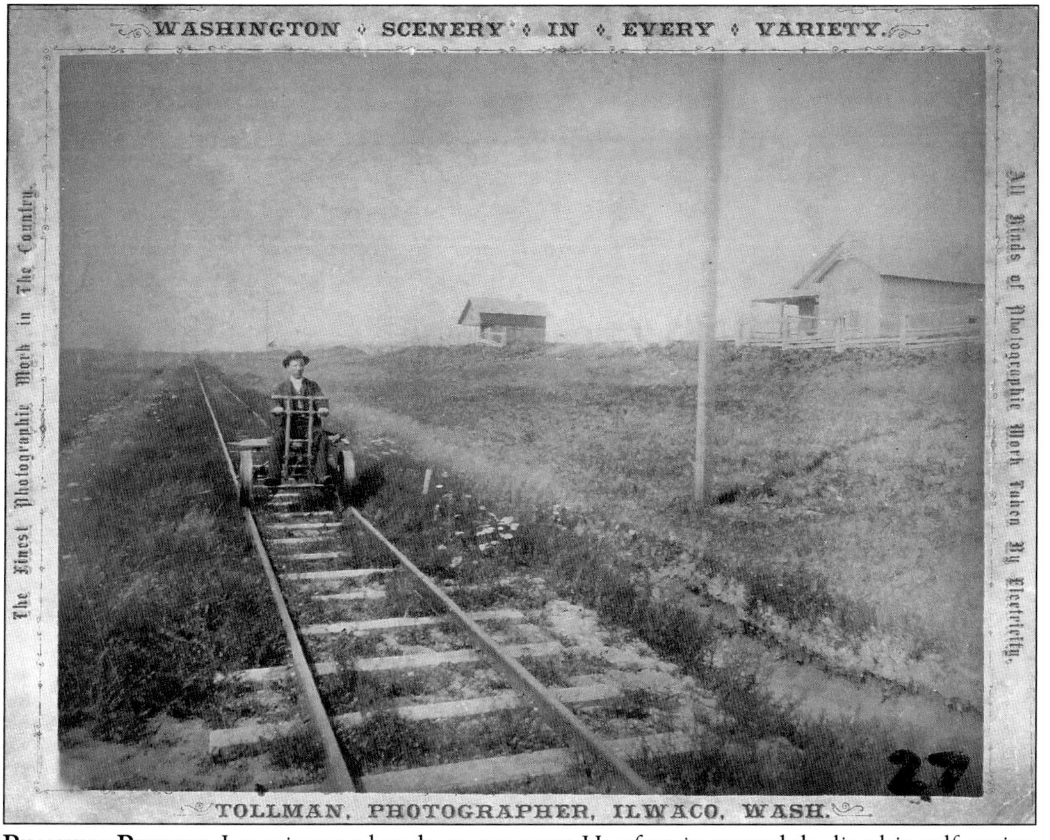

Pinching Pennies. Loomis was a hands-on manager. He often inspected the line himself, acting as his own section boss, and would not allow replacement of any tie unless it was so rotten that the tip of his gold-headed walking stick went completely through it when he struck the tie with it. He also sold cordwood to the railroad for fuel—cut from his own timberland. (Sydney Stevens.)

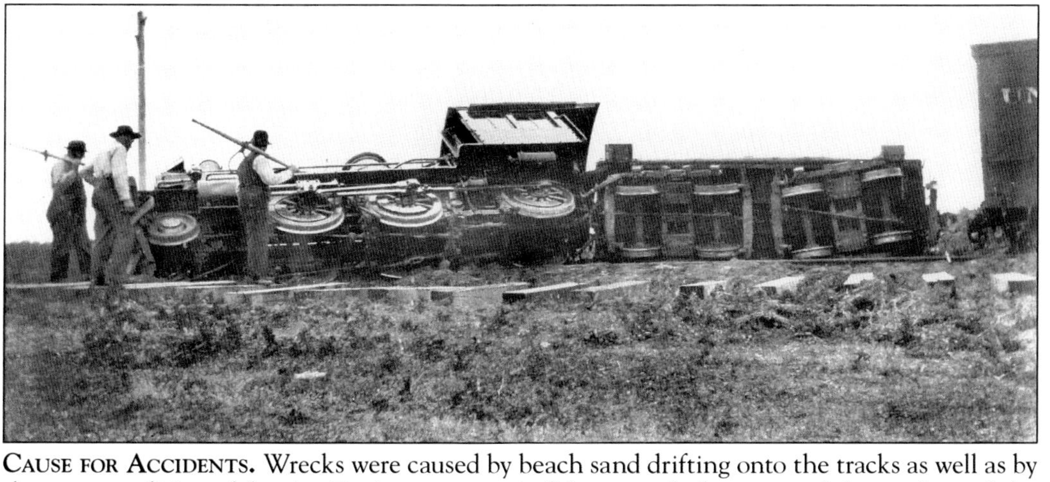

Cause for Accidents. Wrecks were caused by beach sand drifting onto the tracks as well as by the poor condition of the ties. During storms, windblown sand often covered the tracks, and the train stopped while crew members cleared it off. Once, however, the engineer miscalculated the power of his locomotive to push through a drift, and the locomotive turned over. Thankfully, there were no injuries. (Edna Pearson.)

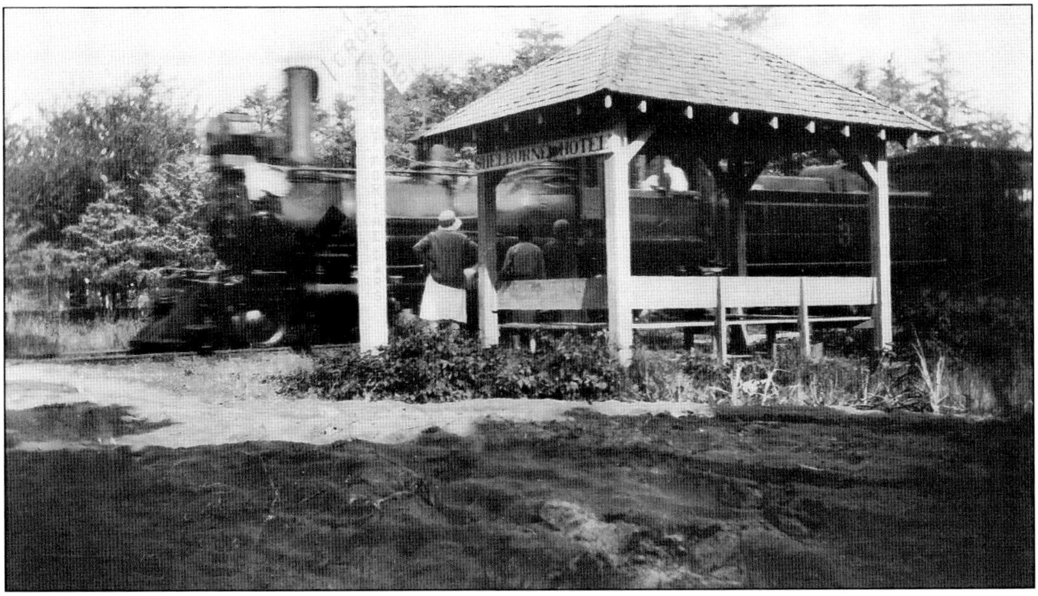

Train Stops. Depots and waiting sheds were built along the route, although during winter when business was slack, the engineer might stop anywhere along the line just to be neighborly. Sometimes the train stopped to pick up a family carrying tired children. Or the journey might be halted so the crew could capture a runaway horse or shoot a bear that was after a farmer's cattle.

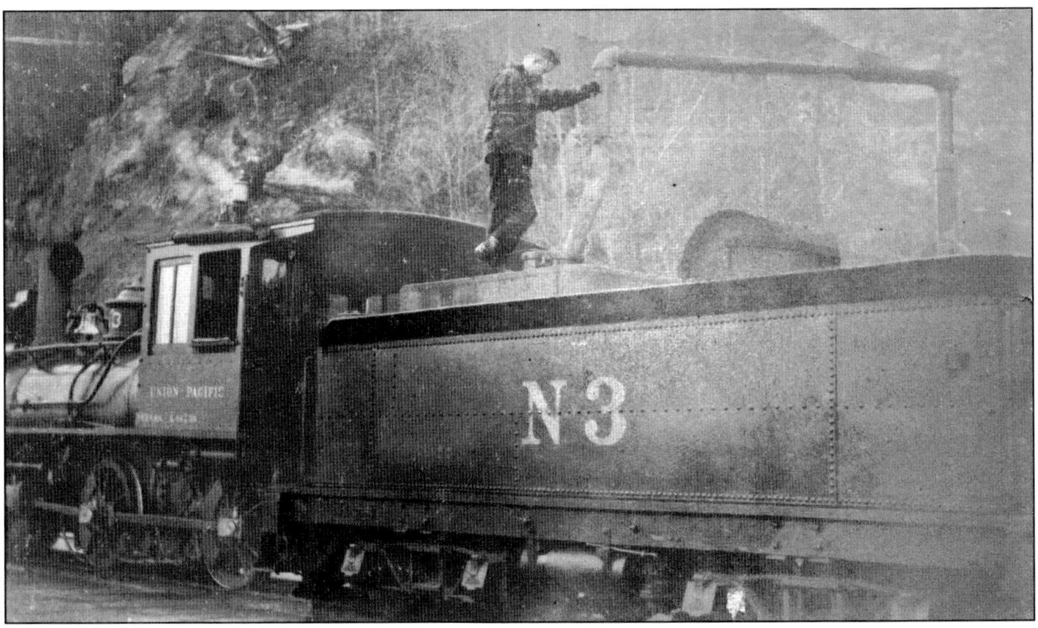

Water Sources. Like its bountiful wood supply, the North Beach Peninsula had easily accessible water. The high water table ensured that by digging just a few feet one would reach fresh water enough to supply innumerable locomotives. Water tanks were located at each terminus and at several points along the route. After the extension was built to Megler, there was a water tower there as well. (Charles Mulvey.)

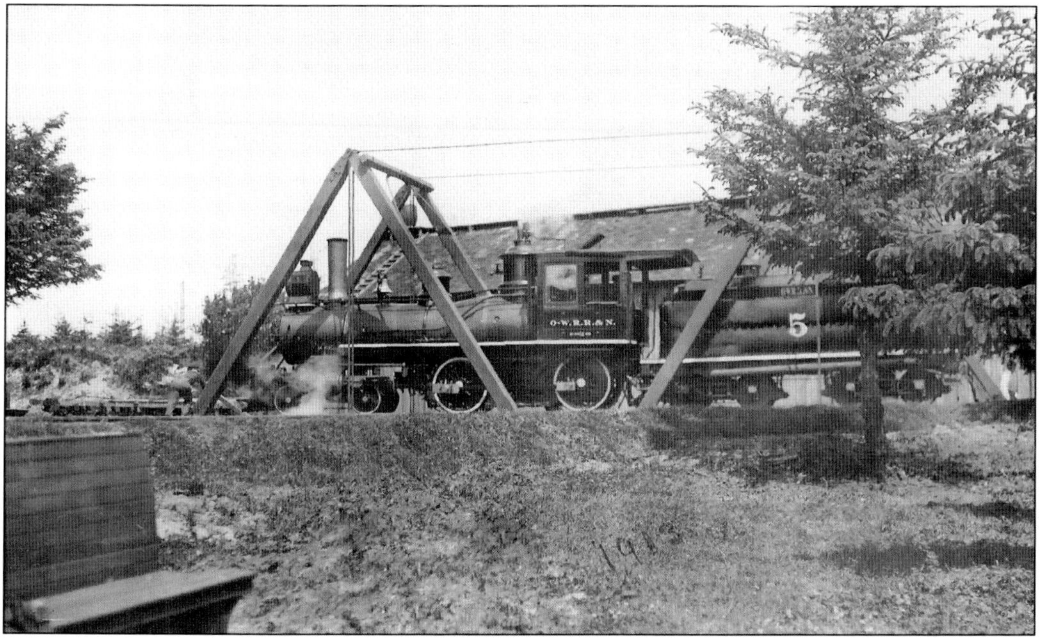

The Flying Switch. As the train rounded the curve heading north out of Ocean Park, there came what Edith Slingerland Olson described as "the best remembered train whistle of all—two longs, one short, one long." The train was on the homeward stretch, downhill into Nahcotta. With the train yard and turntable to the south and the long wharf directly ahead, it was a chance for the crew to have some fun. "A flying switch was illegal even then," Les Wilson would chuckle. "The fireman would uncouple the locomotive and it would head into the yard. Quick-as-a-wink someone would throw the switch so the train would roll straight onto the dock. After the locomotive was turned around, the engineer would back to the train, we'd hook her up, and be ready for the next run." (Above, Edna Pearson.)

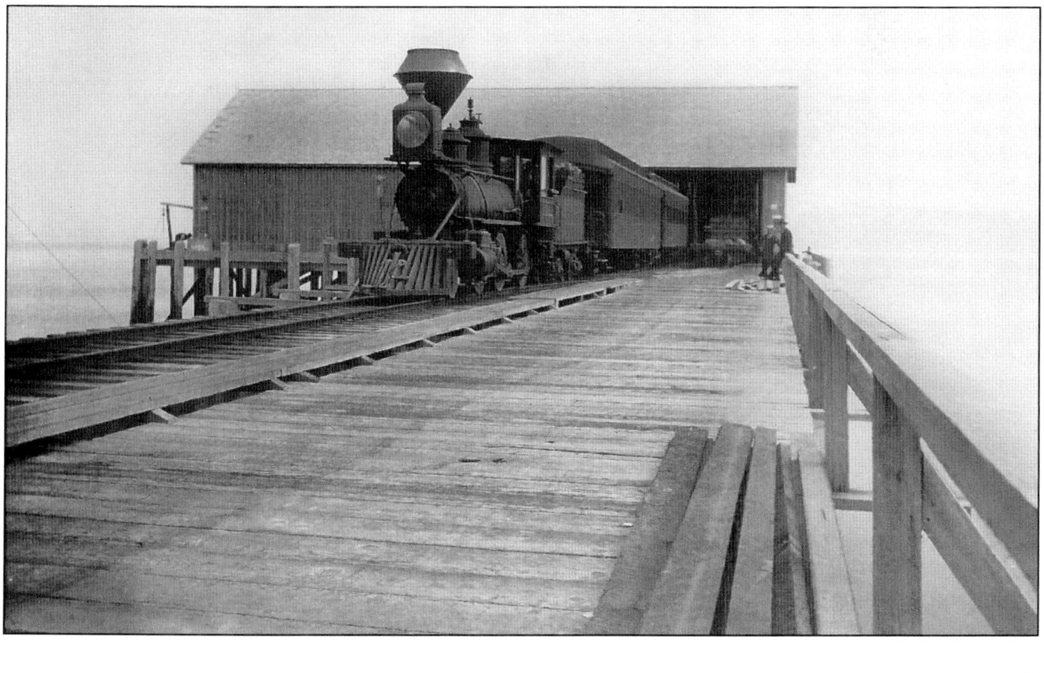

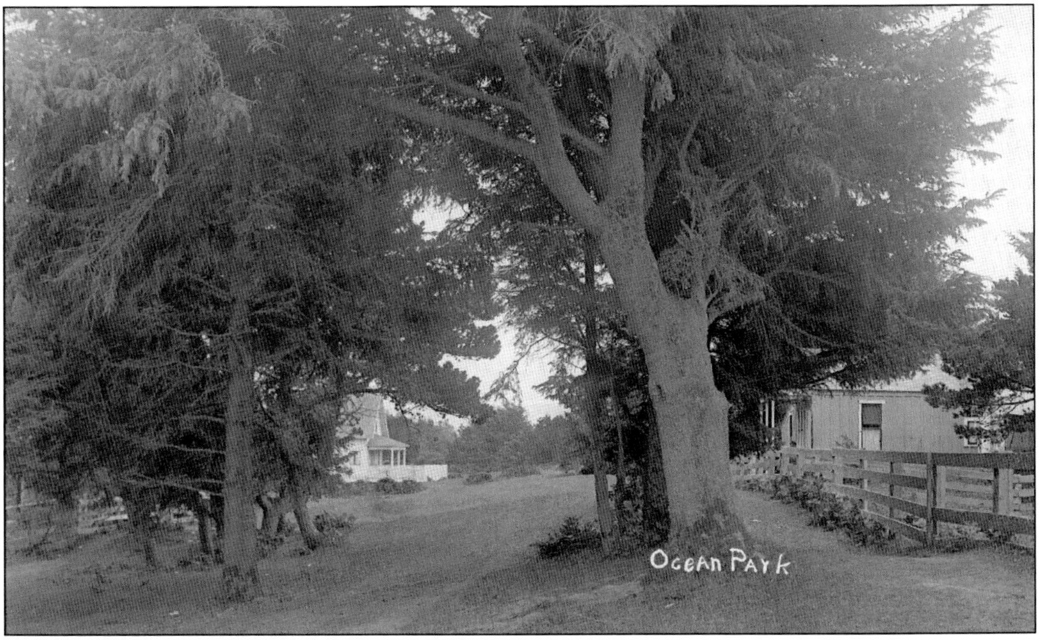

Tree-Shaded Lanes. The quiet residential streets of Ocean Park came to life in the summer when school was out. Dozens of families, escaping from the heat of the inland valleys, arrived to spend the holidays in their cottages by the sea. Some families brought along dogs, horses and buggies, and their own cows to supply milk. Slats were placed on flatcars for transporting the animals. (Sydney Stevens.)

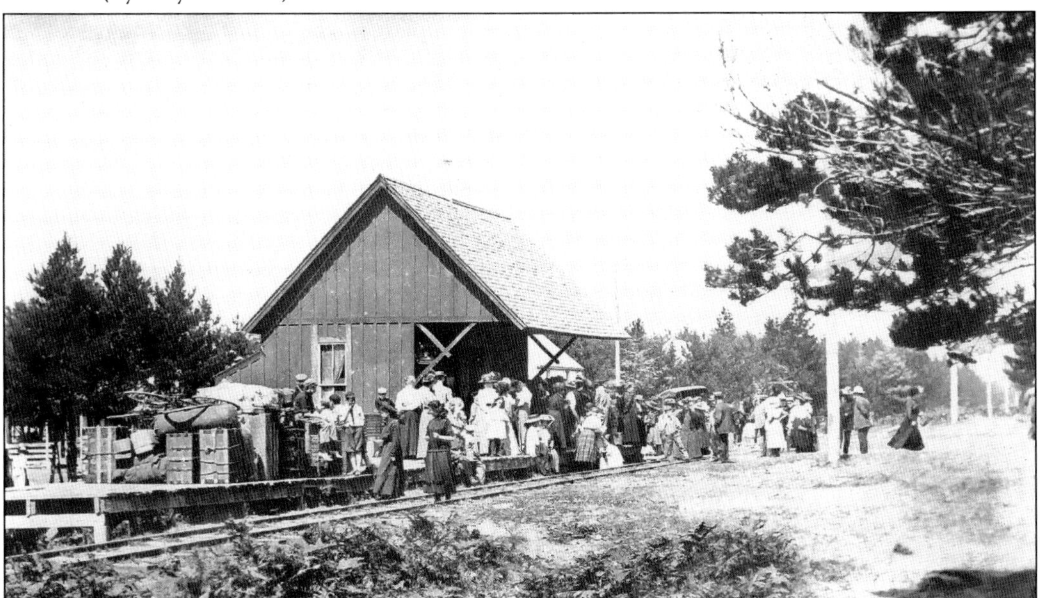

Ocean Park Depot. Ocean Park old-timers still remember that the depot was the center of activity at train time, especially in the summer. Located on the corner of present-day Ridge Street and Bay Avenue, the depot did a booming business in freight and passengers. Tom Beechey, the baggage man, met each summertime train with his horse and wagon, loaded up the luggage, and delivered it to the vacationers' homes.

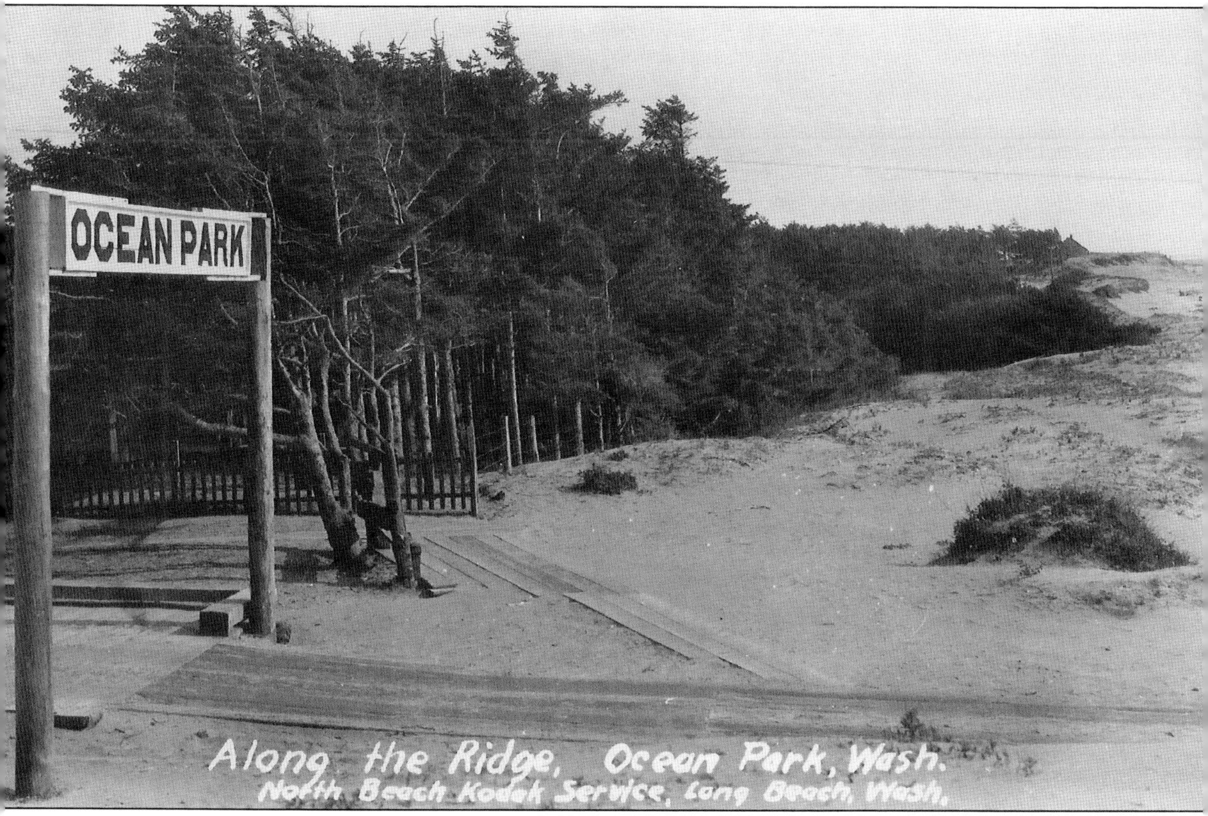

THE OCEAN BEACH. The focal point of Ocean Park was its wide, sandy beach. There summer visitors enjoyed picnic lunches, frolicked in the surf, and partook of the plentiful and readily available seafood—especially Dungeness crab and razor clams. Driftwood brought in by high winter tides was available for the taking and provided an easy source of firewood, for bonfires as well as for home use. (Dobby Wiegardt.)

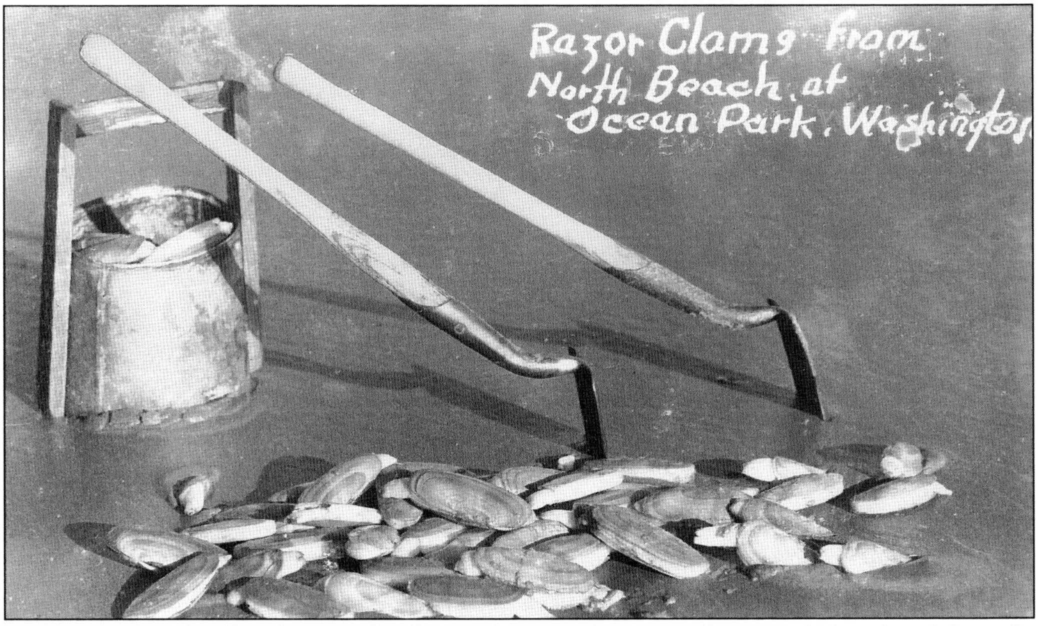

Razor Clams. The abundant supply of razor clams on the peninsula's 28-mile-long beach brought good business to the railroad. Each summer, the promise of clams drew hundreds of tourists to the beach. For some, it was enough to enjoy the delicate flavor of clams fried or in chowder at a favorite hotel dining room. For others, clamming was a sport enjoyed for its own sake. Full-time residents, too, enjoyed these aspects of the razor clam, but there were also those who dug clams commercially for local canneries. Hundreds of boxes of canned clams from Ocean Park canneries were shipped by rail each year. (Below, Dobby Weigardt.)

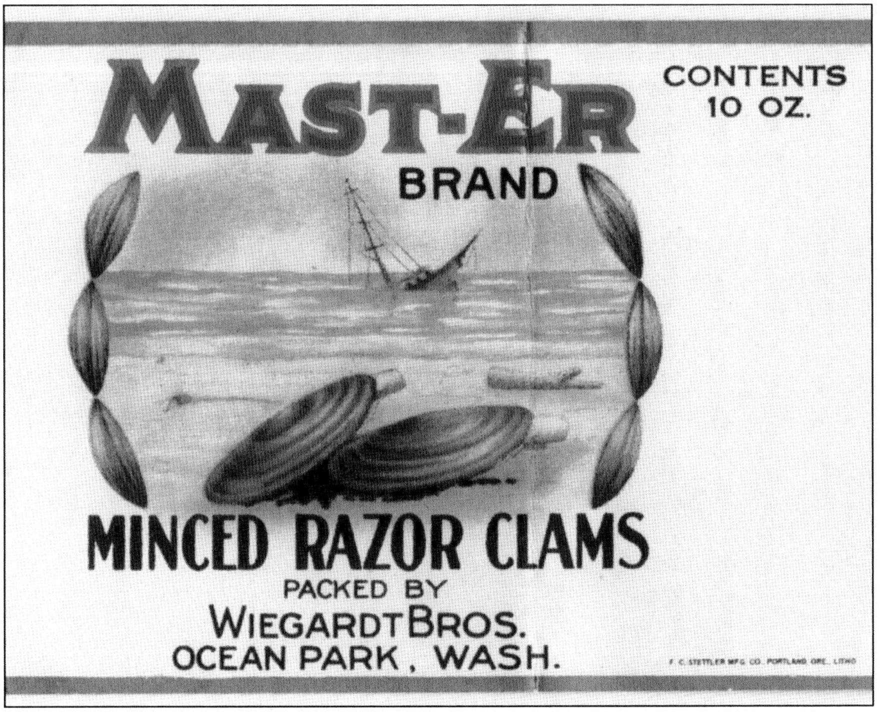

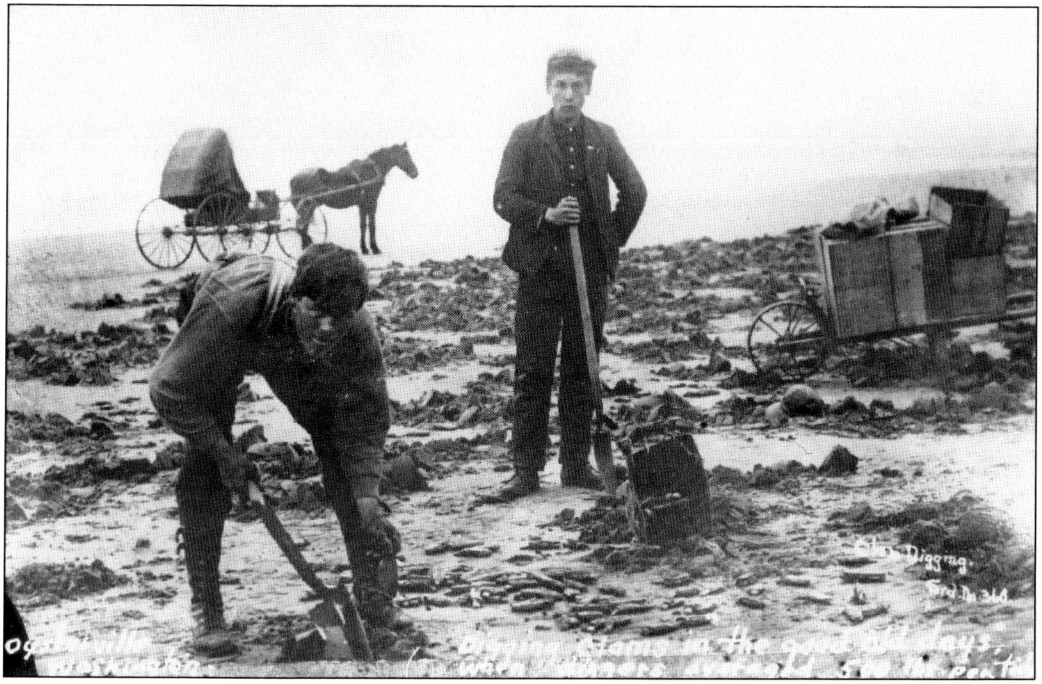

Cash on Delivery. A few hours before low tide, commercial diggers headed for the beach armed with clam shovels they had fashioned from ordinary garden shovels—sides cut off and tapered with the shank bent so that the handle came out at an angle. Diggers claimed such a tool allowed them to work comfortably just by bending over. The cannery trucks threw boxes out along the beach so diggers could pick their spots and get to work. Portable weigh stations were set up where the clams were weighed and paid for on the spot. An experienced clam digger could dig 500 pounds of razor clams on a tide. (Above, Sydney Stevens; below, Dobby Wiegardt.)

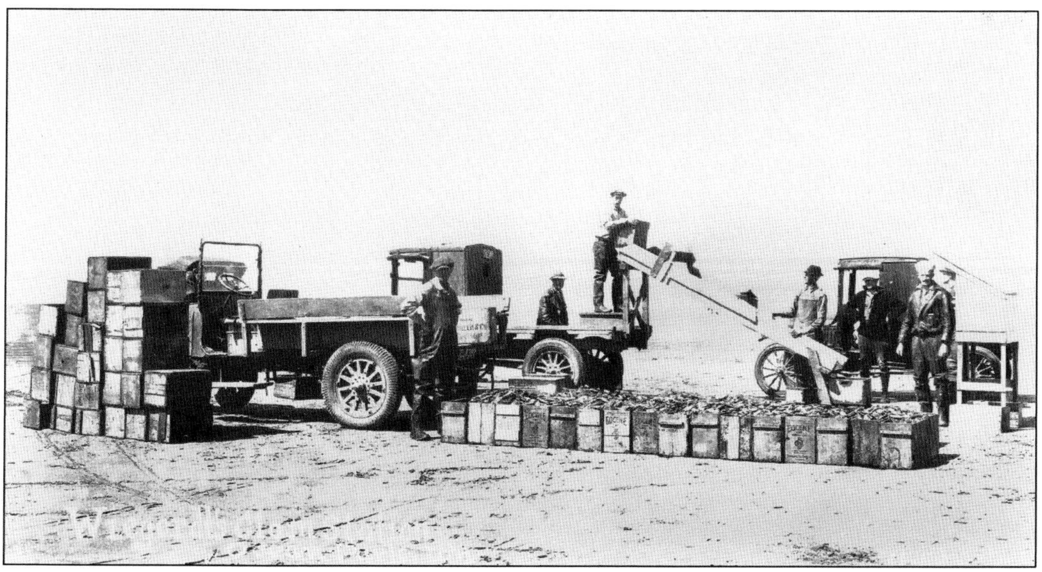

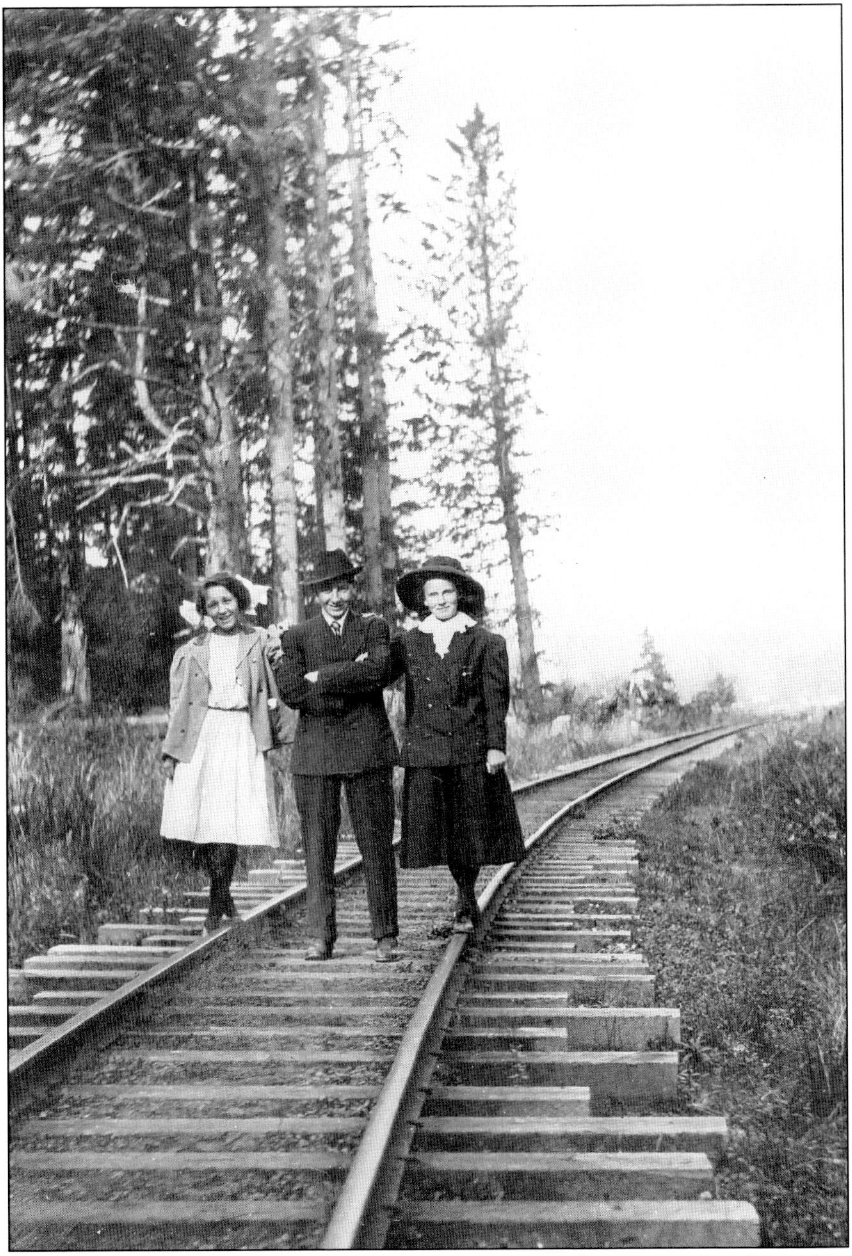

PEDESTRIAN WALKWAY. With few roads of consequence on the peninsula, the railroad tracks became a convenient walkway for pedestrians. "I'm sure we were told not to walk on the tracks," says Dorothy Trondsen Williams, "but we did. My friend Bobby Venable and I used to put our ears to the rails every once in awhile to see if we could hear the train coming. I don't remember if we ever did hear it. Once, when we had walked and walked for what seemed hours and hours, we heard Bobby's mother call us from their porch! I can remember how chagrined we felt to still be so close to home. We must have been five or six." Verna Smith Oller remembers walking along the tracks from her home near Cranberry Station: "We kids walked to Sunday School in Long Beach—three miles down and three miles back. We also went at times to the movies in Long Beach, walking home in the dark."

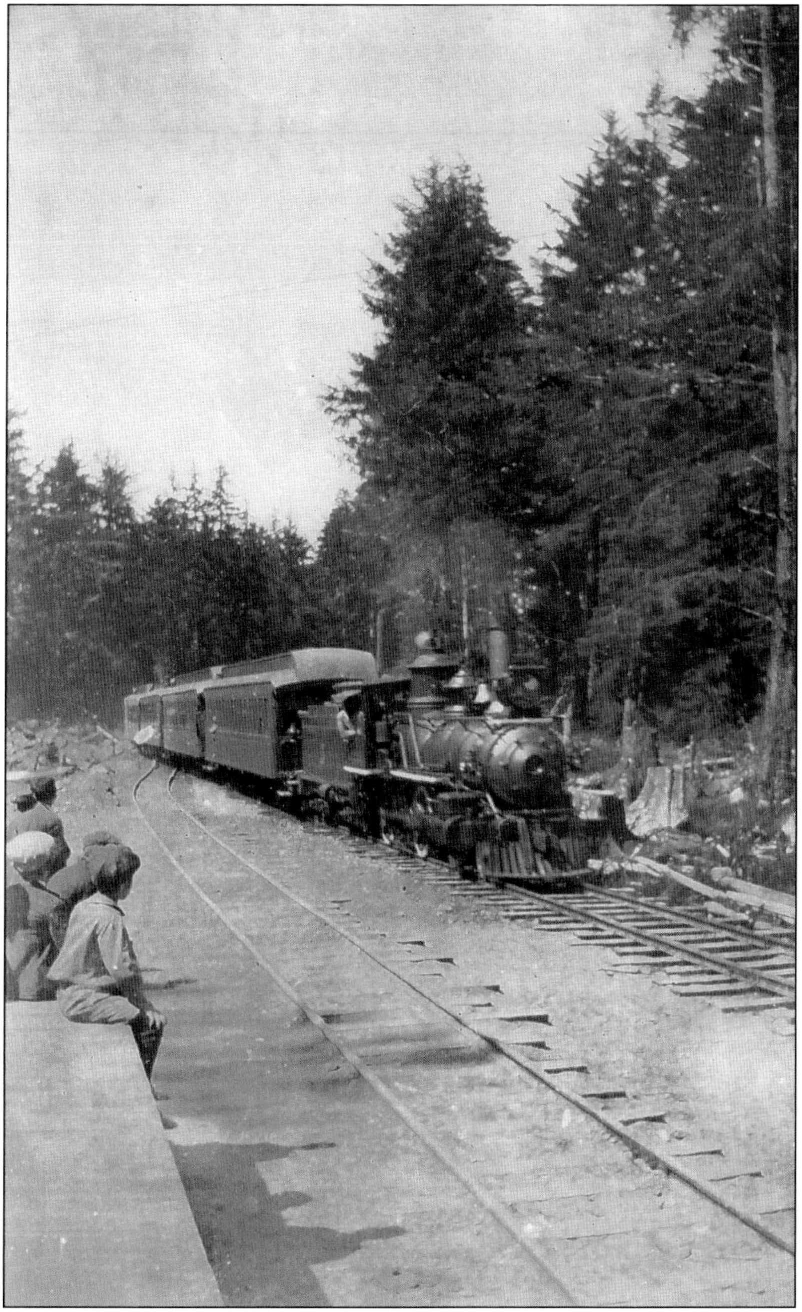

WAITING TO WAVE. Although riding the train left indelible memories, watching it go by was also a highlight for the children of the peninsula. "When I was a little kid we always loved to wave to the engineer when the train went by," remembers Adelle Redfern Beechey, who grew up in Long Beach. "On our way to the beach we'd put bottle caps on the train tracks and then collect them after the train had flattened them. That was a big deal!" Virginia Williams Jones lived in Seaview as a child and has a similar train memory: "The track ran right in front of our house. We would lay pins on the track prior to its arrival. One straight pin, after being run over, became a beautiful small flat sword; two pins crossed were worthy of a decoration on any wall!"

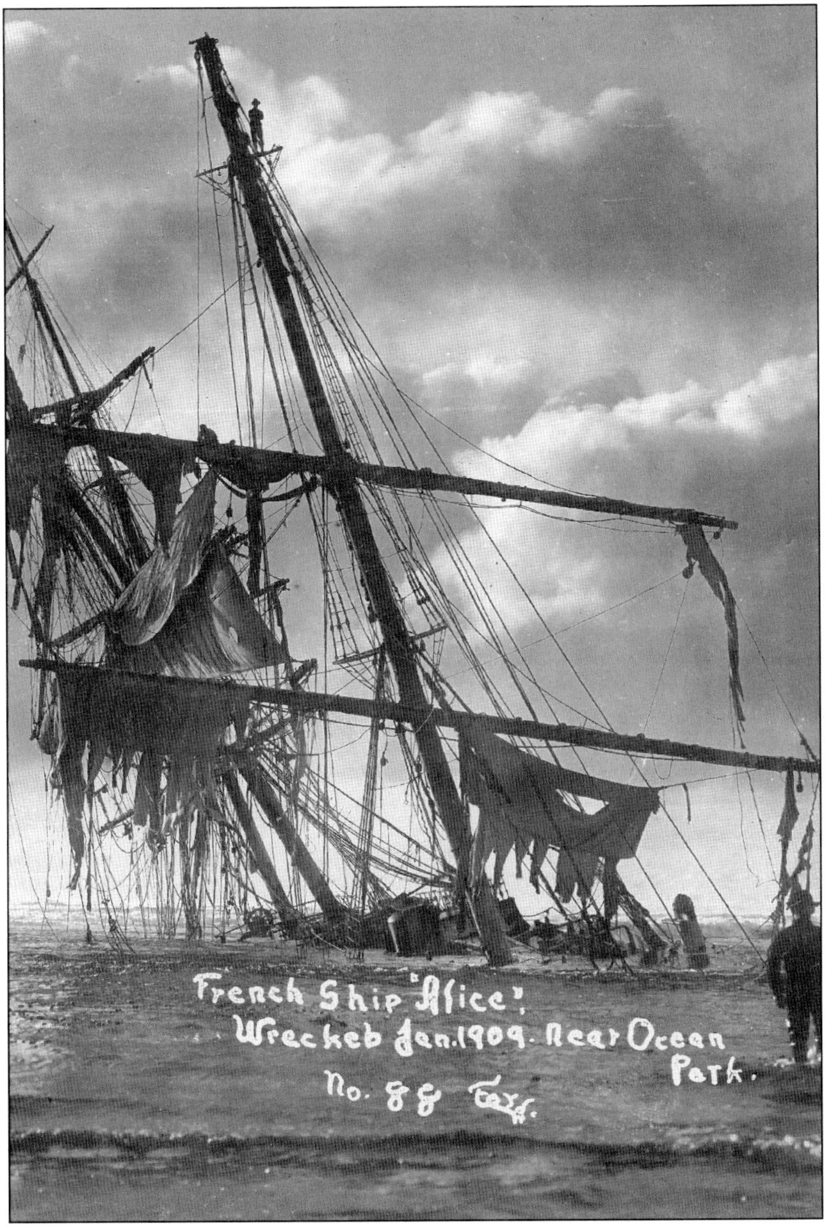

The *Alice*. Before the development of modern navigational aids, shipwrecks were a fairly common occurrence along the North Beach Peninsula. A case in point was the graceful French sailing ship *Alice*, which blew onto the beach just north of Ocean Park early in the morning of Thursday, January 15, 1909. Her cargo of 2,200 tons of cement was immediately catalyzed into hard packets by the saltwater. Plans for her salvage were not even considered. All hands reached shore safely using their own lifeboat, and all live animals and the portable articles of any value were salvaged. Her French crew stayed at the Taylor Hotel in Ocean Park until they could arrange transport home. At Oysterville and Nahcotta, school was let out early that Thursday, giving students a holiday to go see the wreck. During the days that followed, the train ran special excursions, coordinating with the steamers *Shamrock* and *Reliable* so the spectacular sight could be seen by residents from across the bay.

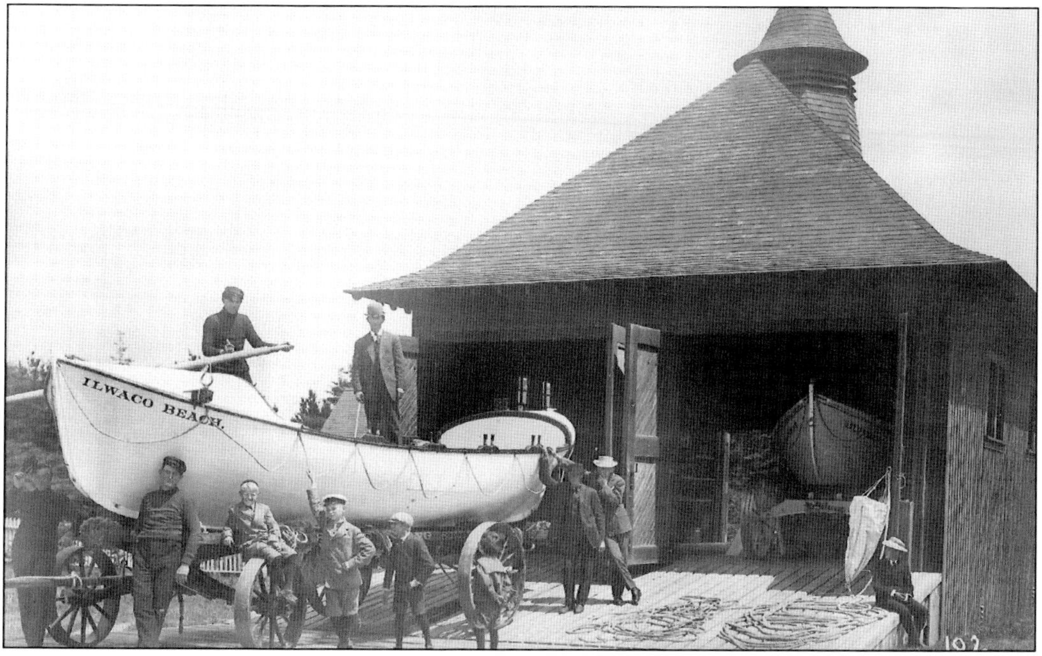

KLIPSAN BEACH LIFE-SAVING STATION. In 1889, due to increasing numbers of shipwrecks along the peninsula beach, the federal government placed a life-saving station on a 2-acre compound at Klipsan Beach, 3 miles south of Ocean Park. A barracks and boathouse were built to accommodate a keeper, his six-man crew, and two New Jersey–style lifeboats. A popular summer Sunday excursion offered by the IR&N was to watch the lifesaving crew drill with breeches buoys and with horse teams trained for surf rescue. More importantly, when a vessel was in peril, the train hauled the lifeboat and its crew from Klipsan to whatever point along the ocean beach they might be needed. For such emergencies, the train could be chartered at any hour of the day or night at a maximum charge of $15. (Below, Sydney Stevens.)

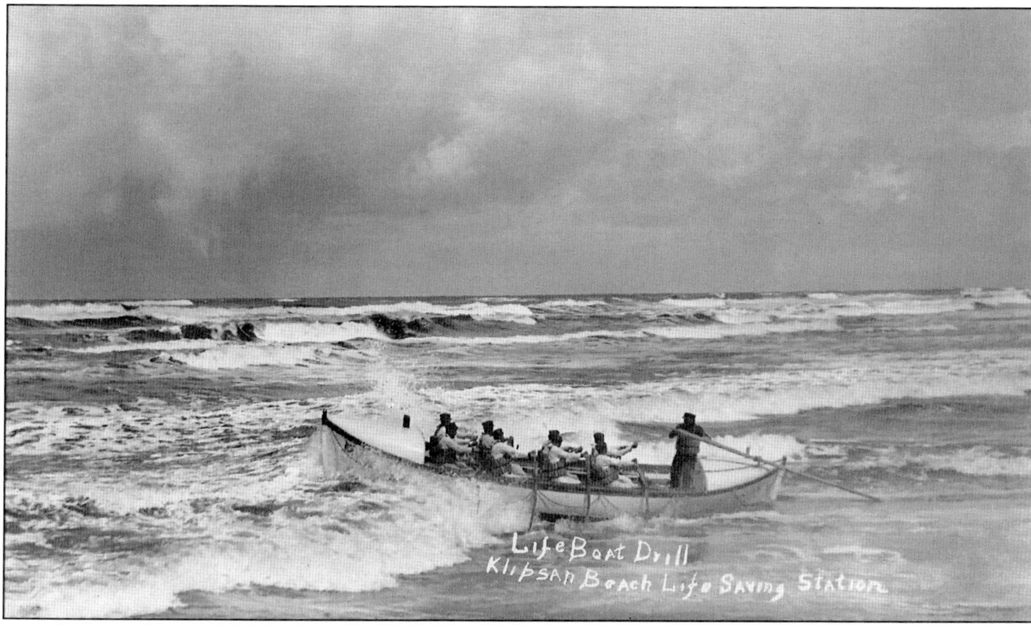

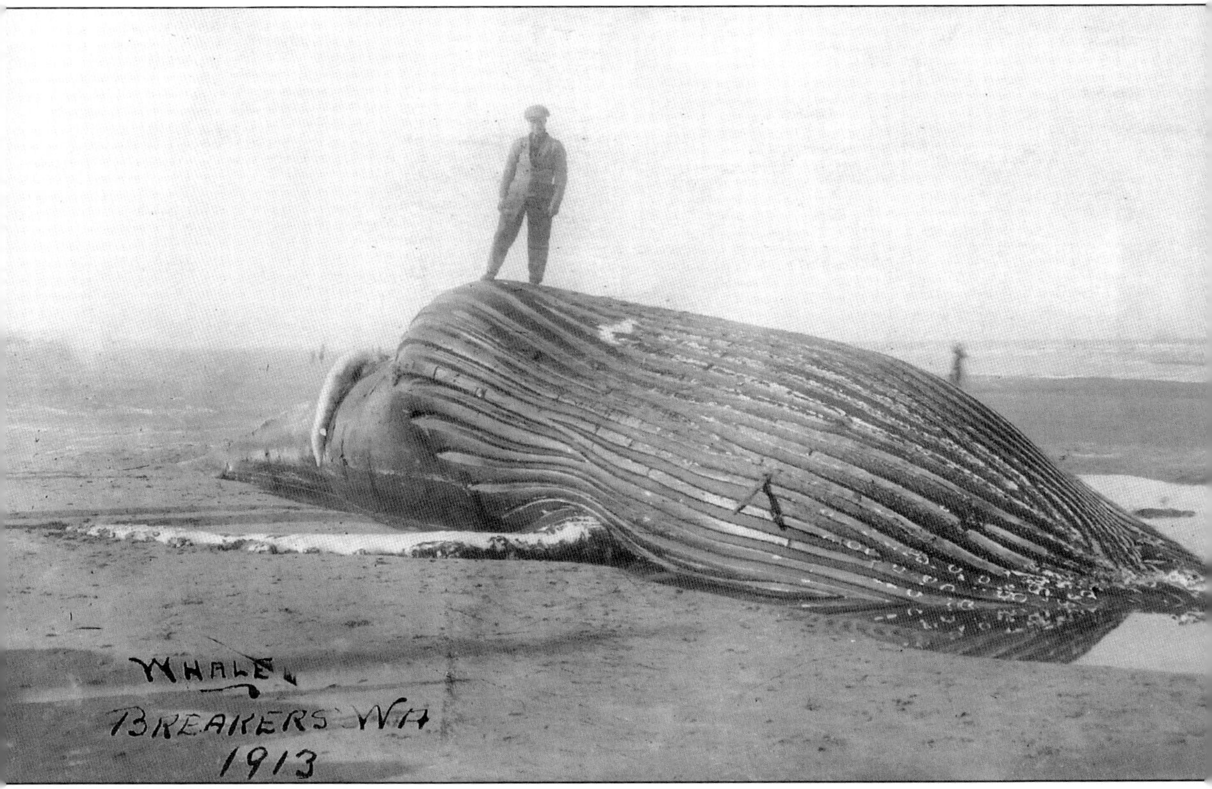

WHALE STATION. From time to time, whales also washed up on the beach. In August 1913, a 47-foot humpback whale washed in near Cranberry. A special boat and rail excursion was offered from South Bend at a combined fare of $2.05. The railway company built a station platform, and a boardwalk was laid to where the leviathan rested. The stop became "Whale Station" and was a popular attraction, even after it became exceedingly odiferous. Loomis finally succeeded in having the carcass removed by the Ocosta Whaling Station. Twenty years earlier, another humpback floated in on the beach south of Ocean Park. John Hudson, a tailor and taxidermist in South Bend, took possession of the beast at Loomis's invitation and, with the help of four Native Americans from Bay Center, prepared it for exhibition at the Columbian Exposition in Chicago. For a month, they worked at their smelly task while nearby residents used disinfectants and burning rags to offset the odor. The purified skeleton was loaded on a flat car, provided by Loomis, and made the journey to Chicago.

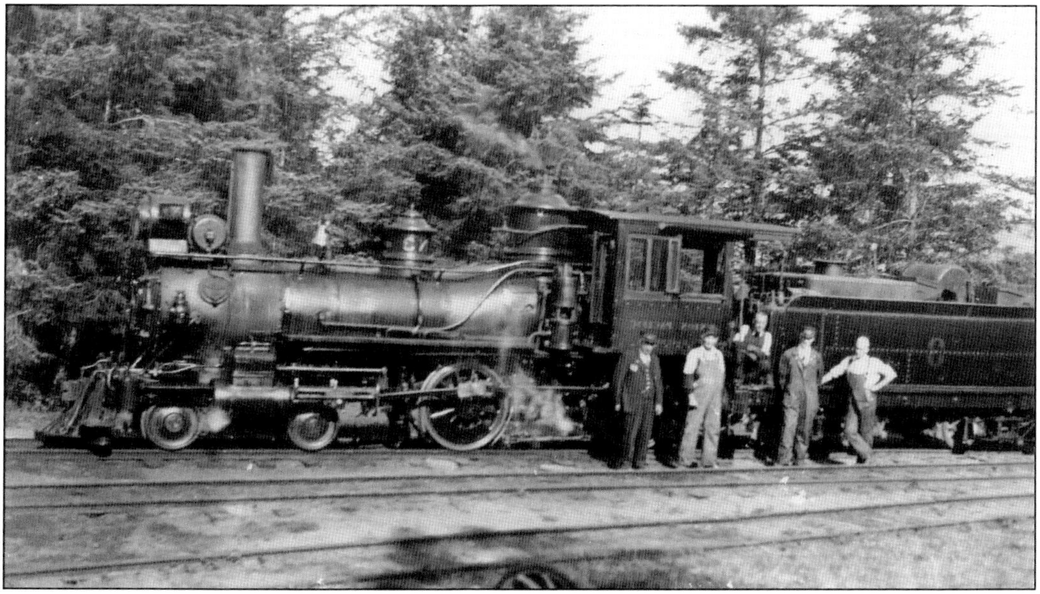

Off Season. Winter was usually quiet on the peninsula and on the railroad. Visitors were few and far between, and full-time residents had little reason to ride the train. A business trip or doctor's appointment in Astoria or South Bend might call for a train trip, but most day-to-day activities occurred close to home—even work. The railroad, instead of running four round-trips a day as it did in the summer, cut back to two—a morning and an afternoon run, one from Ilwaco north and one from Nahcotta south. Train crews sometimes had a bit of time on their hands and were happy to strike a proud pose or even to take time to decorate a locomotive in the spirit of the Christmas season. (Below, Matt Winters.)

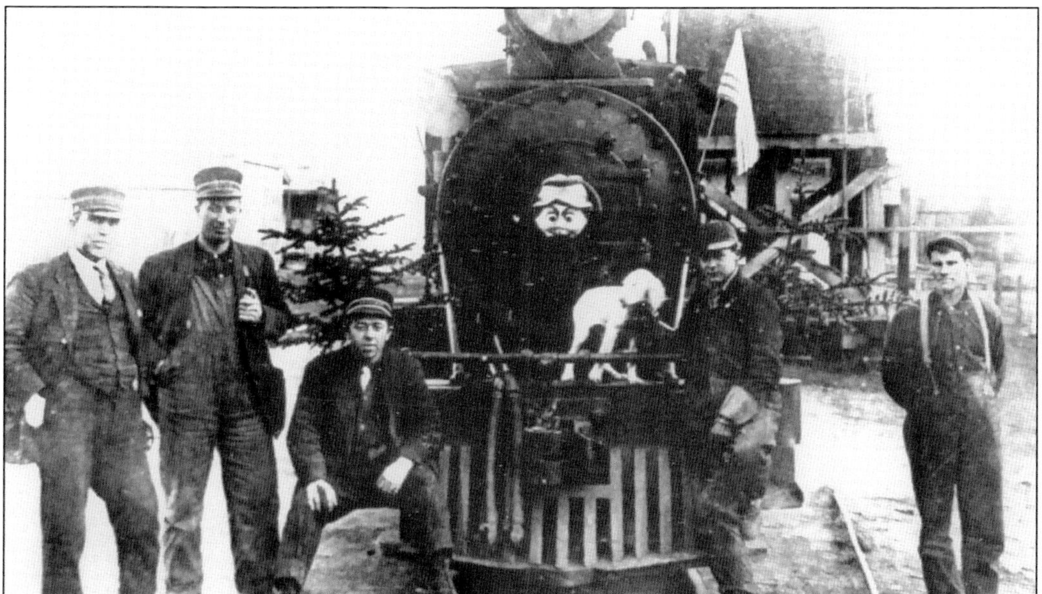

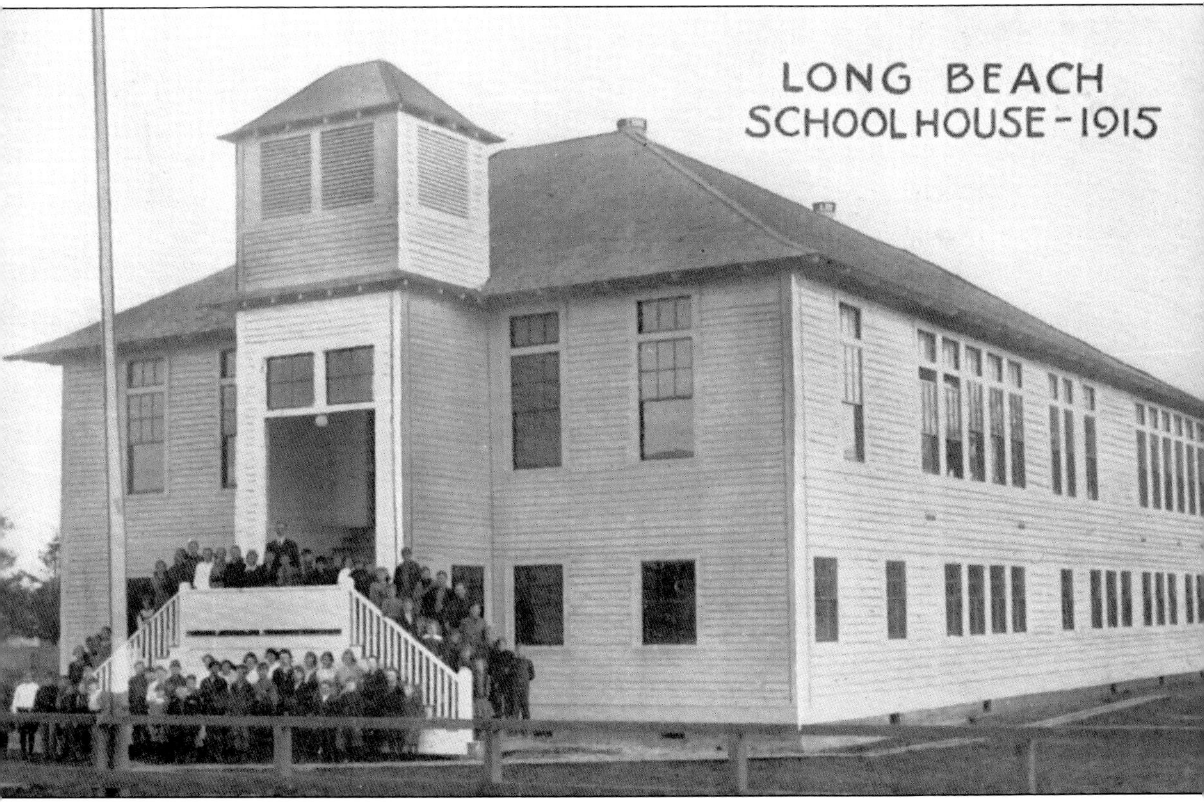

GRADE SCHOOL RIDERS. For students who lived near the rail line and could afford the price of a ticket, there was the possibility of getting to school by train. Verna Smith Oller and her older brother and sister rode from Cranberry Station to Long Beach School. "The connections were pretty good," she remembers, "but we had to leave school a little early. I had misbehaved at school one day, and the teacher locked me in the closet, which had a window in it. As I looked out the window, I saw my brother and sister heading for the train. I sure started crying. I don't know if the teacher heard me or remembered; anyway, she let me out and we all caught the train for home. There were two girls from Ocean Park who also rode on the train going to high school in Ilwaco. And one boy rode the train to Chinook School."

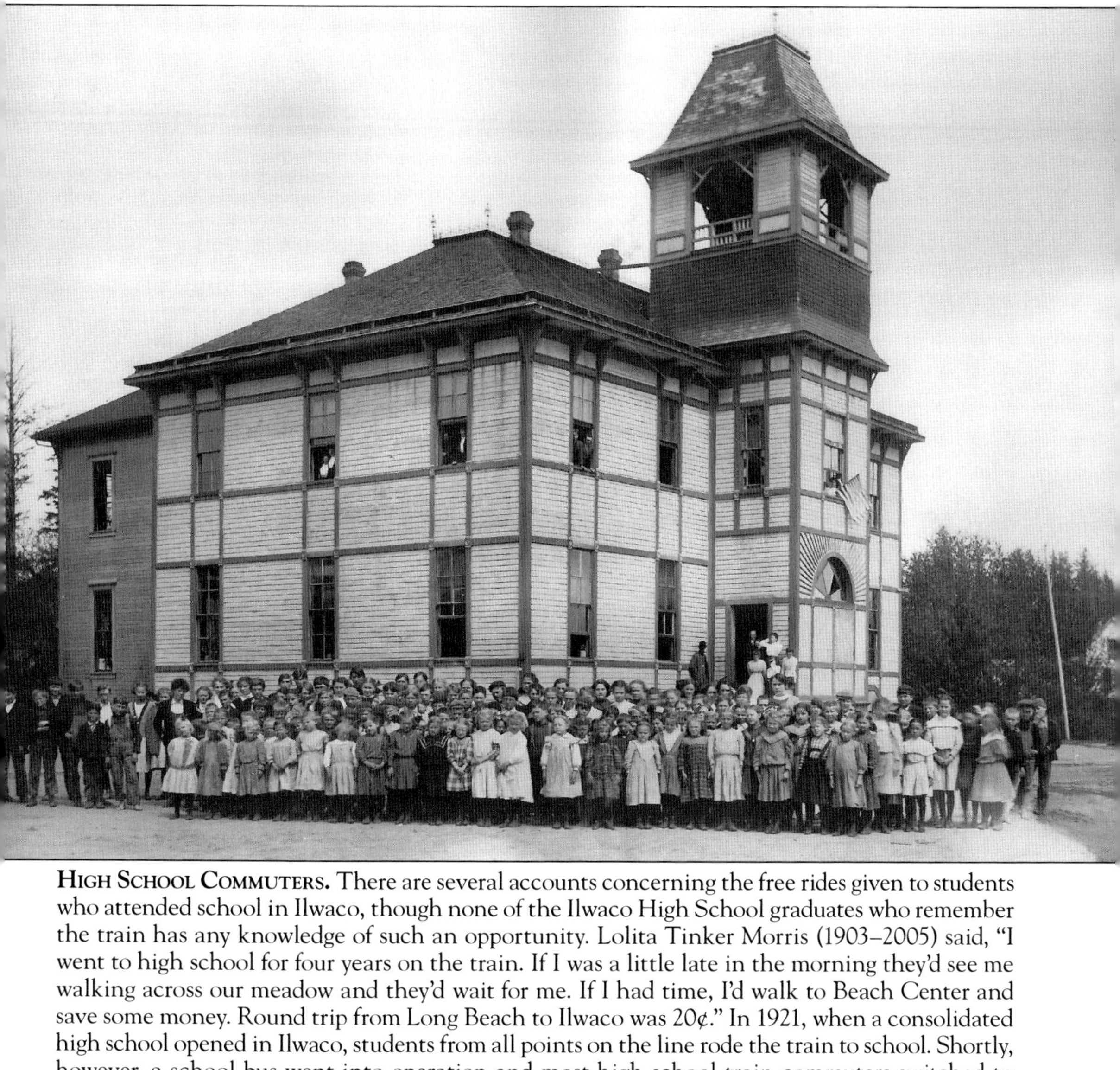

High School Commuters. There are several accounts concerning the free rides given to students who attended school in Ilwaco, though none of the Ilwaco High School graduates who remember the train has any knowledge of such an opportunity. Lolita Tinker Morris (1903–2005) said, "I went to high school for four years on the train. If I was a little late in the morning they'd see me walking across our meadow and they'd wait for me. If I had time, I'd walk to Beach Center and save some money. Round trip from Long Beach to Ilwaco was 20¢." In 1921, when a consolidated high school opened in Ilwaco, students from all points on the line rode the train to school. Shortly, however, a school bus went into operation and most high school train commuters switched to free transport. Said Virginia Williams Jones, "We wished we could take the train to school, but it was too expensive, so we rode the school bus."

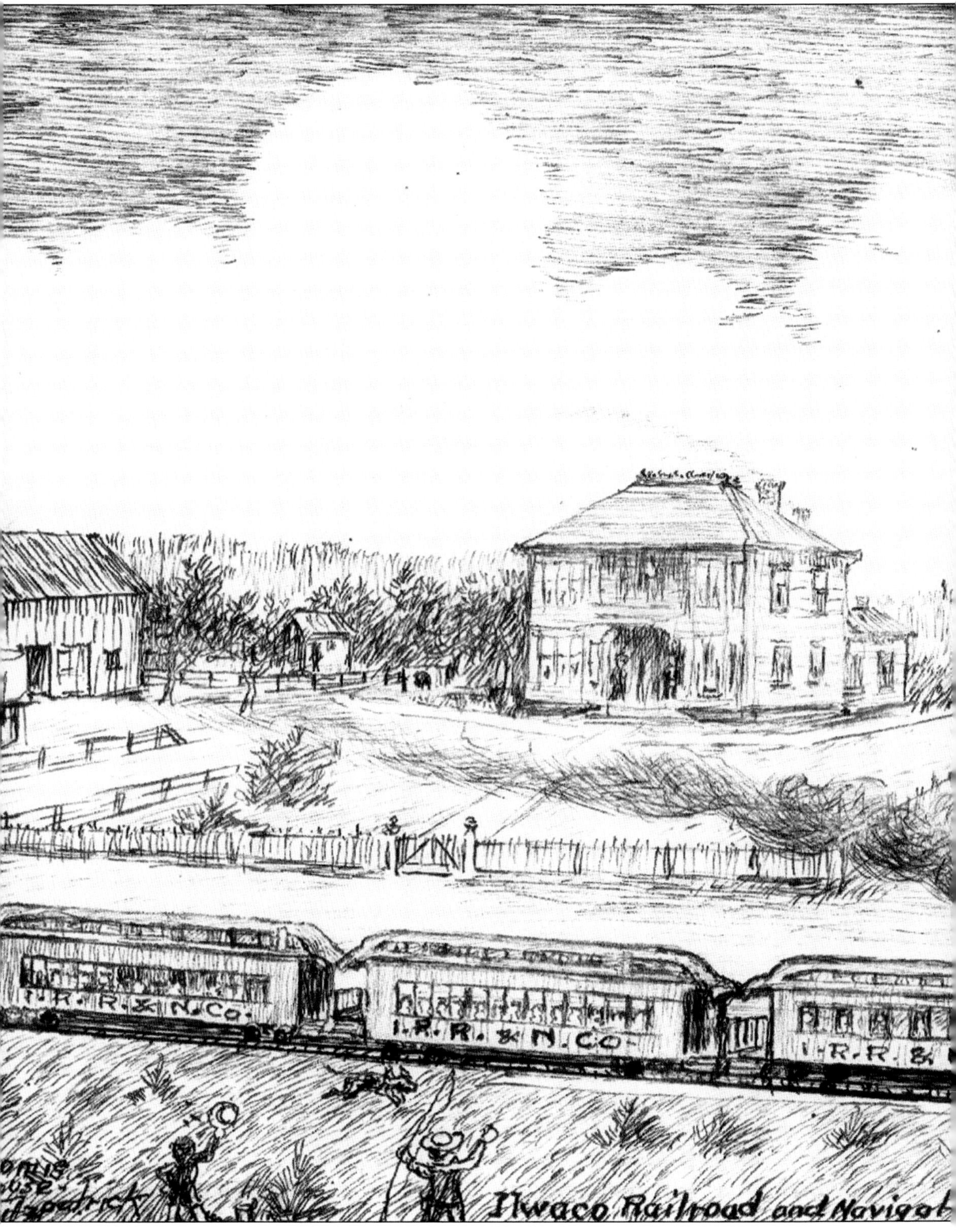
I.R.R.&N.Co.
I.R.R.&N.Co.
I.R.R.&
Ilwaco Railroad and Navigat

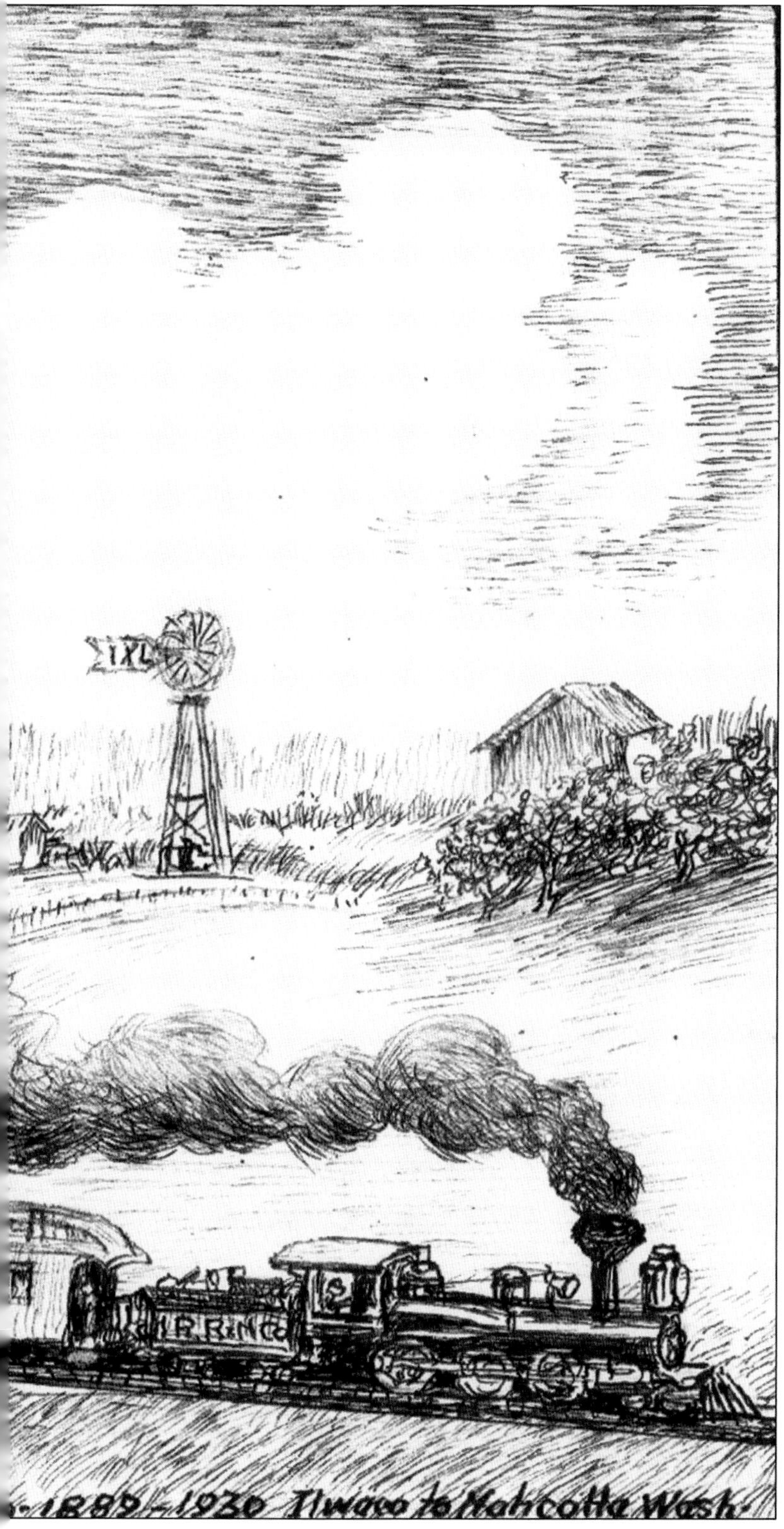

Loomis Station. While he was building his railroad, Loomis was also building a grand Victorian mansion just south of Klipsan Beach. Four tall bay windows faced the ocean, heavy cornices adorned the roof, and a quartette of ornate fireplaces heated two stately parlors and two masters' bedrooms. With 12-foot ceilings, polychrome scrolls around the main light fixtures, paneled walls topped with decorative moldings, a conservatory, and eight bedrooms, it was said to be the most magnificent structure in the county—worthy of Loomis himself, who was known for his wide-brimmed hat, black frock coat, and gold-headed walking stick. In the fenced enclosure surrounding the house were barns, blacksmith shop, and lodgings for helpers. The mansion was a stop for the train, but according to Loomis's granddaughter, Ellen Loomis McMurry, it was mostly for the family's convenience. (Sydney Stevens.)

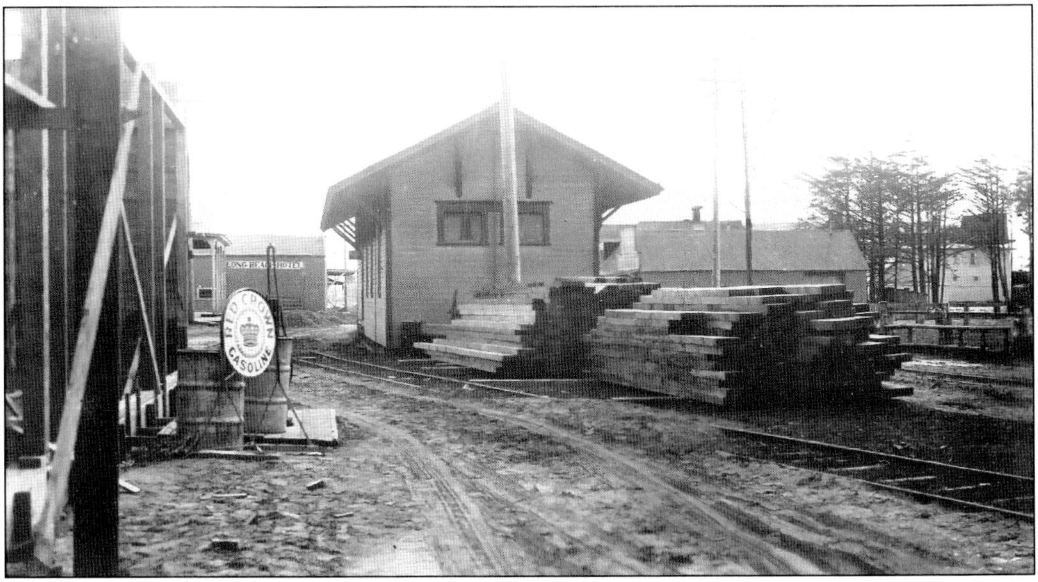

Complying with the Commissioners. In May 1890, the Pacific County Commissioners gave the right-of-way for a railway station on B Street in Long Beach, between First and Second Streets. The condition attached was that the IR&N deed another piece of land to the public and that they pave the street with planks. The requirements were fulfilled, a station was built, and a side track was laid. In a later order, the commissioners, concerned about equestrian and pedestrian traffic on the rights-of-way, ordered the IR&N to construct a fence between the two grade crossings in the Black Lake area. The commissioners specified that it be a tight board fence, not less than 5 feet high, and that it be kept in good repair. Again, the rail line fulfilled all requirements.

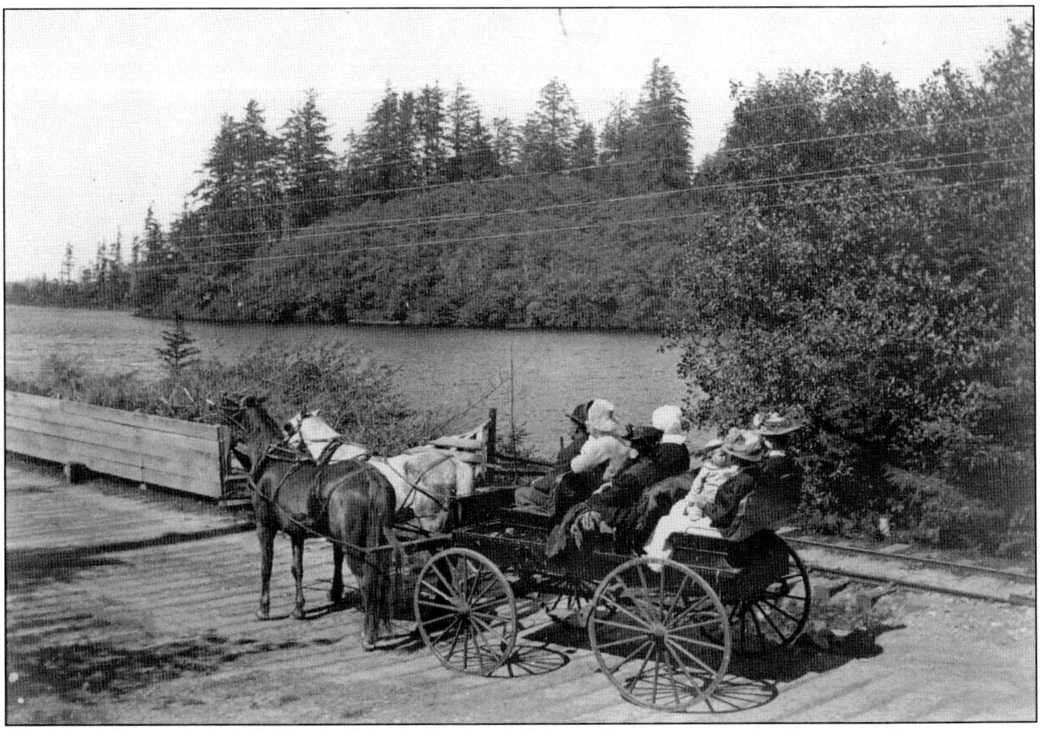

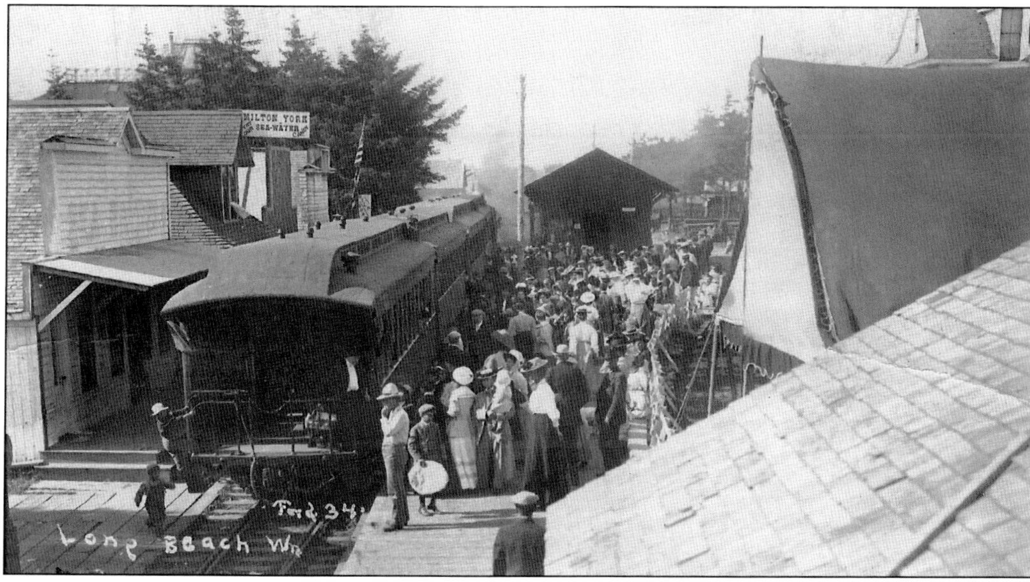

The Right-of-Way. In the early years, the right-of-way was a mere 10 feet in width. Passengers reported that they were so close to the stores in Long Beach they could make purchases through the windows of the coach. At Tinker's Hotel, it was possible for the train crew to lay a plank directly from the car platform to the hotel door—a distinct advantage in rainy, muddy conditions. In areas where high wooden fences bordered the track, there was only a space of 18 inches between the 7-foot-wide narrow-gauge cars and the fence on either side. After an incident involving a pedestrian being "rolled" along the fence, the right-of-way was widened to 15 feet.

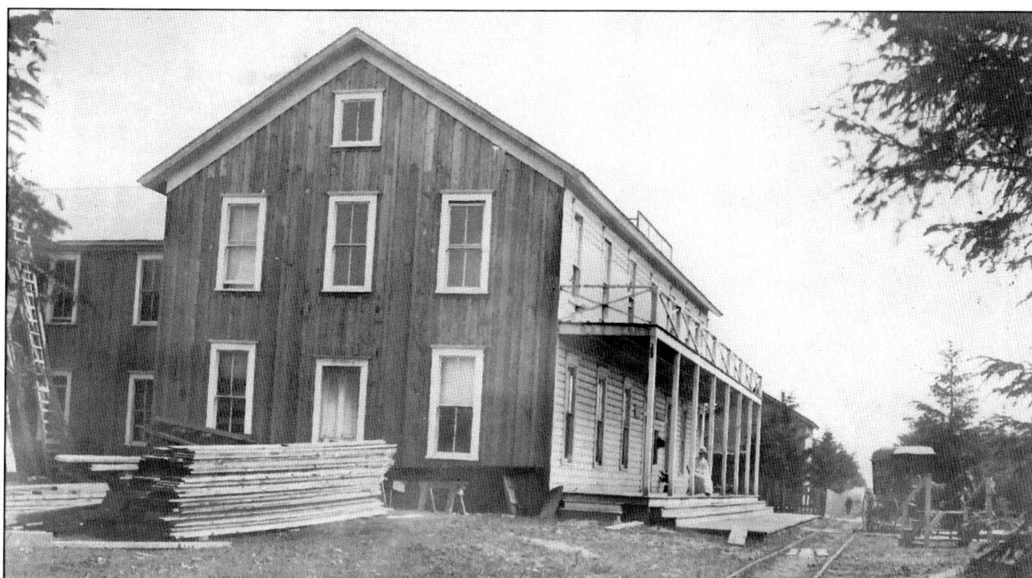

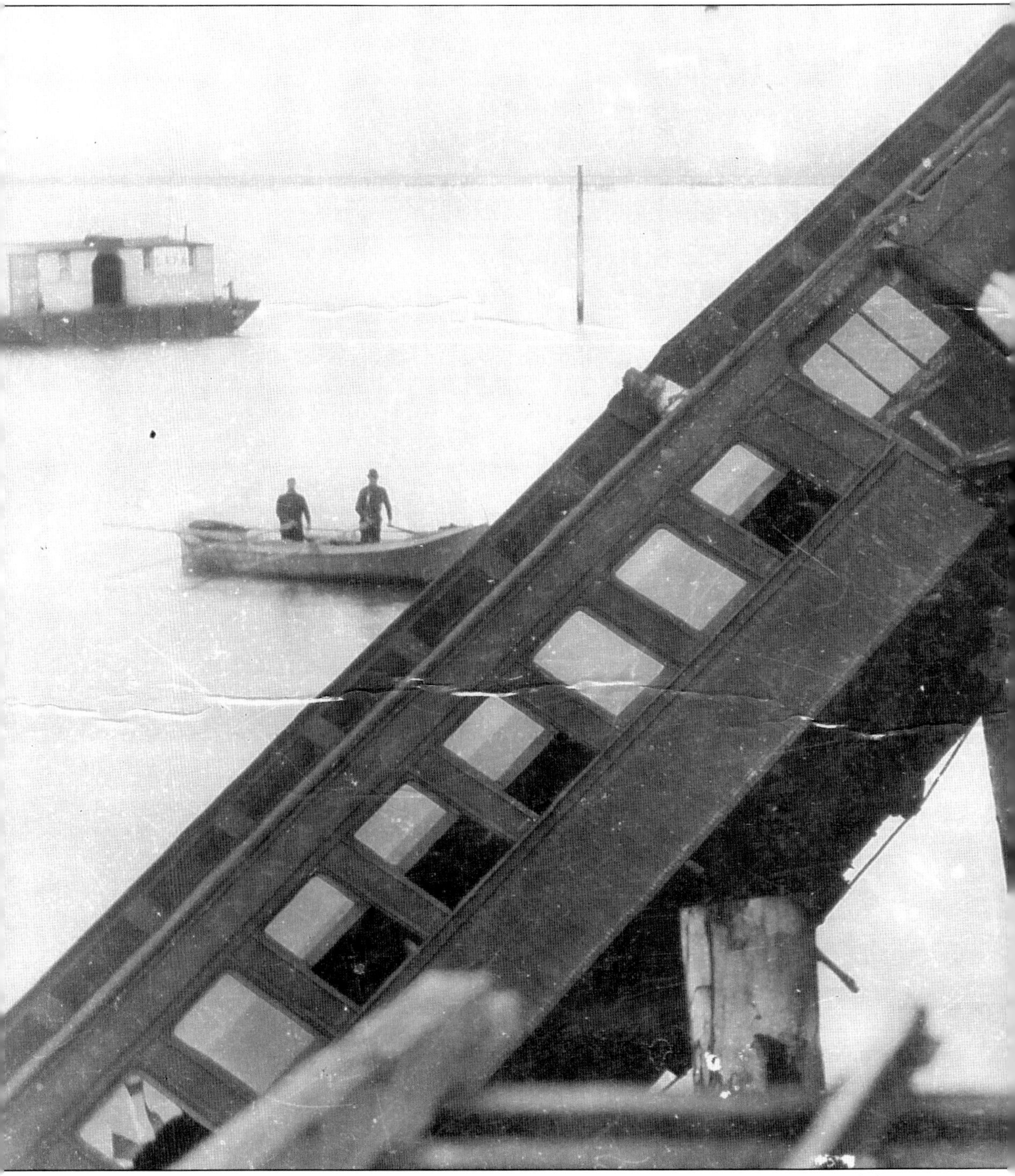

Spectacular Wreck. A wreck at the Ilwaco dock on May 22, 1899, could have had disastrous results but ended, instead, by giving local residents a chuckle. A train, consisting of locomotive, boxcar, and the combination boxcar–passenger coach, was backing onto the wharf when some pilings gave way. The locomotive toppled into about 6 feet of water in Baker's Bay, pulling the tender and boxcar with it. One end of the combination car caught on the dock and was only

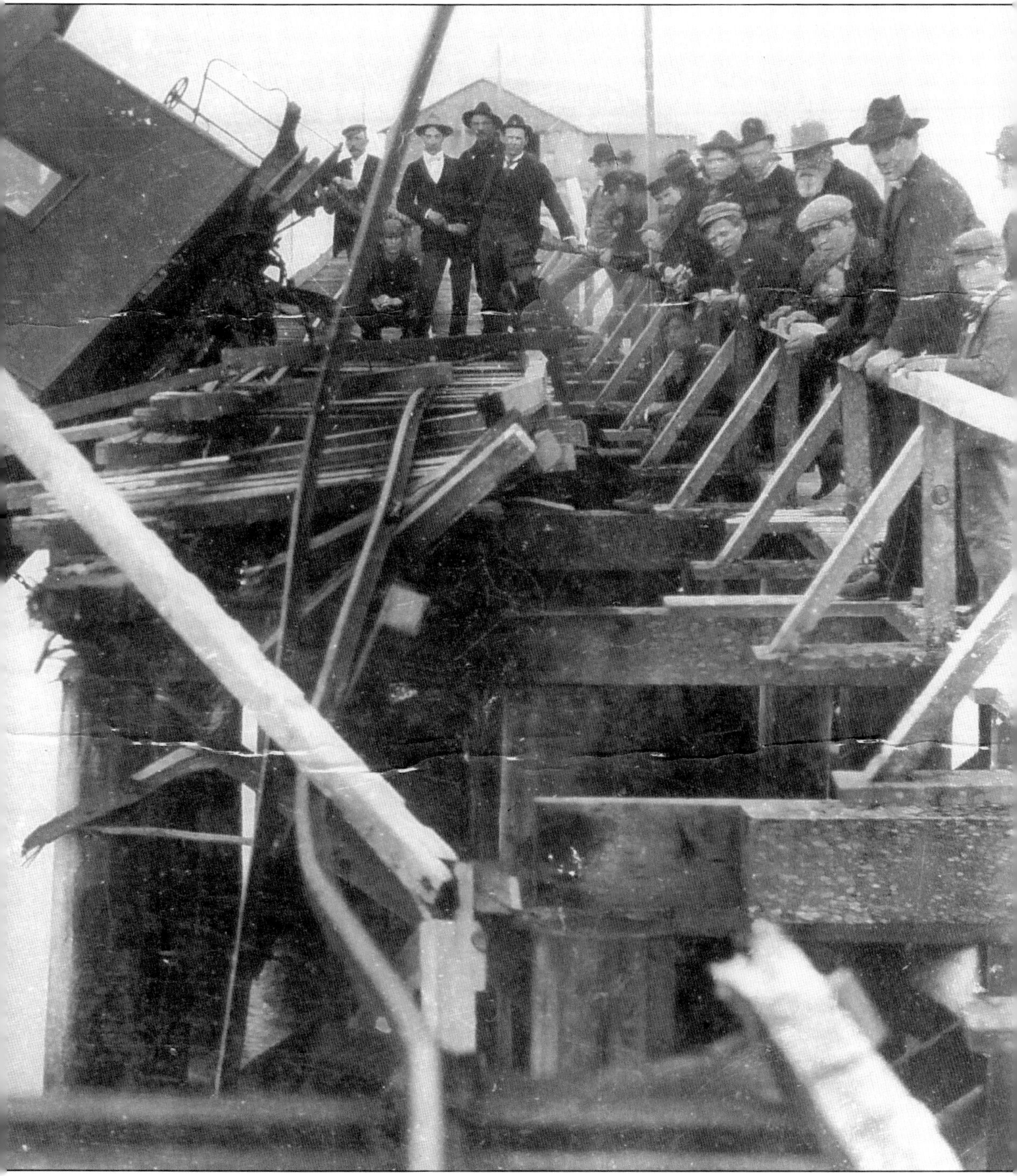

partially submerged. The engine crew and some passengers on the front platform of the combination swam ashore, but eight others were trapped inside for a short time until they could be helped to safety. During the rescue operation, an IR&N official gained fleeting local notoriety by calling out, "Save me first! I'm a company officer."

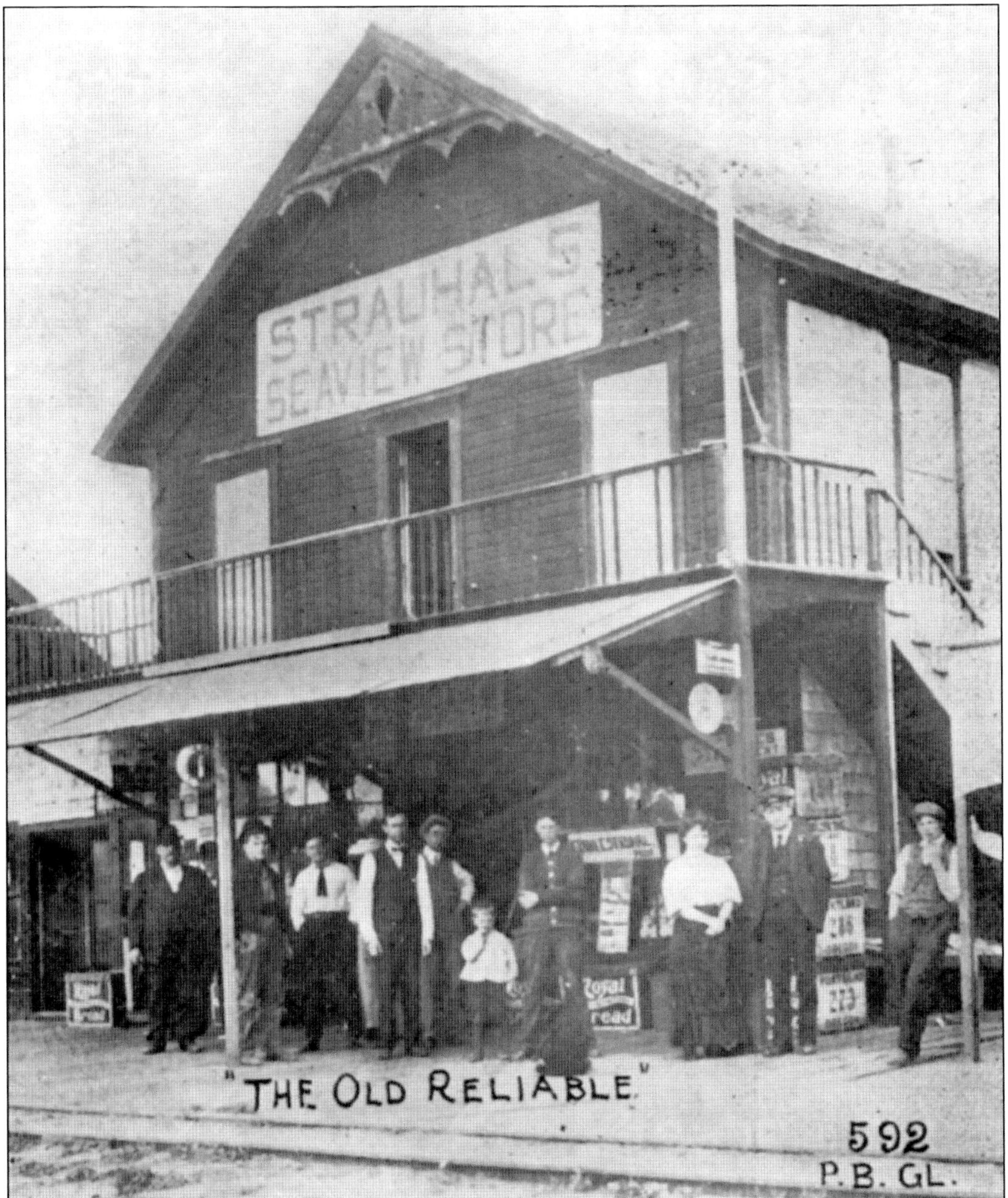

INTEGRAL PART OF LIFE. Despite the teasing at the railroad's expense, the line was beginning to be thought of as "Old Reliable" by its clientele. As the 1890s drew to a close and a new century began, it was clear the IR&N had become a part of everyday life on the North Beach Peninsula. Train arrivals and departures governed the way people planned their days. Years later, Helen Espy would remark, "It was so much easier when the train ran. You knew when visitors would arrive. If they weren't on the morning train, you had a few more hours to tidy up before their arrival on the afternoon train. Nowadays, with automobiles, people seem to just drop in any time." No longer were communities so isolated from one another and from the world beyond. Now it was possible to reach a doctor in a timely fashion, plan periodic shopping trips to Portland, or have a visit with friends and relatives who lived at the other end of the peninsula.

Four

Change and Growth

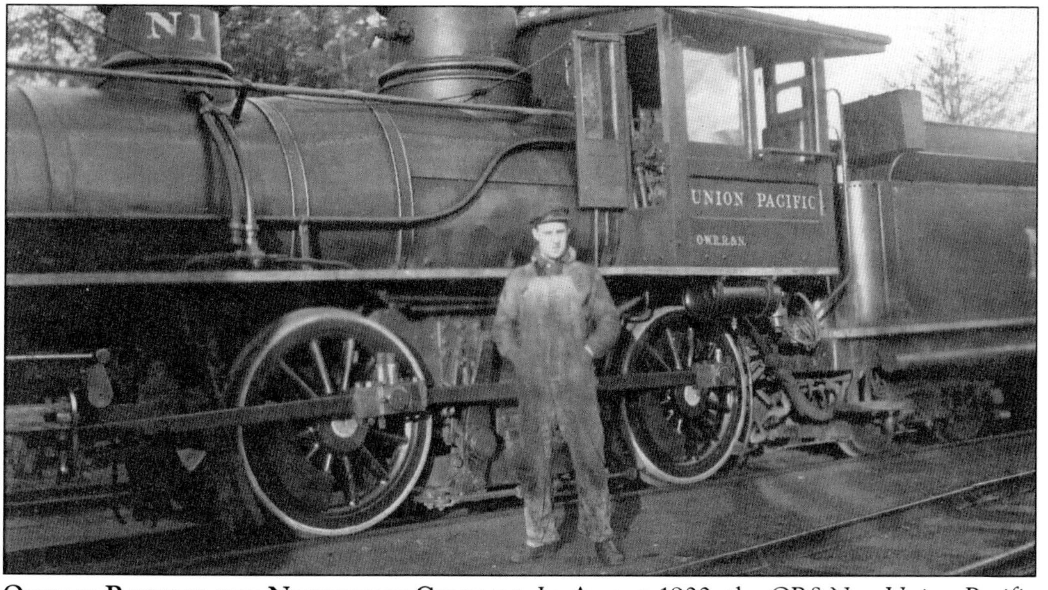

Oregon Railway and Navigation Company. In August 1900, the OR&N, a Union Pacific subsidiary, quietly completed its buyout of the IR&N by paying Loomis $142,000 for his interest in the company. The deal included 3 locomotives, 8 passenger cars, 12 boxcars, 8 flatcars, 2 river steamers, docks at Ilwaco and Nahcotta, all railroad tracks, and numerous parcels of property, the total valuing $248,000.

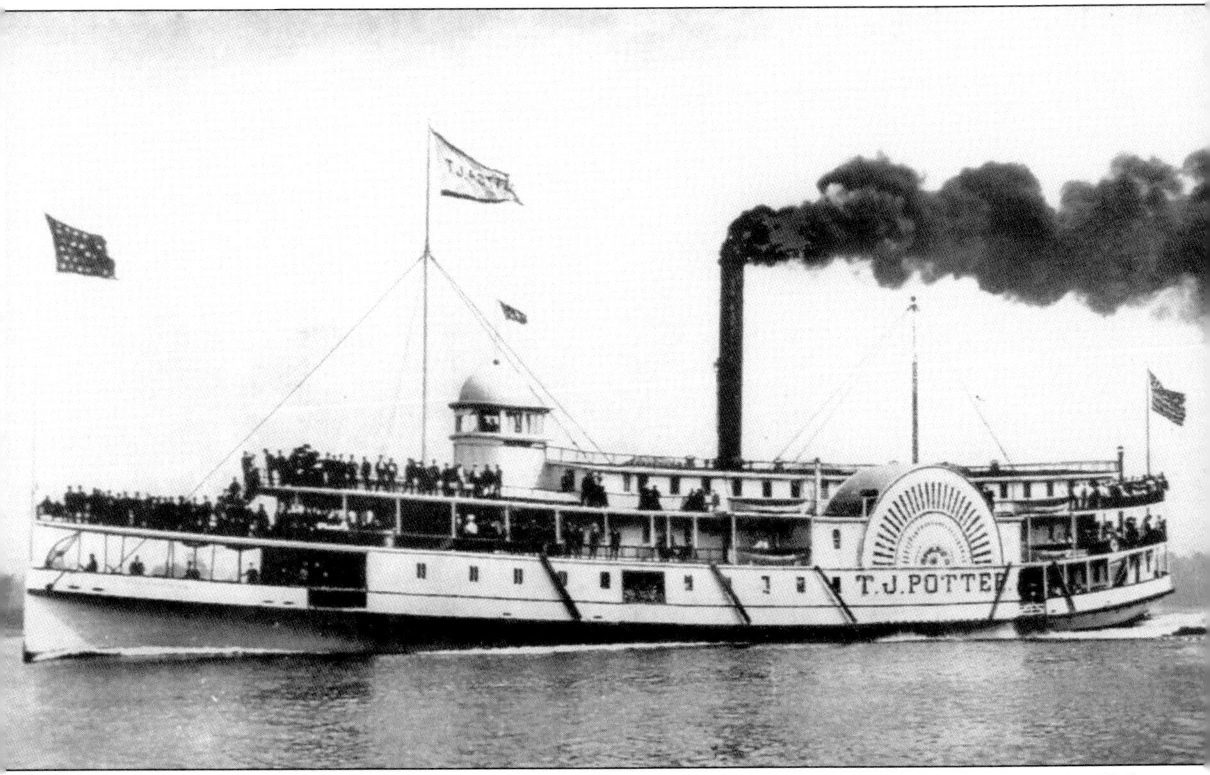

THE *T. J. POTTER*. One of the OR&N's first orders of business was to remodel its steamer, the *T. J. Potter*. The company invested $86,000 in the graceful 230-foot-long side-wheeler and immediately put her on the Portland-Ilwaco run. During the four-hour voyage to the North Beach Peninsula, passengers enjoyed luxurious surroundings. Leading up to the grand saloon was a curving staircase behind which, the company claimed, was the biggest plate-glass mirror in the West. Light filtered through the stained-glass windows of the clerestory, and the mellow tones of a grand piano provided background music during the voyage. The elegant ship, nicknamed the "Daddy Boat," left the Ash Street Dock in Portland at 1:00 each summer Saturday, often carrying more than 600 passengers. Most were husbands and fathers of families vacationing at the beach. Special trains, usually using every piece of available rolling stock, met the boat Saturday evening, and a late train was run out of Nahcotta Sunday night to accommodate those who wanted to stay as long as possible at the beach.

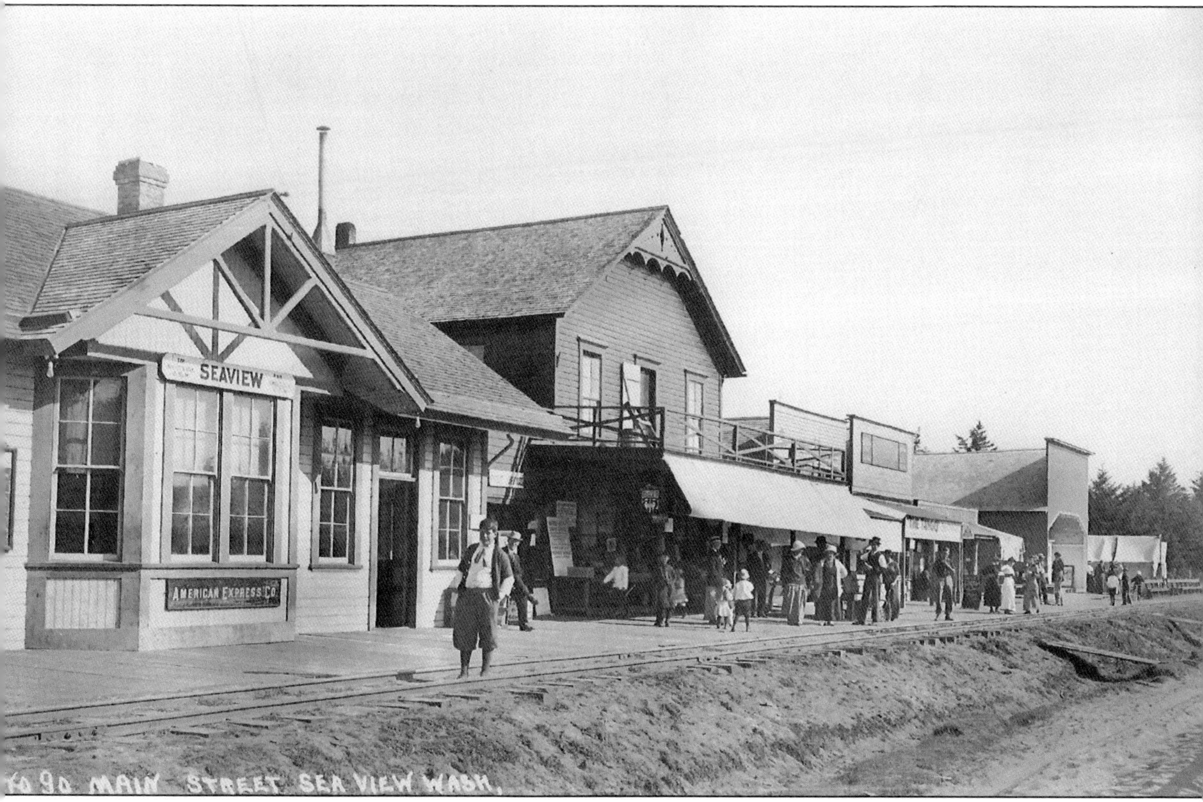

MORE CHANGES. The OR&N's new superintendent of the line, Dorsey B. Smith, immediately began to apply more structure and discipline to the railway. Train crews were required to wear uniforms, and a telephone line was installed from Ilwaco to Nahcotta to improve train dispatching. In 1903, air brakes and knuckle couplers became standard equipment in compliance with new Interstate Commerce Commission regulations. Several new cars were added, and two cabooses were built for the expanding freight business. In addition, the shed-like structures serving Seaview and Long Beach were replaced by regular depots. Even with these improvements, when Edward Budd was sent to replace Smith as superintendent, his assessment after his first inspection was, "Humph! Clamshell Railroad!" Although clamshells had no part in the construction of the roadbed or in any other aspect of the railway, the name tickled the fancy of the local residents and it stuck.

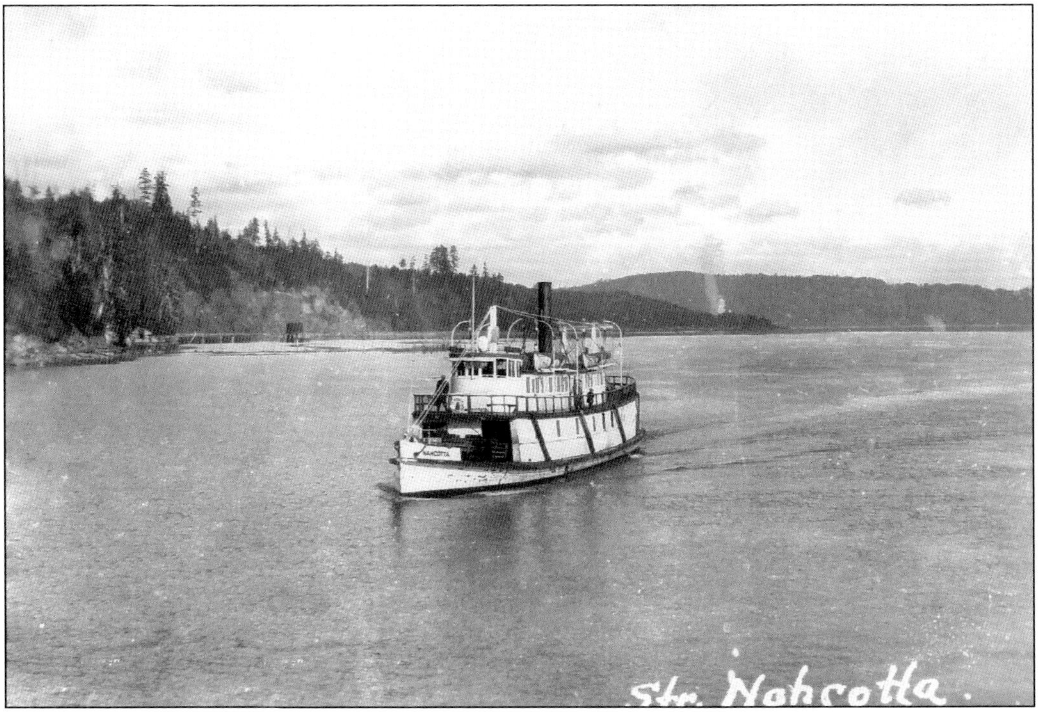

THE NAHCOTTA. The two last steamers built specifically for the Ilwaco Railway and Navigation Company, the *Nahcotta* and the *Canby*, were acquired by the OR&N as part of its purchase agreement with the IR&N. In 1904, the OR&N directors determined that just the *Nahcotta*, with the able assistance of their larger steamers, could handle all the traffic on the Columbia, and it was decided to sell the *Canby*. The *Nahcotta* was sent to Portland in 1908 to be refurbished. With oil burners installed and outfitted as a passenger ferry, she continued to work for the railway for another 20 years before she was dismantled. Her hull eventually became a floating fish store in the upriver community of Cathlamet. (Below, CRMM.)

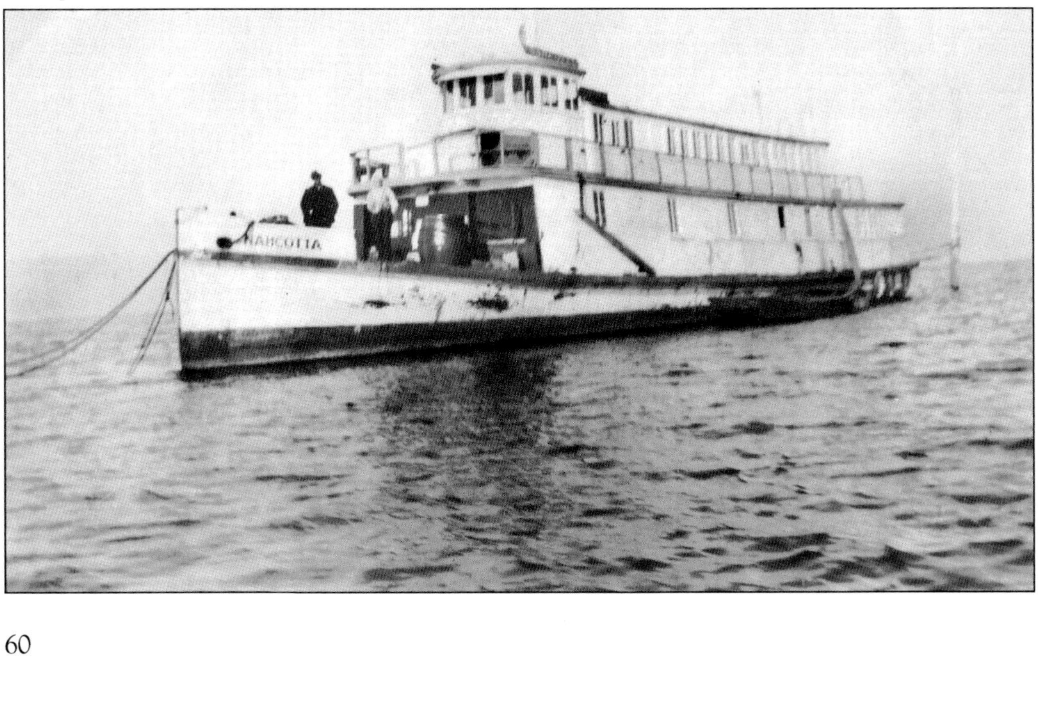

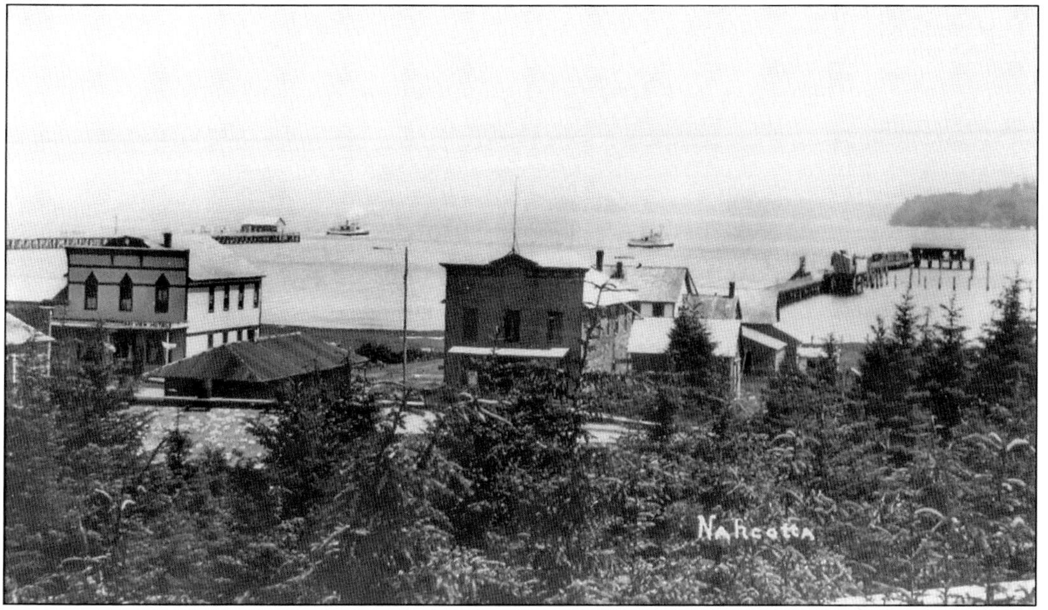

STEADY GROWTH. Nahcotta had been named by John Peter Paul in honor of Shoalwater Bay Indian chief Nahcati, who had lived in the area in the mid-1800s. The town, created specifically to serve the rail line, flourished as the railroad became established. Soon, besides the railroad buildings, it boasted two general merchandise stores, two hotels, and, for a short time, the weekly newspaper, the *Pacific Journal.* (Matt Winters.)

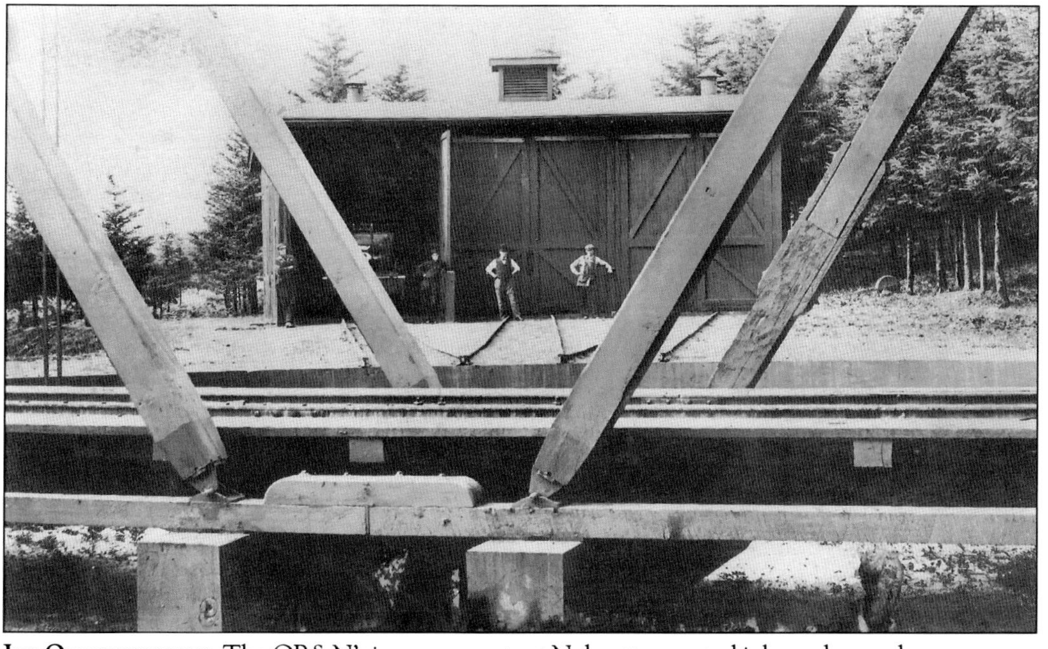

JOB OPPORTUNITIES. The OR&N's improvements at Nahcotta created jobs and caused a resurgence of activity within the community. The trestle and dock were re-timbered, the turntable was repaired, and the shops and grounds were cleaned up. Now the shop payroll included two machinists and a helper, two boilermakers, two car repairers, and a painter. In addition, there were eight laborers on the dock and roadway. (Charles Mulvey.)

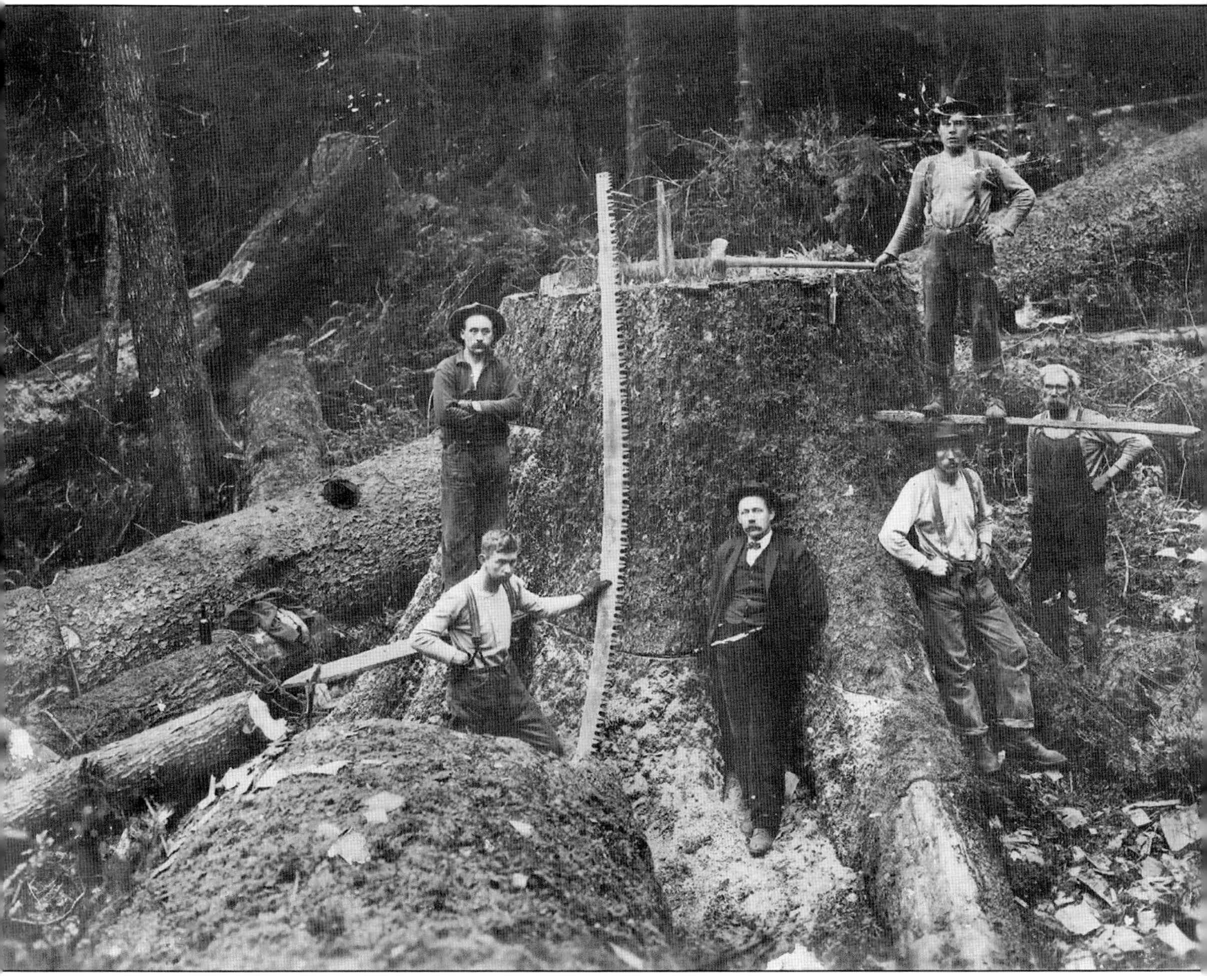

MASSIVE TREES. Though many of the first settlers in Pacific County had arrived intending to farm, they found the thick forests of the area a challenge to clear. Oysterville pioneer John Marshall wrote, "I go in the woods and look for trees suitable for a house but can't find them they are so big. They are from 150 feet to 200 feet high and from 3 feet through to 6 feet and it is so much labor to get them and they stand so close together that we can't hardly get through them. I never saw such woods until I came to this country. . . . People here own claims of 100 acres and . . . can't get land enough cleared to raise a few potatoes to eat." Erstwhile farmers soon turned to logging. At first, they used teams of oxen to haul logs to tidewater on corduroy "skid roads." Around 1900, steam power replaced the bull teams, and steam donkeys and ground-lead cables were used to haul logs great distances through the forests. Logging for profit became one of the area's primary industries.

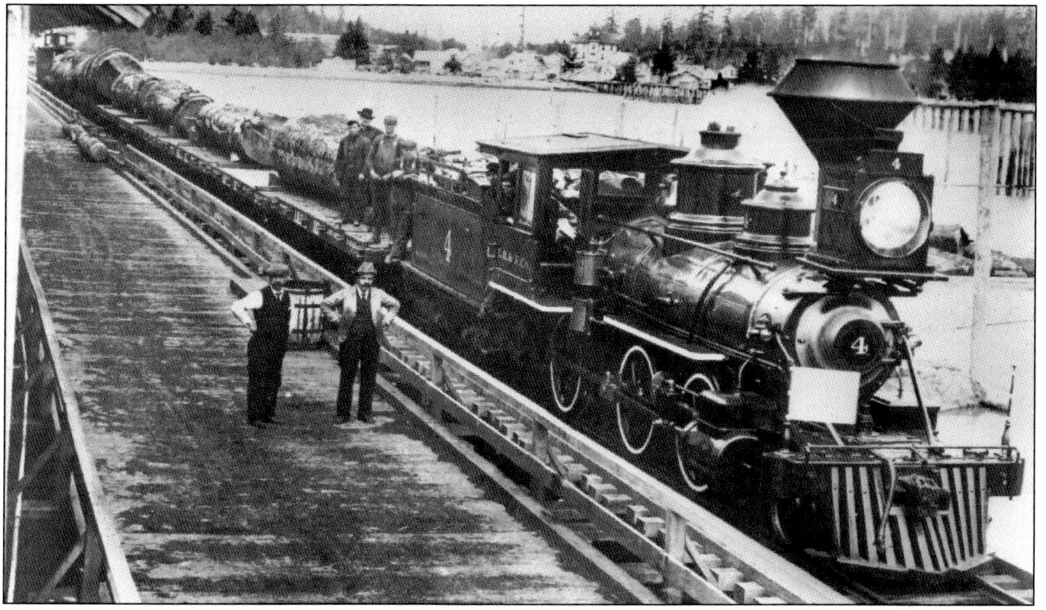

Logging Transfer Business. In 1902, in order to increase freight revenues, the OR&N opened a logging transfer business. From the Palix and Naselle River logging operations, logs were towed across the bay to Nahcotta, then moved to Ilwaco by rail where they were dumped into the Columbia River for towing to a mill. A logging dock was built at Nahcotta, and a number of small log-buggies were added to the railroad to handle this business. At Nahcotta and Ilwaco, booms were constructed and winches and derricks were erected for transferring logs to and from the cars. Good profits were made for two years, but when huge seagoing log rafts were introduced, the OR&N's business declined and the log-buggies became rock and work cars. (Above, OHS-9611; below, PCHS.)

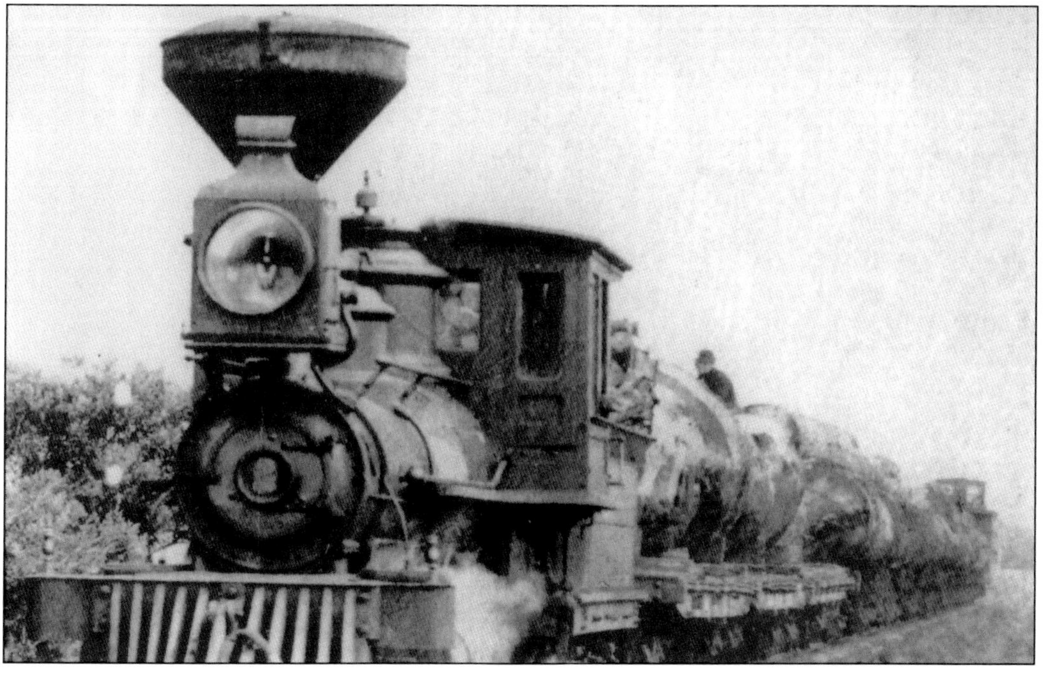

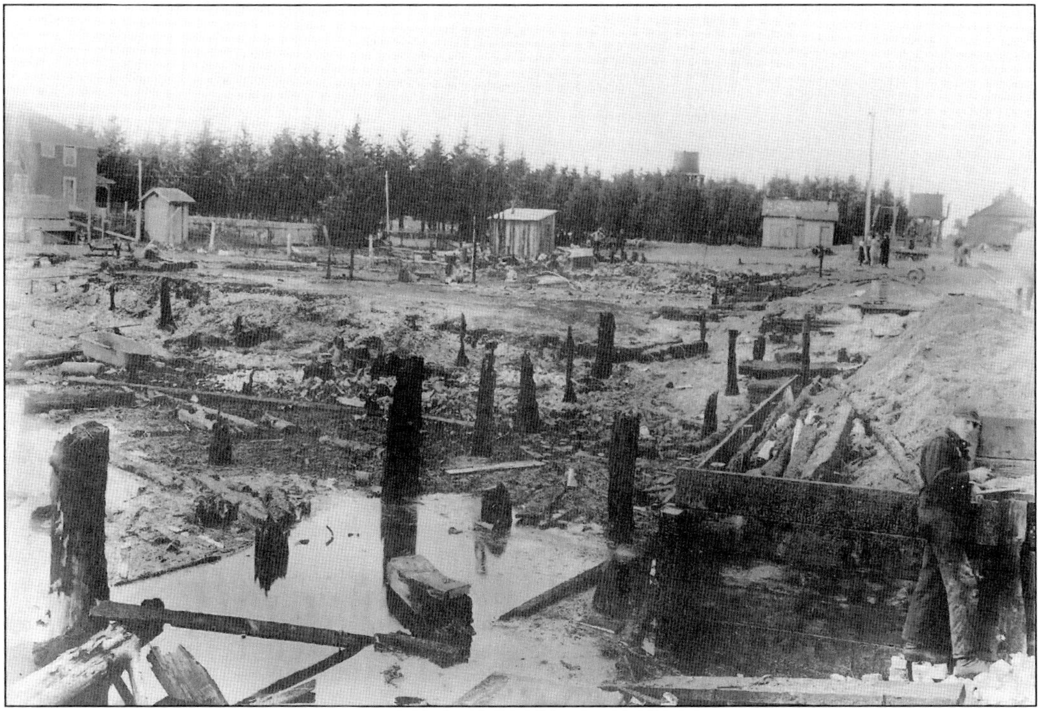

Town Disaster. On Friday, January 29, 1915, Helen Espy of Oysterville wrote, "Maybe you have heard that Nahcotta burned to the ground day before yesterday. Everything gone. It started in the old Petit Hotel, spread to Morehead's store, thence to the other hotel across taking depot, post office, and Duggans'." Though the telephone building was one of the first to burn, the operator valiantly put through a call for firefighters before leaving his post. The afternoon train was in Chinook when the crew received word of the fire. News spread quickly, and within a half hour, three carloads of men were on their way northward, picking up firefighters all along the way. They reached Nahcotta just in time to pull several cars away from the burning depot. (Above, the Les Wilson family.)

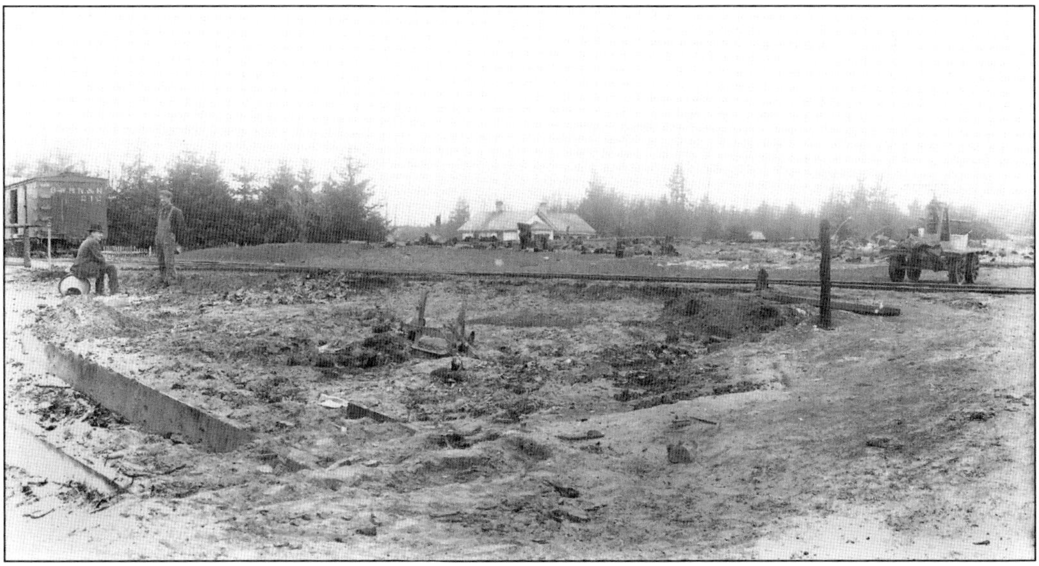

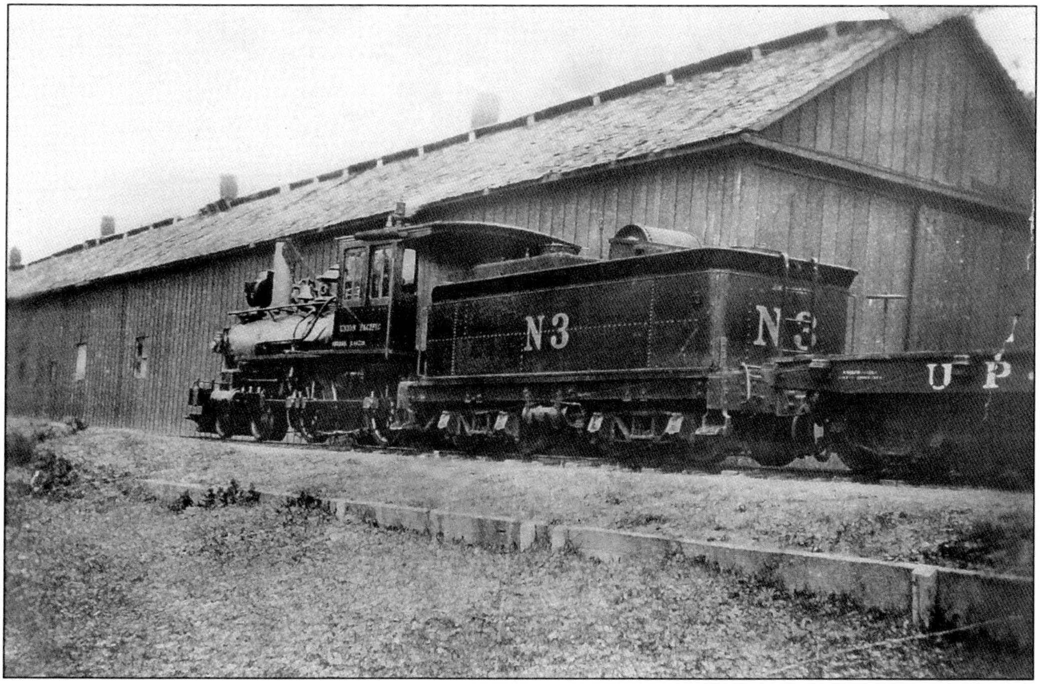

Railroad Fared Best. Firefighters rushed to save Nahcotta's residential district and the OR&N's rolling stock and buildings. Actually, the rail line fared better than most other businesses. After the fire, the only building of importance still standing in the business district was the railroad's carbarn, the cars within unscathed. Damage to the town was estimated at $32,000, most of it not covered by insurance. Gone were Trondsen and Brown's store, the Bay View Hotel, Petit's Hotel, a saloon, a meat market, the train depot, and more. By March, the depot had been rebuilt, but very few other businesses were ever replaced. (Above, Adelle Beechey.)

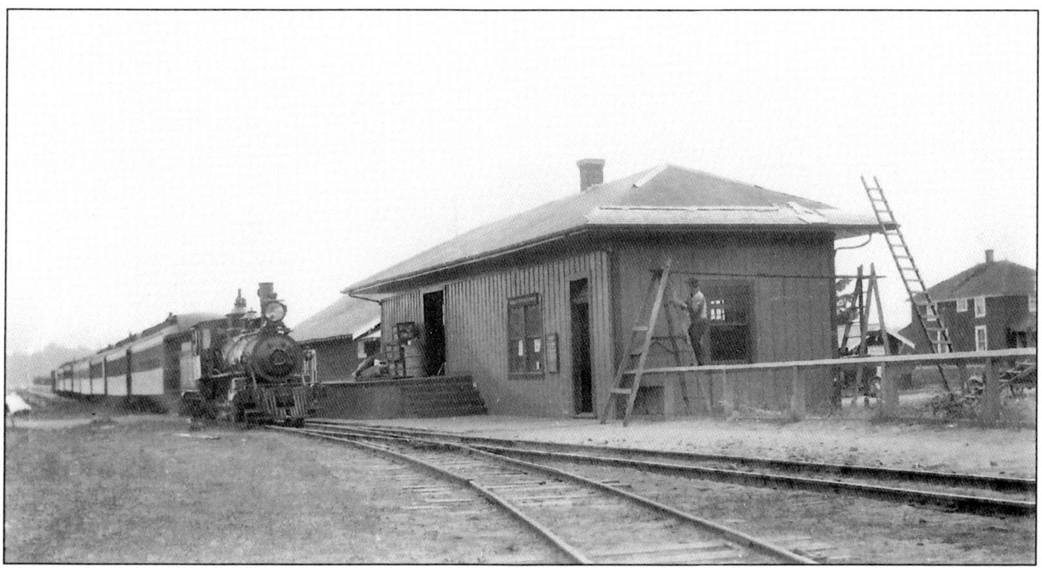

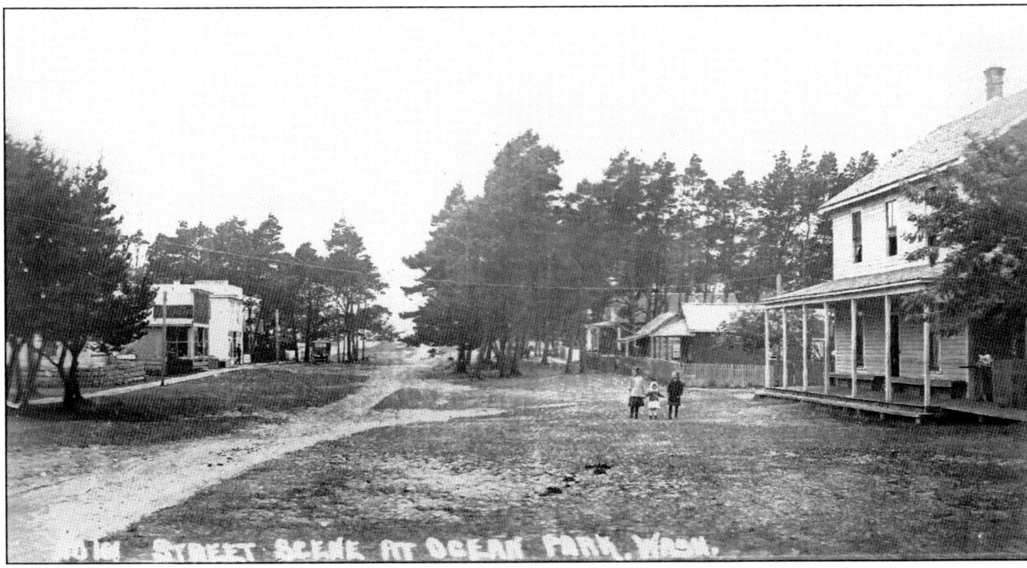

ANOTHER NORTH END COMMUNITY. Less than a mile west of Nahcotta was Ocean Park, the only other settlement at the peninsula's north end besides Oysterville and, of the three, the only one built facing the ocean. Platted in 1883 by Oysterville's cofounder I. A. Clark, Ocean Park's 250 acres became a summer retreat for religious camp meetings of the Methodist Episcopal Church of Portland.

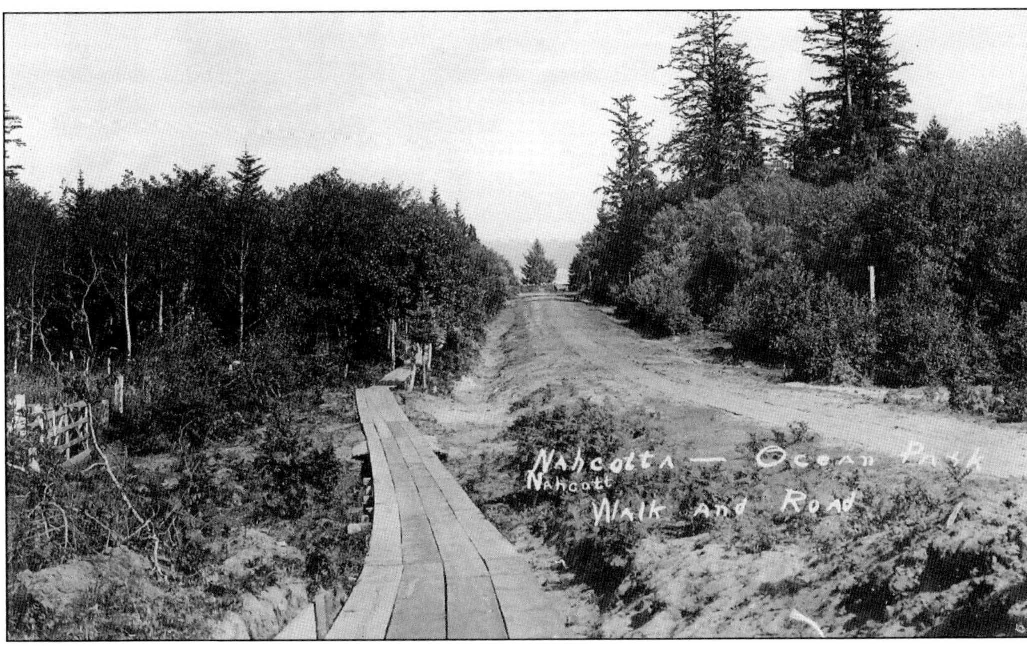

SUMMER HOMES. By 1900, the Ocean Park camp meetings had been discontinued and property was being sold to vacationing Portlanders who began to build summer homes there. Few year-round residents meant not enough children to warrant a school. Until 1936, when the Nahcotta School burned, students from Ocean Park walked the mile to and from the Nahcotta schoolhouse along the planked lane beside Bay Avenue. (Dobby Wiegardt.)

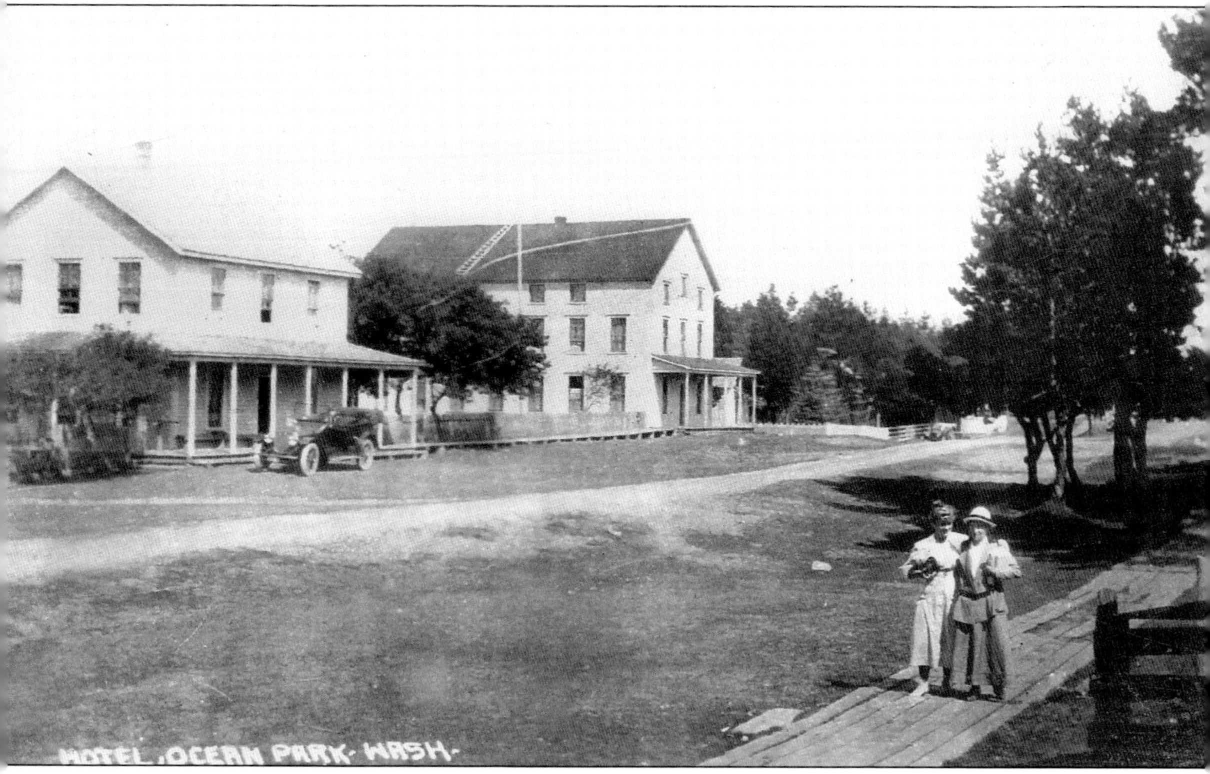

Hotel and Annex. Adelaide and William Taylor moved to Ocean Park in 1886, just three years after the town's beginnings. They had most recently been residents of Oysterville, where Taylor had served as sheriff and assessor of Pacific County and had worked for Lewis Alfred Loomis as stagecoach driver. Taylor had undoubtedly delivered many a passenger to the Methodist Camp Grounds during his years as stage driver, so it is easy to speculate that, when the Taylors established their Ocean Park business, they located their hotel close to the beach with the stagecoach in mind. Within three years, however, the narrow-gauge railroad was up and running. Even though the train could not offer front-door delivery as the stage had done, it soon became apparent that the six upstairs guest rooms of the hotel would not be up to tourist demand. The Taylors lost no time in building a 36-room annex in the block to the east of their hotel. (Eileen Weidner.)

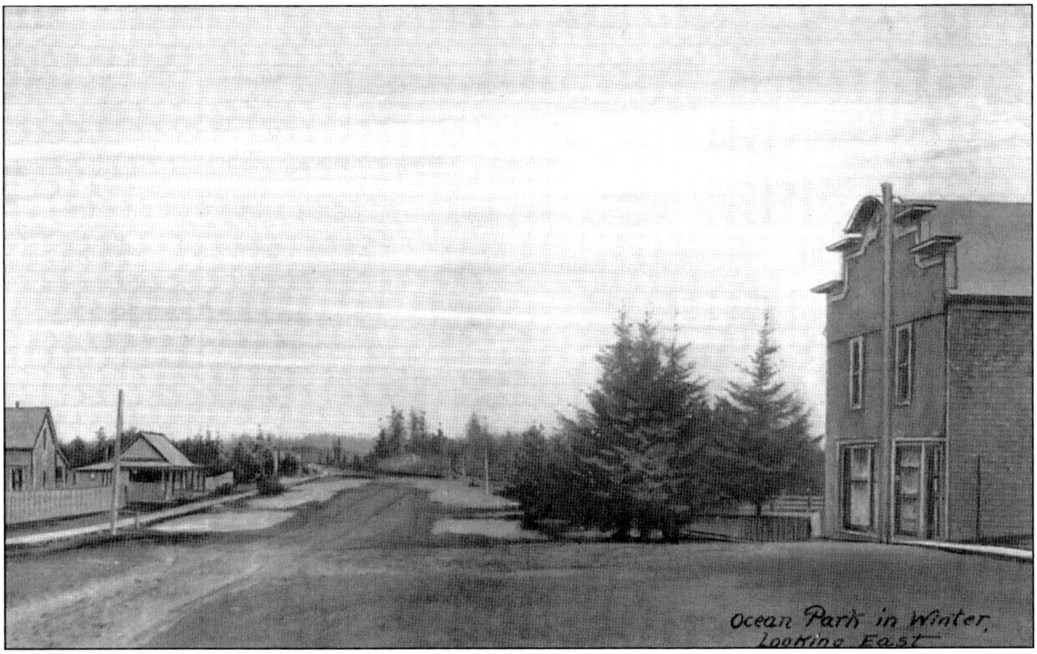

NORTH END HUB. Ocean Park's broad, tree-lined main street, Bay Avenue, crossed the peninsula from the Pacific Ocean to Willapa Bay and soon became the business center of the town. As residential districts developed to the north and south, the town gradually took on an air of permanence, though for many years it was primarily a summertime community. All the same, Ocean Park residents were content to let Long Beach, their neighbor to the south, promote the carnival, resort atmosphere popular with visitors. Ocean Park remained residential in character, and not until after Nahcotta's 1915 fire was it looked to as the new north end shopping hub, increasingly frequented by householders from Leadbetter Point to Klipsan Beach. (Eileen Weidner.)

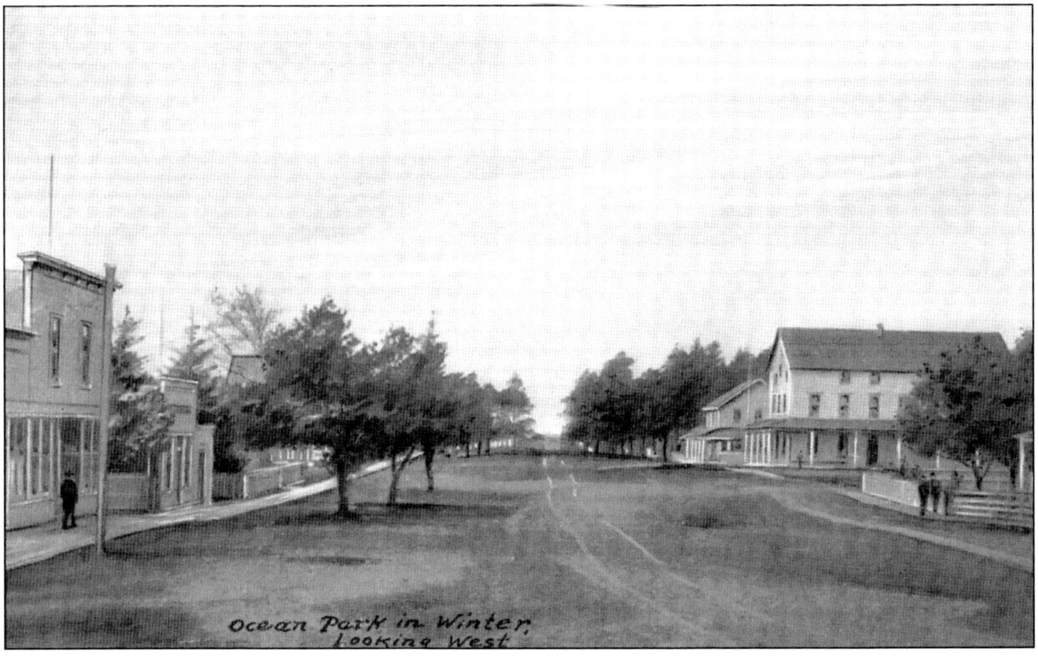

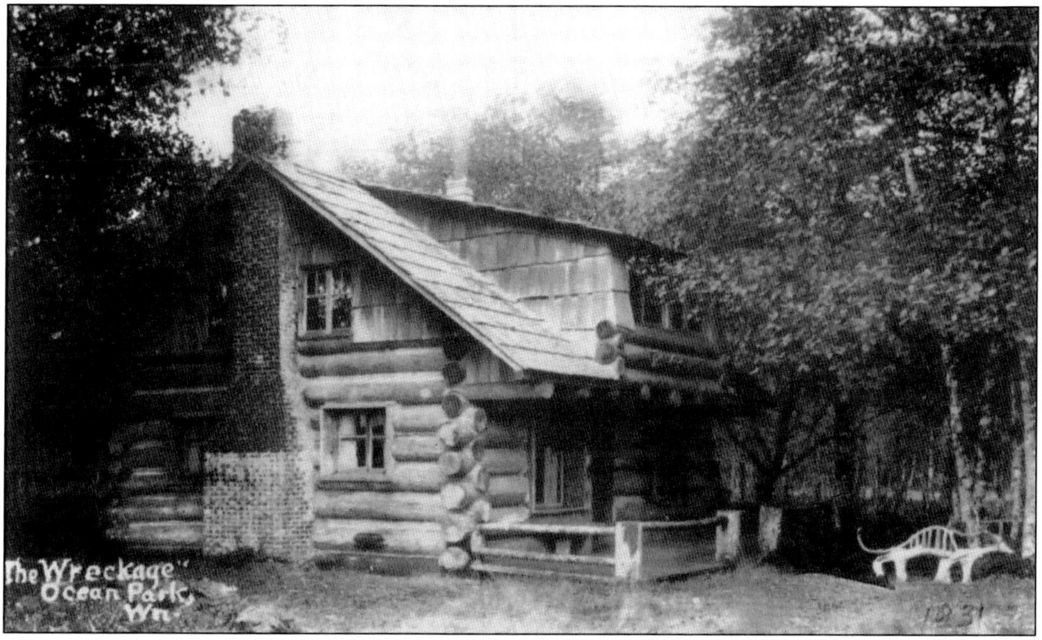

OCEAN PARK CREATIVITY. Ocean Park property owners were creative in their use of building materials. One homeowner called his place the Wreckage, having utilized driftwood for house, furniture, and yard art. Another summer cottage was built entirely of cedar-paneled doors salvaged from a pavilion at the 1905 Lewis and Clark Exposition in Portland. Deeds to property still reflected the original requirements of the Ocean Park Camp Meeting Association of the Methodist Episcopal Church—prohibitions against the use and manufacture of intoxicating drinks and against gambling and other immoral practices. As the residential and business districts grew, deed restrictions were relaxed and finally overlooked entirely. Over time, more and more people took up full-time residence and Ocean Park began to lose its "summertime only" character. (Below, Dobby Wiegardt.)

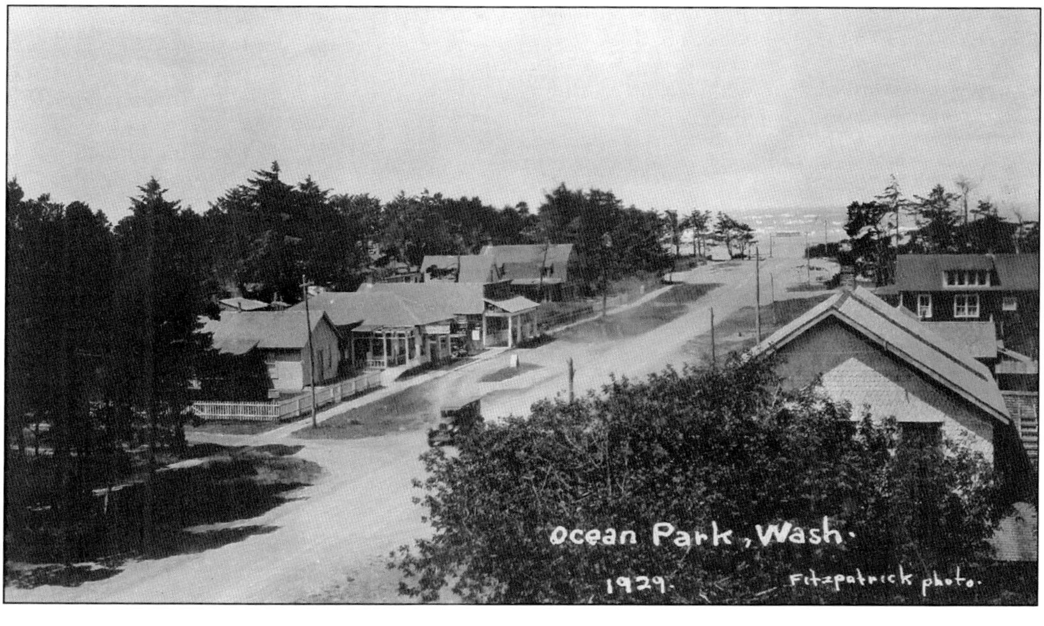

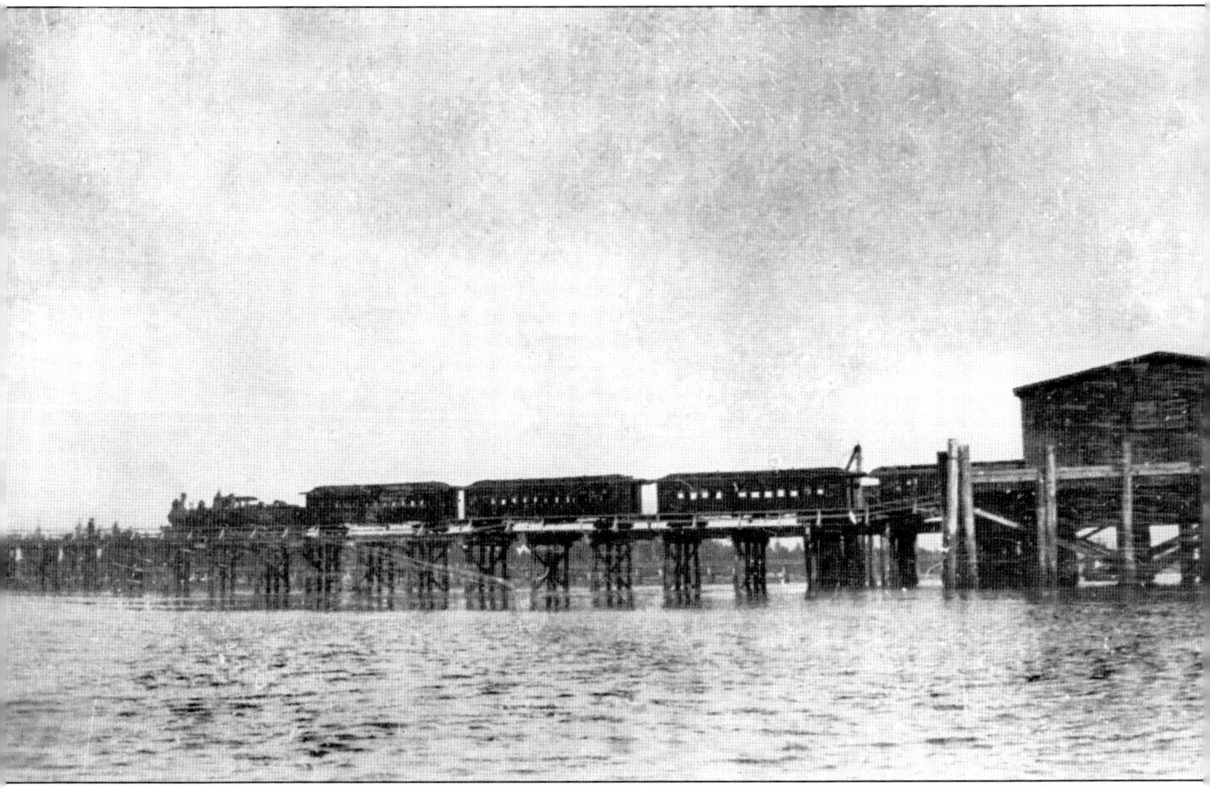

STRIVING FOR IMPROVEMENT. As an additional improvement in service, the OR&N began a policy of running separate passenger and freight trains. This cut down on delays to passengers while waiting for freight to be loaded or unloaded. Even so, the more orderly train service did not preclude an occasional unscheduled stop, perhaps to net a salmon along the river or to try for one of Loomis's turkeys seen wandering along the right-of-way. As much as Superintendent Budd strived for a more professional and structured company, the train crews fell back on their comfortable, fun-loving ways. One order to the train crew concerned "sliding the wheels," which was the result of excessive braking. The order asserted that there "were more flat wheels caused by sliding on this line than any other section of the Union Pacific System." For all of the line's efforts at improvement, the trains continued to take a ribbing in the local newspapers, but in general, peninsula residents appreciated the friendly, informal atmosphere. (OHS-CS39172-3.)

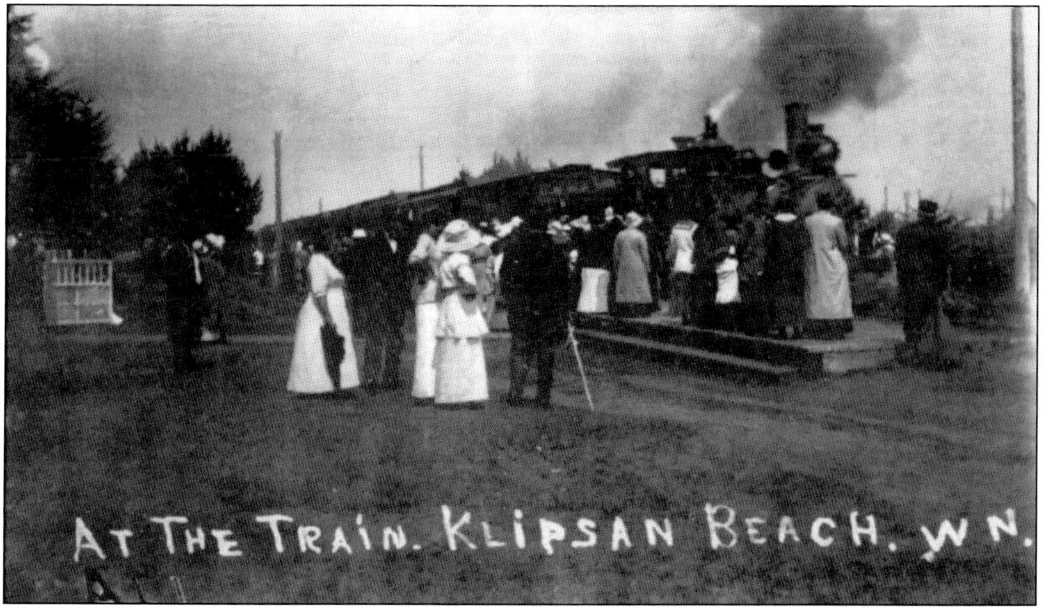

KLIPSAN BEACH. This picture taken at Klipsan Beach in the summer gives an idea of the crowds who took advantage of the excursion trips to watch the life-saving crew drill on Sunday afternoons. There was no actual depot at Klipsan, just a waiting platform, and, except for the special excursions or life-saving emergencies, the train did not stop there on a regular basis.

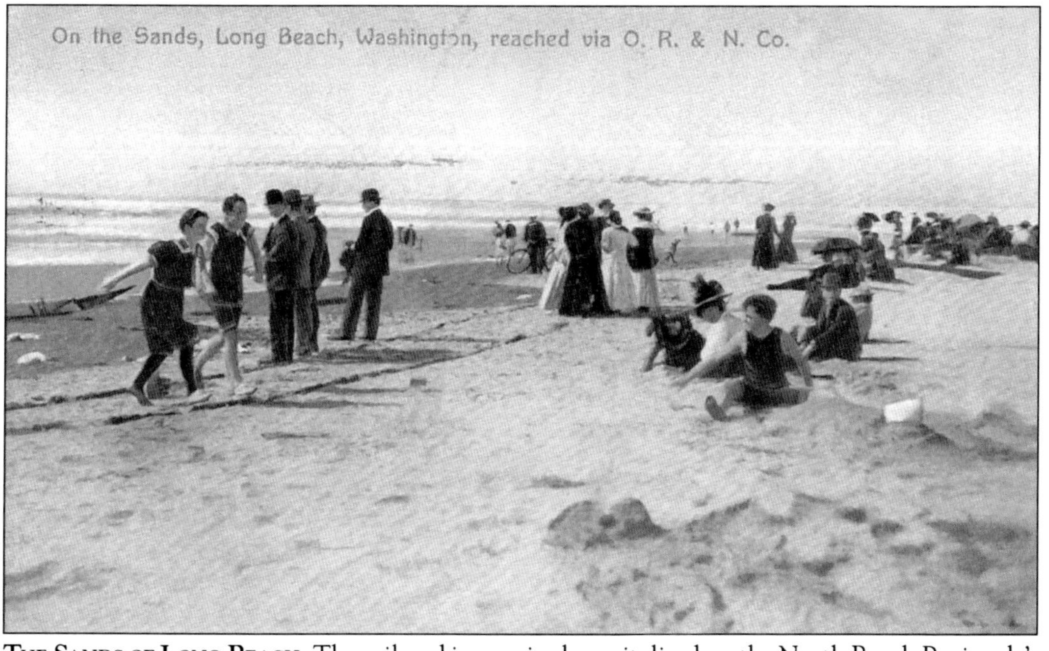

THE SANDS OF LONG BEACH. The railroad increasingly capitalized on the North Beach Peninsula's long, sandy beach with its lighthouses and other attractions of interest to summer visitors. Postcards, brochures, and newspaper and magazine advertisements urged vacationers to take advantage of the OR&N's "unequalled service for close connections with Portland trains and boat" and promised "speed and comfort in traveling."

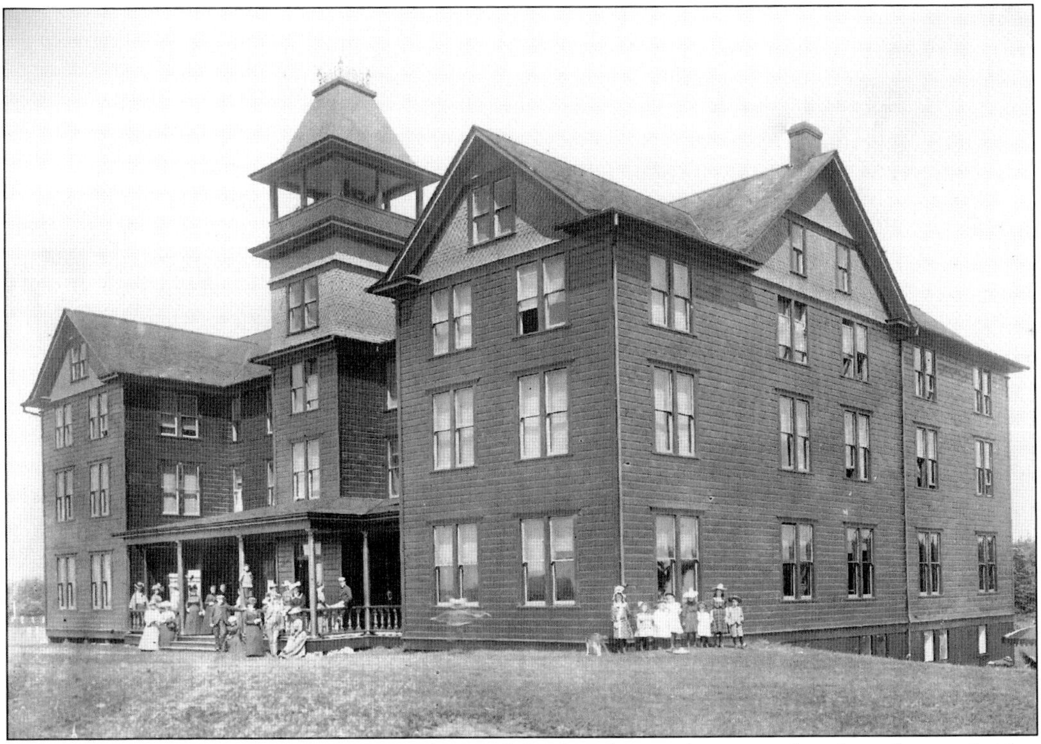

The Breakers. Just north of Long Beach stood the Breakers, a four-story hotel on the sand ridge overlooking the ocean. Built by J. M. Arthur, a Portland real estate promoter, it was named for its excellent view of the breaking surf. The hotel had 200 rooms with accommodations for 300 guests at rates of $12, $14, $16, and $18 per week. Special rates were given for "families, societies, and large delegations." Special conveniences included telephone and telegraph service, and from August 17, 1905, through March 31, 1919, there was a post office at the hotel. The Breakers was a regular train stop during the summer season, and the railroad provided a covered waiting platform for use by hotel guests and visitors.

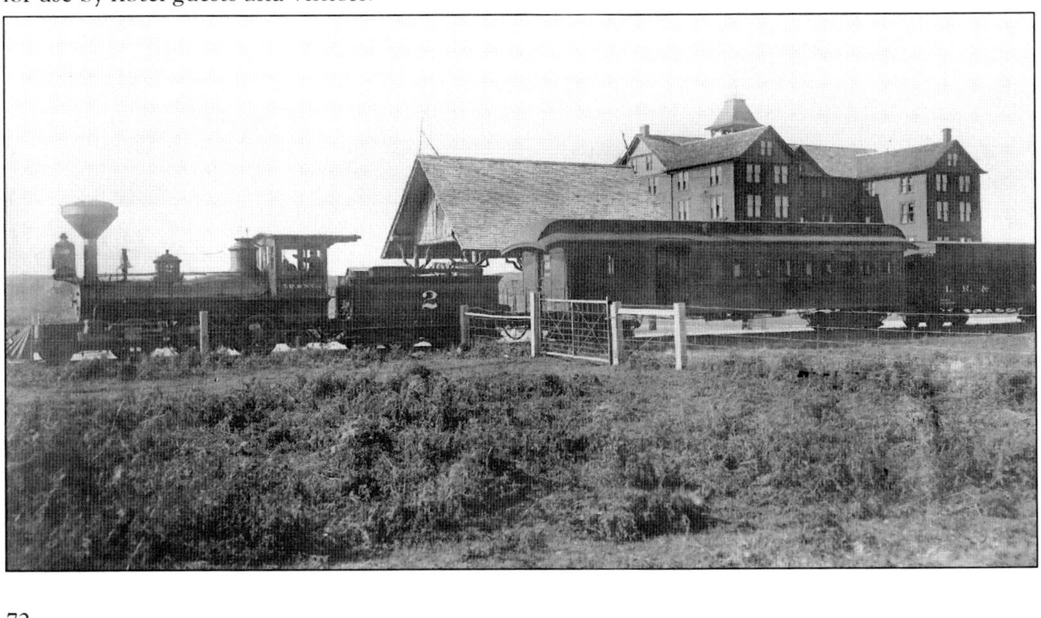

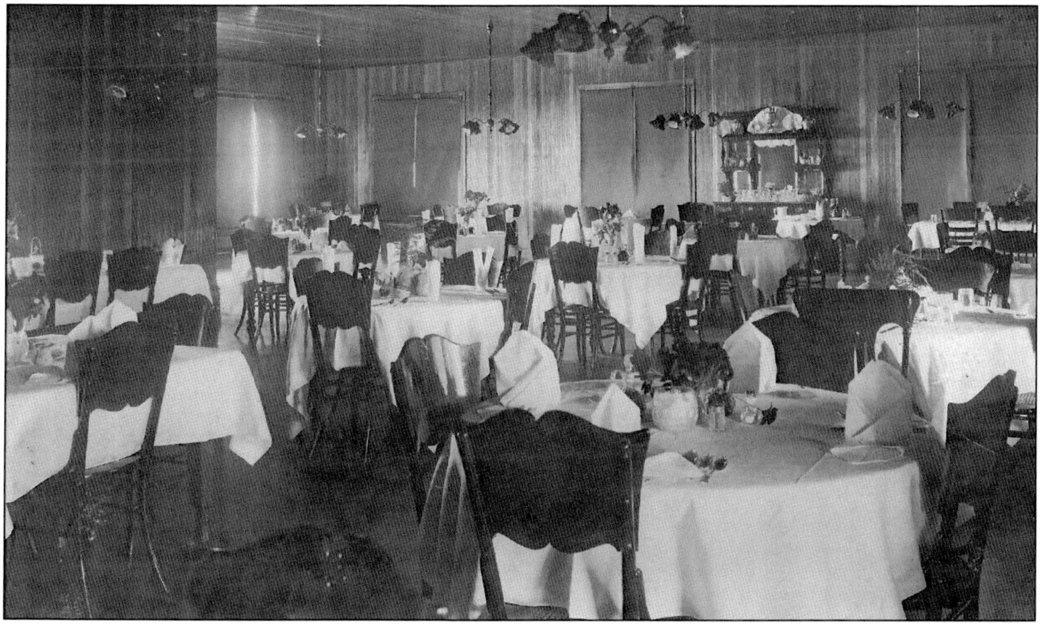

The American Plan. Meals were served in the Breakers' dining room according to the American plan—three meals a day, which were included in the quoted weekly rate. On September 15, 1904, shortly after the hotel had closed for the season, the big wooden-framed structure was destroyed by fire, which started in a faulty kitchen flue. Volunteer firefighters arrived by locomotive from Ilwaco to find, according to the newspapers, "the finest summer hotel on the North Pacific coast a mass of smoking ruins," an estimated $70,000 loss. All that was saved were the orchestrion (a large music box that simulated orchestra music), the player piano, and a few pieces of furniture. Though the hotel was rebuilt and continued to boast amenities such as the well-furnished library pictured below, it never entirely recovered its initial grandeur and finally closed in 1920.

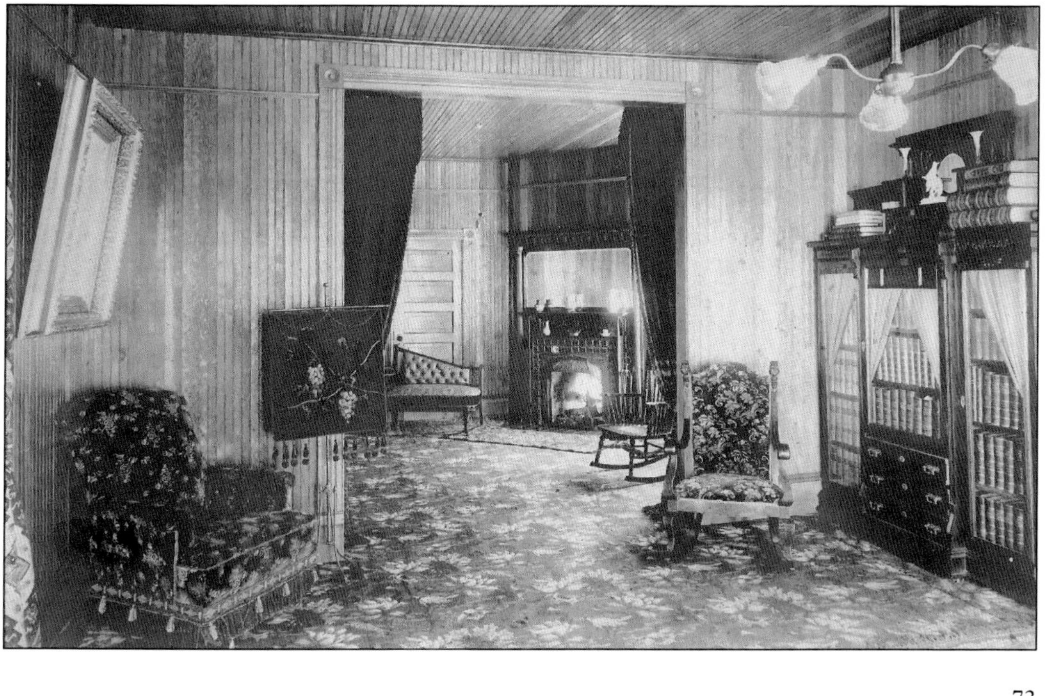

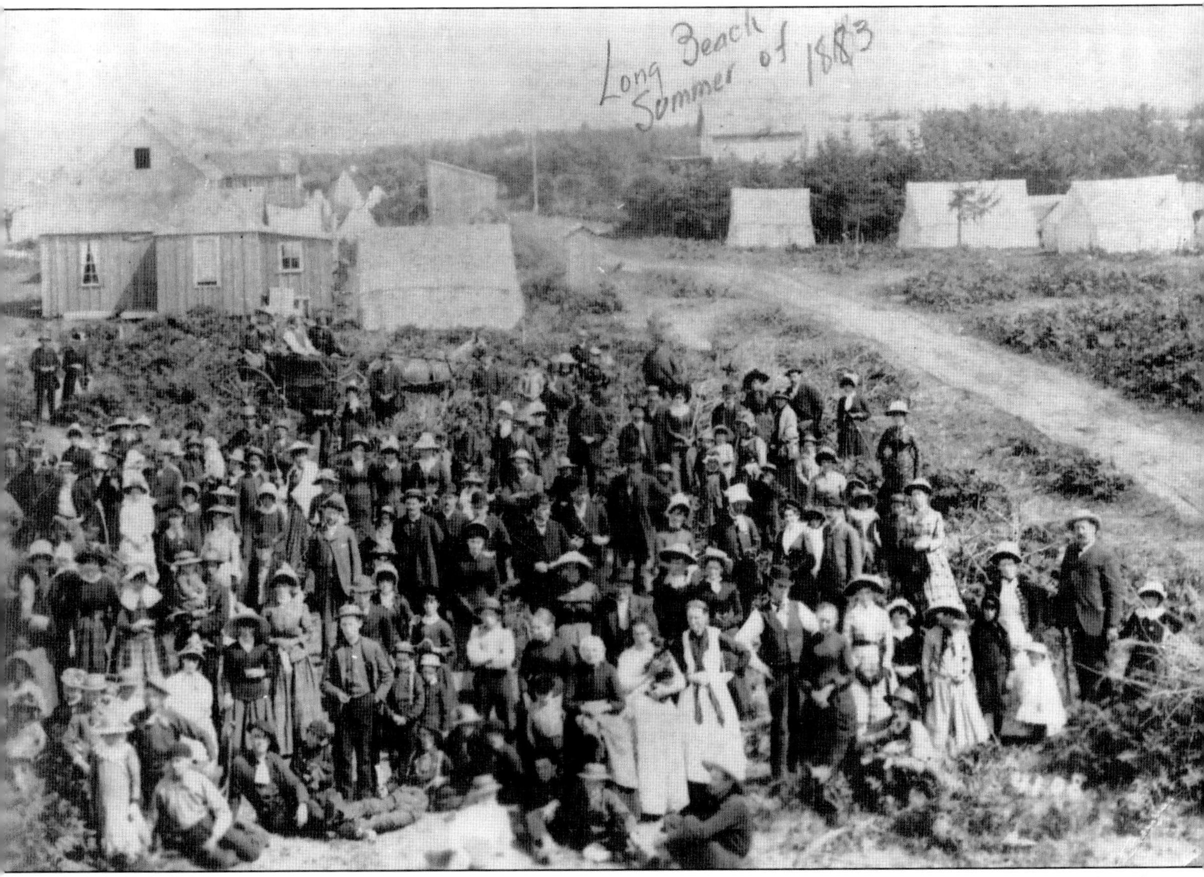

TINKERVILLE, A TENT CITY. In 1881, H. H. Tinker purchased a large tract on the ocean side of North Beach Peninsula and platted a town, which people called Tinkerville in his honor. He envisioned his town becoming a resort destination for the many tourists who were beginning to arrive by boat and stage each summer and who were camping anywhere there was an open space. At his invitation, a group of summer visitors from the city set up the East Portland Camp, a "tent city" that served as a camping area for many years as town was developing. A tent site could be purchased for $2.50 for the season. Meanwhile, Tinker set about clearing away trees and brush and filling marshy spots on his future town site. He laid out streets, house lots, park and school areas, and even barn lots where visitors could tether horse and buggy while enjoying the beach. As the town developed, its name was changed to Long Beach.

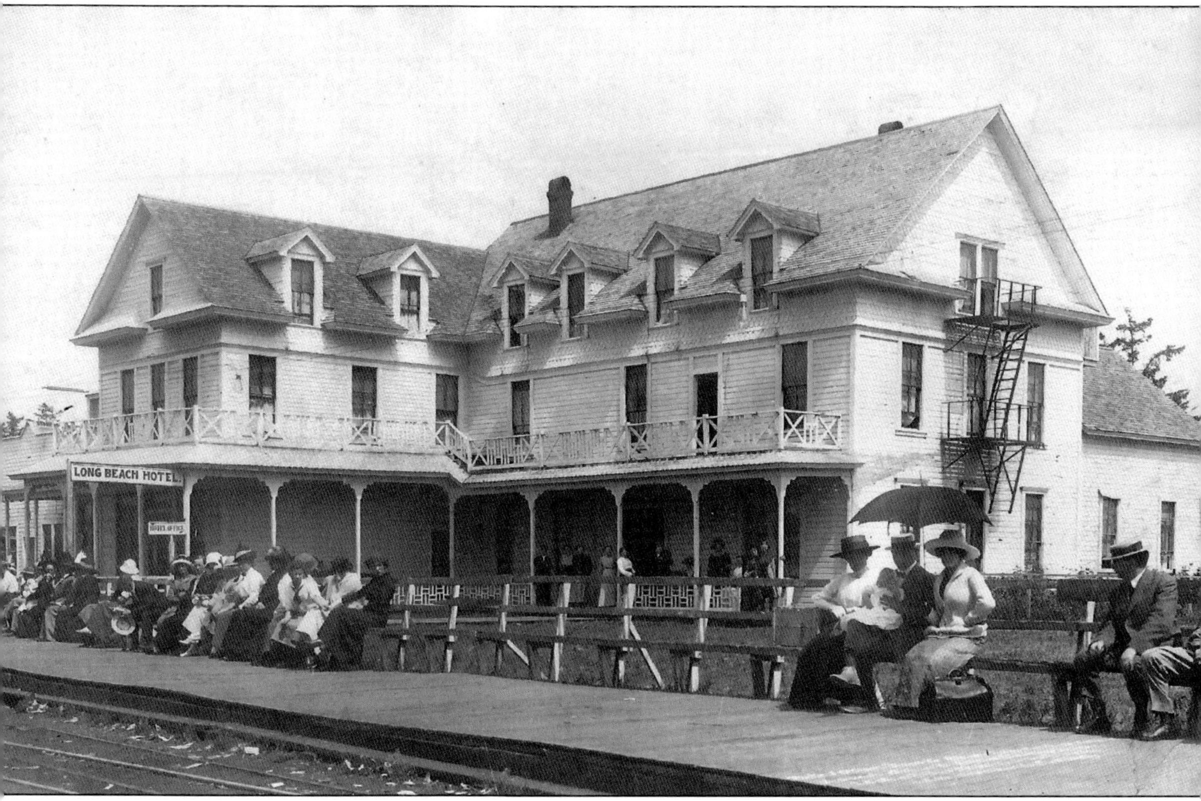

THE FIRST HOTEL. Tinker built Long Beach's first hotel, an imposing white building of 40 rooms located in the center of town. When the railroad was established, it ran right down the main street of town, the tracks just a few feet from the front door of Tinker's hotel. The train, with its direct connection with boats from Portland, brought hundreds of visitors, who soon began to build summer cottages in the developing community. Other large hotels, residential districts, and a variety of stores were built as the area prospered. In 1896, when Tinker's hotel burned, he replaced it with another, which was called "the most striking building in Long Beach" and continued to be the town's centerpiece until it was demolished in 1964. In the early 1900s, rooms in Tinker's Long Beach Hotel cost $9 to $12 with three meals a day included in the price. The bathroom was down the hall.

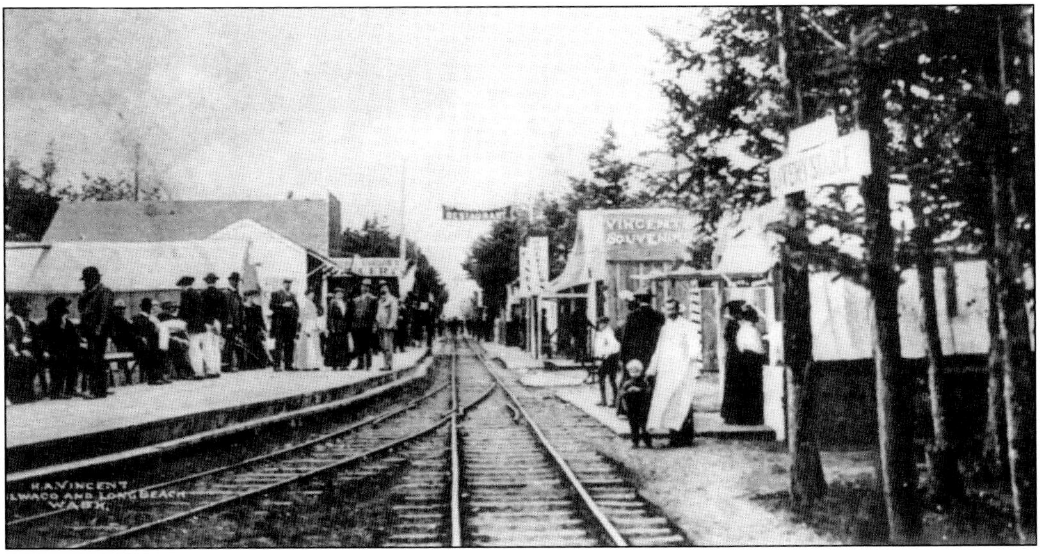

Rubberneck Row. The best seats in Long Beach for watching the comings and goings of the summer crowds were in front of the Long Beach Hotel. Residents and visitors alike gathered at train time to "meet and greet" and to generally enjoy the excitement of the throng. It was a time to show off a summer frock, to get the latest news, or to see the occasional arriving dignitary. In winter, however, it was a different story. Most stores in Long Beach were boarded up for the season, few people were on the streets, and Rubberneck Row was all but deserted.

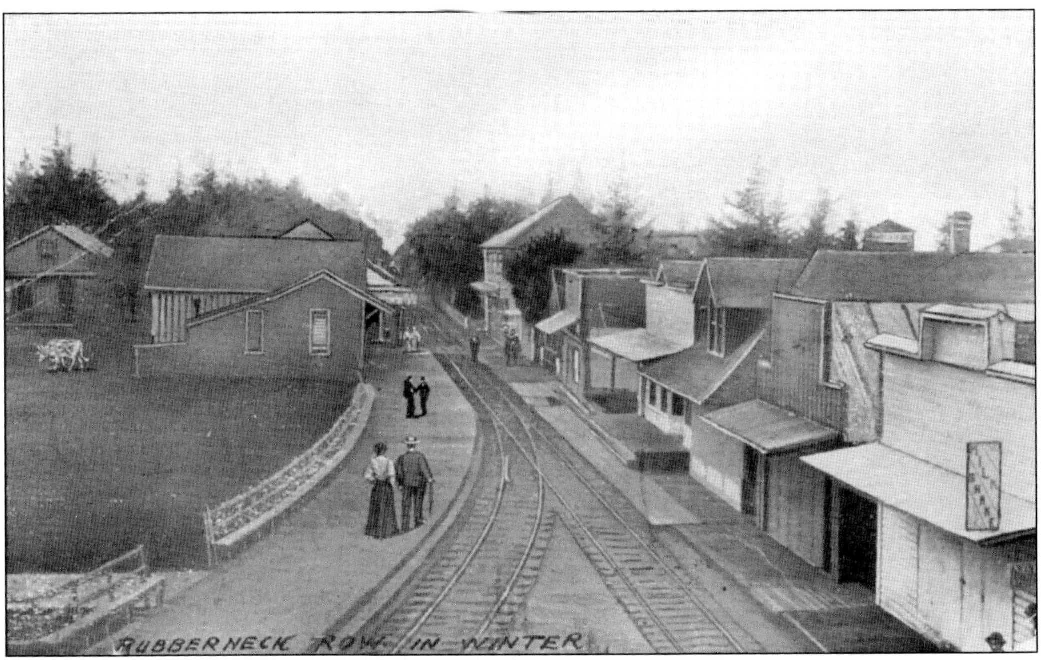

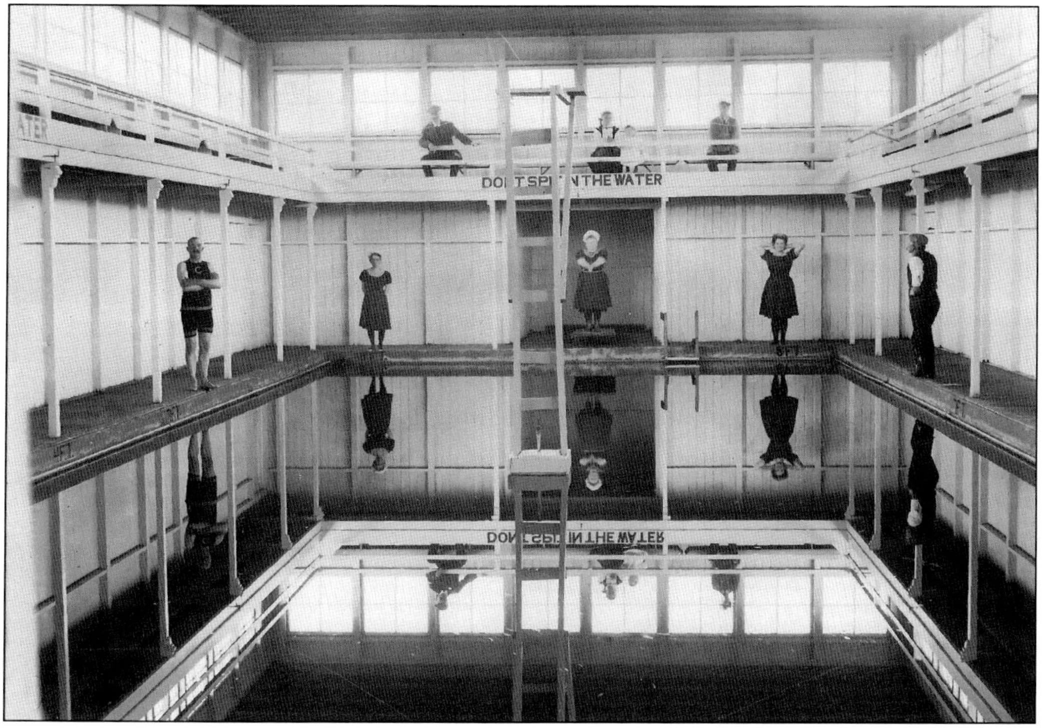

LONG BEACH ATTRACTIONS. While the beach was indeed a major attraction, it was not conducive to swimming. Cold water temperatures, a dangerous undertow, and wave-tossed driftwood made the Pacific Ocean at the North Beach Peninsula a treacherous playground. The solution to this problem was the natatorium. The Crystal Baths, a spacious indoor swimming pool offering piped-in saltwater, a high diving board, and bathing suits at a 25¢ rental fee, was a popular destination. The town abounded with other activities, as well. Parades, dances, horseback rides, souvenir shops, and restaurants provided a jolly, carnival atmosphere. Years later, one visitor reminisced, "It was truly the most exciting place in the world."

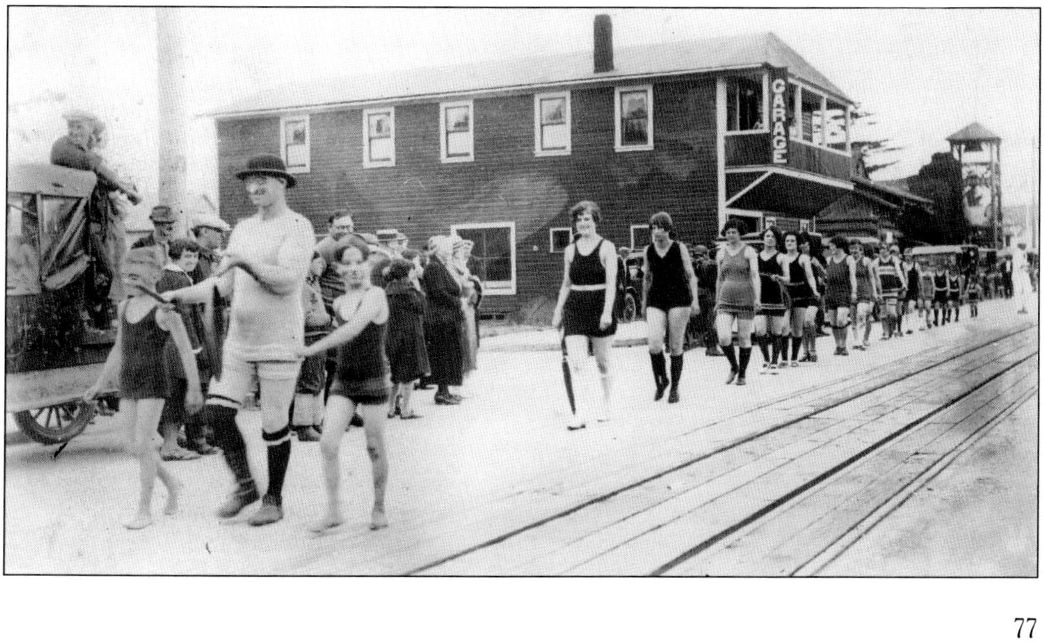

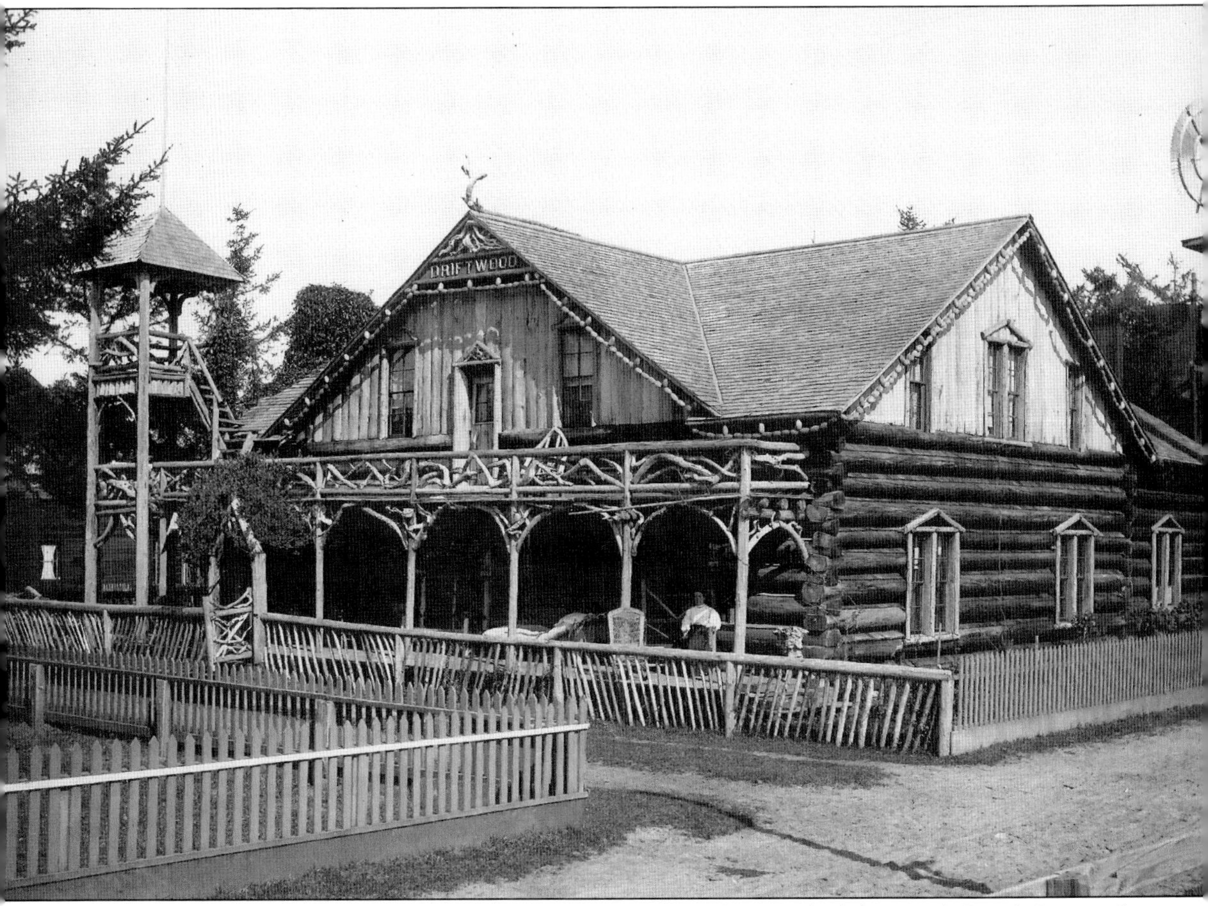

THE DRIFTWOOD HOTEL. One of the most picturesque and unusual of the North Beach Peninsula hotels was the Driftwood, begun in the 1880s by a Mr. Merritt from materials gathered on the beach. When Tom and Molly Lyniff bought the hotel from him, Tom continued the building project, combing the beach for useful odds and ends. Finally, the hotel was considered completed when he incorporated the timbers salvaged from two log rafts that had broken up on the Columbia River bar. Examples of Tom's creativity were everywhere: short, weathered pieces of wood carefully pieced together formed the interior walls; the stairwell was partially enclosed by an intricate pattern of fishing floats. Salvaged materials included remnants of shipwrecks—oars from the *Strathblane*, hinges from the *Frank W. Howe*—and even furniture, including a writing desk from the *Point Loma* and willowware dishes and a bookcase from the *Potrimpos*.

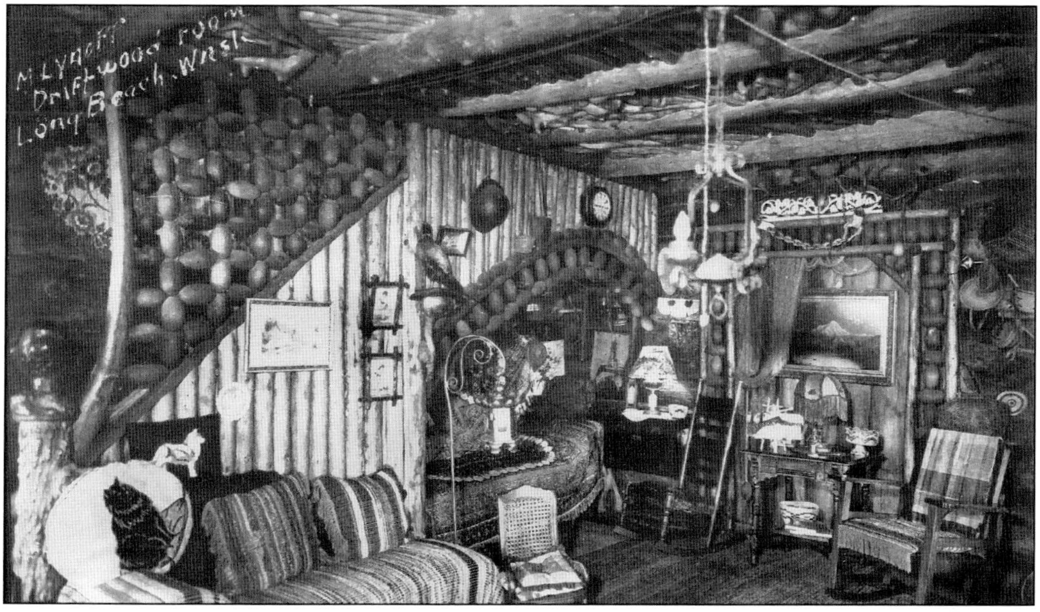

Lobbying for Tourism. While Tom Lyniff continued working on his driftwood masterpiece, his wife, Molly, kept her eye on the legislators in Olympia to make sure that her hotel guests were accorded all the pleasures the beach could offer. In a letter written in January 1911 to Sen. Harry Espy, she wrote, "Kind Friend, I want your advice and help. I cannot buy clams or crabs [in] June, July, August and it works hardship and great disappointment to [the] Public as [they] come and expect seafood. . . . Now can't we have this law changed, if not to be shipped out of state, ship them for our own use in state. . . . I can't keep house without food . . . so please help me as this is for the benefit of Public at large." (Below, Sydney Stevens.)

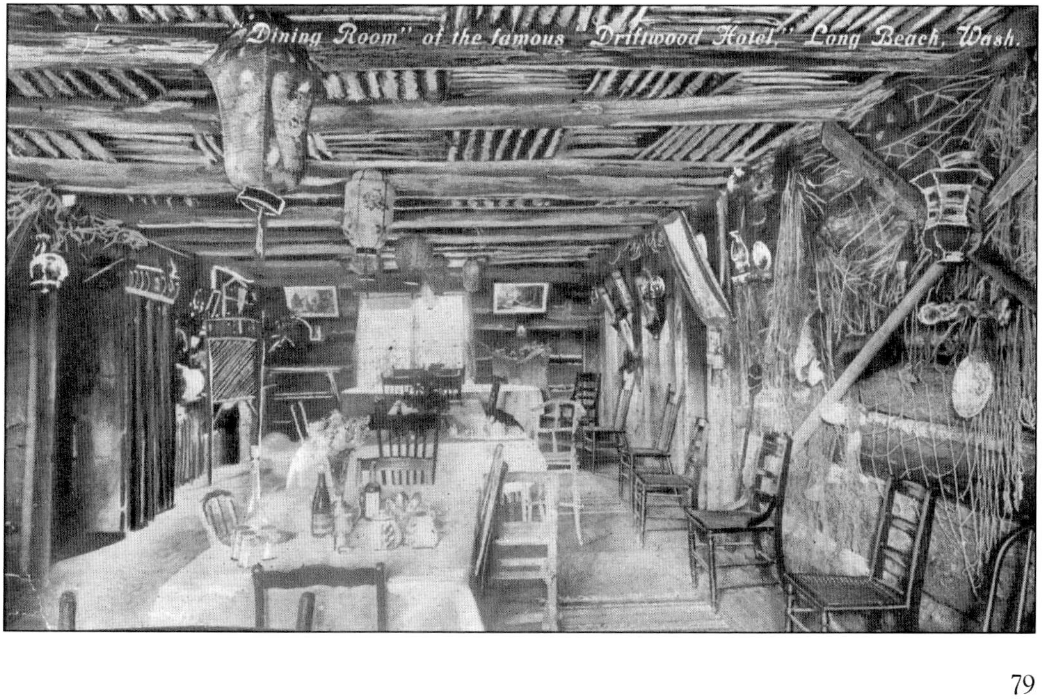

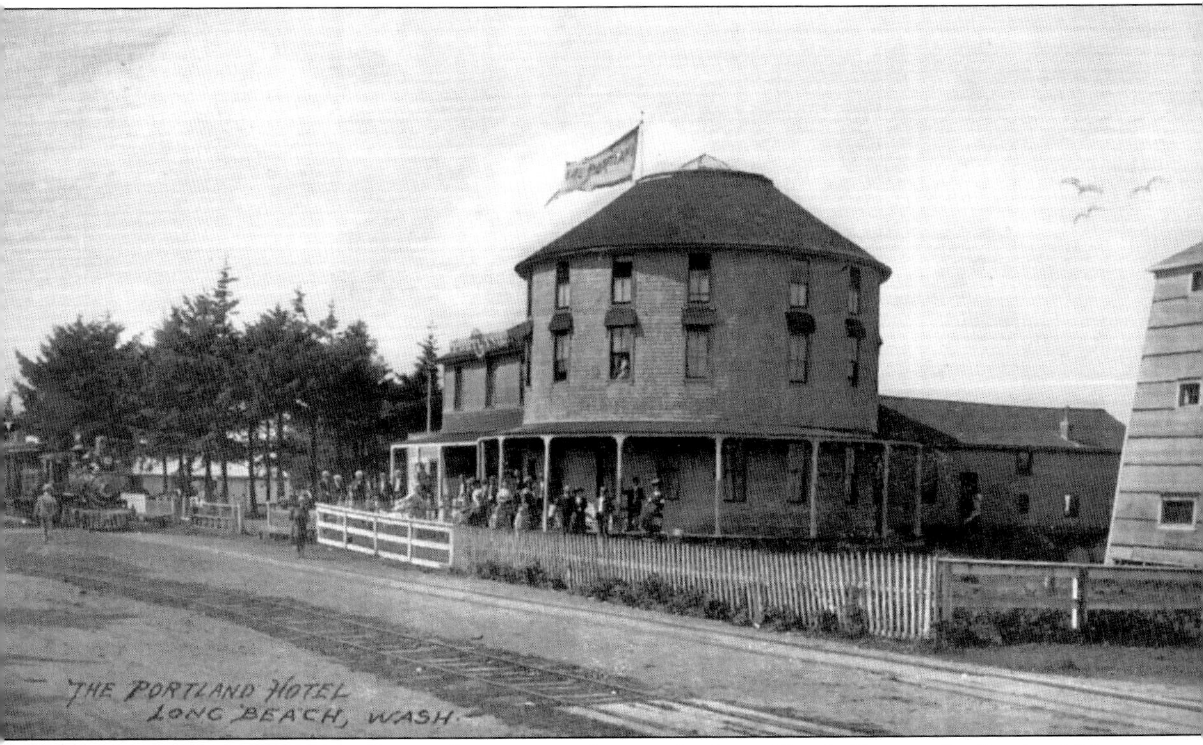

ALSO CLAIMED BY FIRE. Located conveniently near the Long Beach Depot, the Portland Hotel had a distinctive circular tower at one end from which, during "the season," flew a large pennant proclaiming its name. The hotel's front yard featured a fountain complete with an overgrown plaster nymph, and its bar and restaurant were convenient gathering places and well patronized. One evening when the owners were away at the motion picture theater, the hotel burned down—a tragedy all too common at the beach. Like most other structures on the North Beach Peninsula, the hotel was built entirely of wood and depended upon wood to fuel cook stoves, fireplaces, boilers, and pot-bellied heating stoves. The attendant danger was an ever-present reality. The train served as the emergency fire vehicle. Word was sent from depot to depot by the railway's telegraph, and the nearest locomotive was put into service. As it rushed toward the fire, it slowed to allow volunteer firemen, armed with their axes and buckets, to hop aboard.

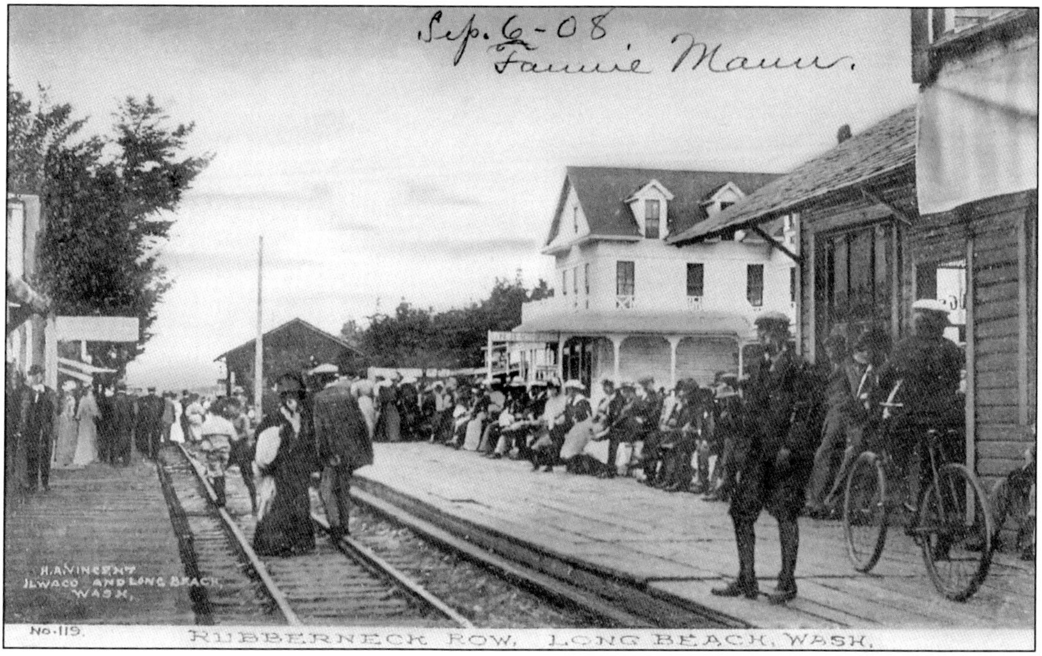

THE BOULEVARD. Since the main street of Long Beach was entirely taken up by the train as it puffed through town, a large boulevard was constructed one block to the west for the convenience of equestrian and pedestrian traffic. The driftwood brought in by high tides accumulated on both sides of Boulevard Avenue and was a convenient source of firewood for Long Beach residents. In 1913, a 2-mile-long jetty was built near Cape Disappointment. In the years following its completion, accreting sands eventually changed the beach so that the tide line was many hundreds of feet to the west and Long Beach was no longer flooded by high winter tides. (Above, Brenda Hill.)

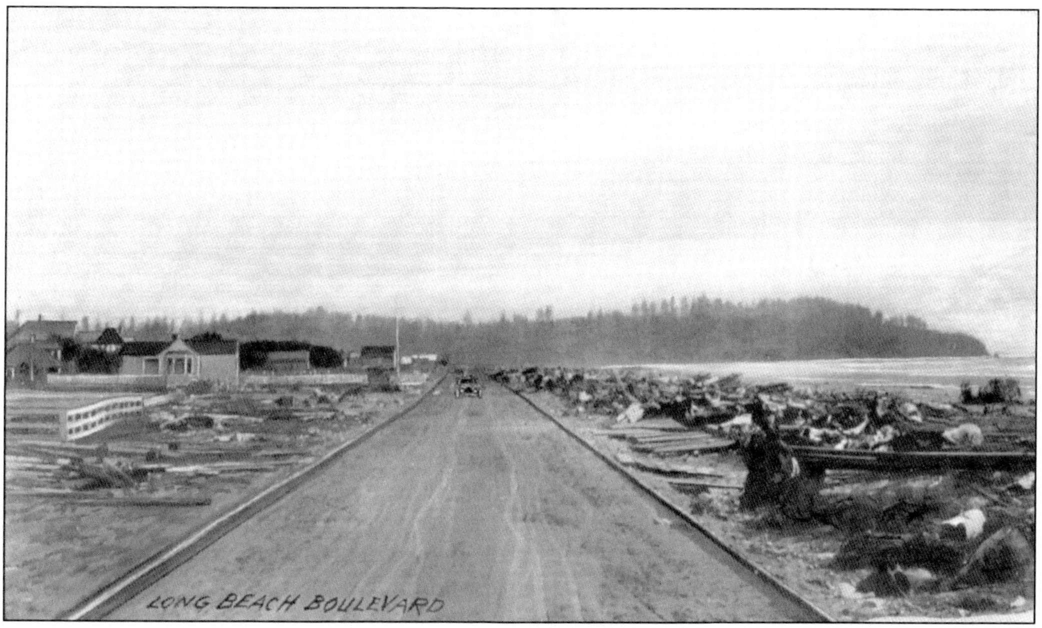

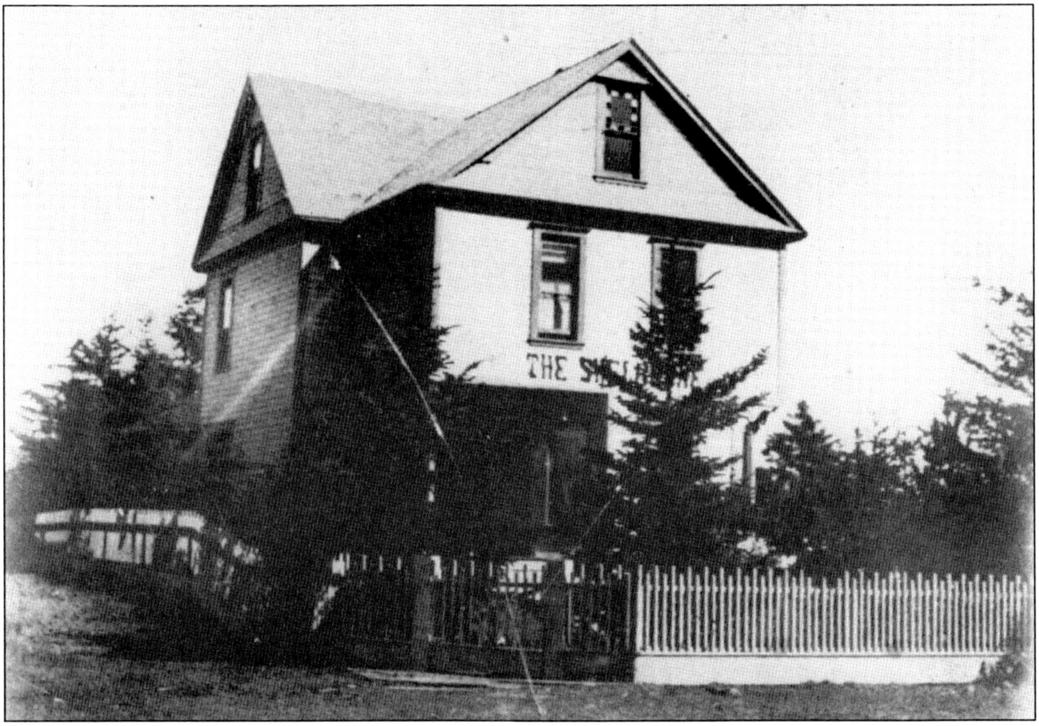

A Move across the Street. The Shelburne Hotel in Seaview was built in 1896 with lumber milled in South Bend, barged to Nahcotta, and transported to Seaview by the IR&N. The two-and-one-half-story structure had 14 rooms for permanent and summer boarders and was spacious enough to accommodate builder Charles Beaver's four-member family. In 1911, it was purchased by Timothy and Julia Hoare, moved across the street to its present location, and joined to another building. Timothy convinced the railroad to put up a covered waiting platform just south of the hotel so that the Shelburne, like the Breakers, had its very own stop for the convenience of guests. (Below, Charlotte Herrold Davis.)

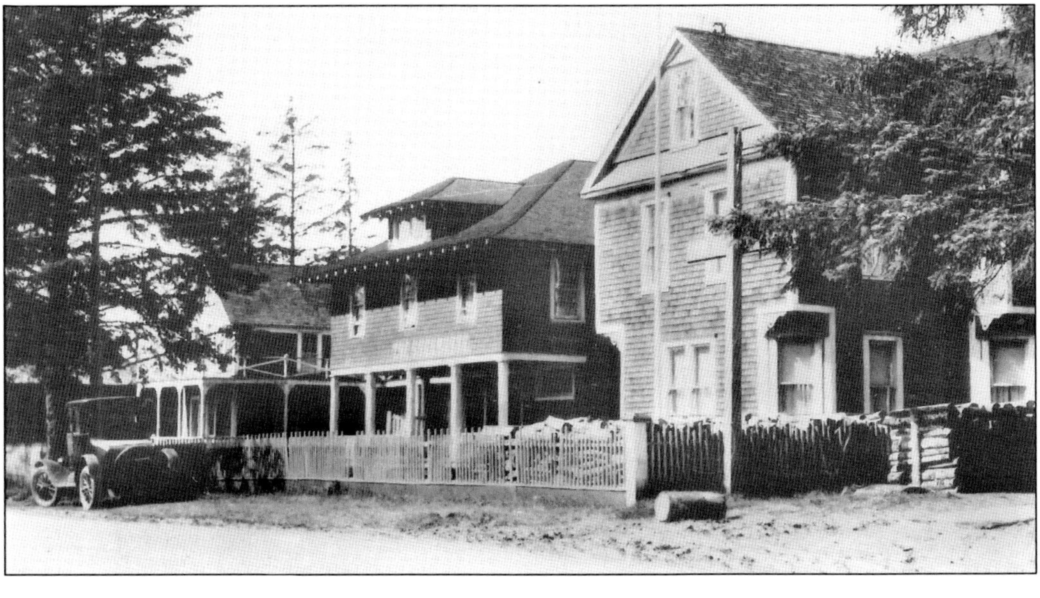

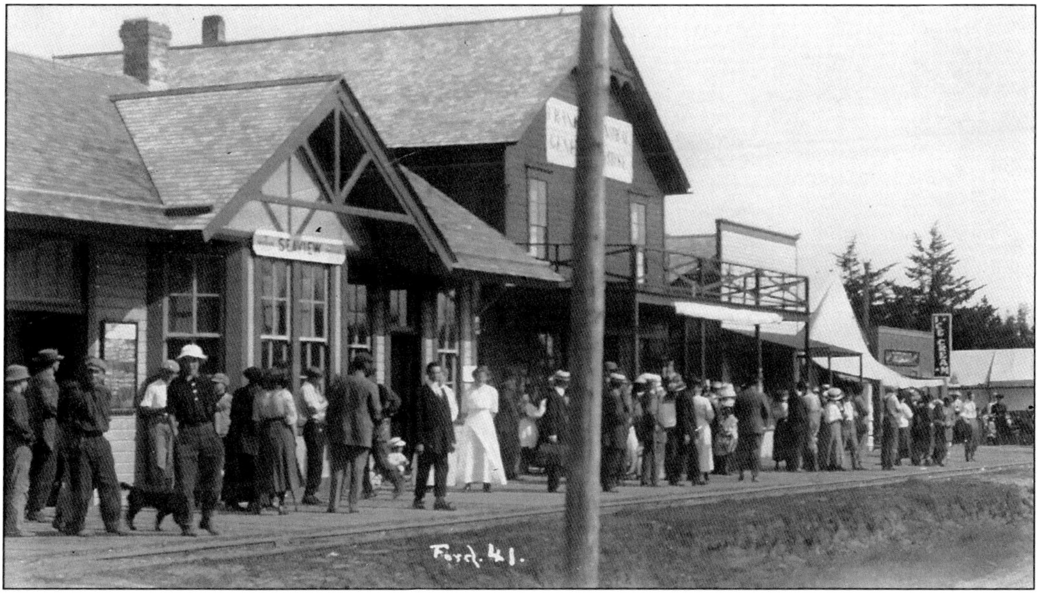

JONATHAN STOUT'S SEAVIEW. In 1880, Jonathan L. Stout purchased 153.5 acres of ocean frontage for a summer resort and the next year had his property subdivided into 50-by-100-foot lots. Hundreds of lots were sold for $100 each, tents suddenly materialized, and Stout built a hotel facing the ocean. It accommodated those who preferred not to rough it in tents or who could not yet afford to build a cottage (though Stout claimed one could be built for $200 to $300). His hotel had an entertainment center and dance pavilion, a bathhouse, and a stable for horses and carriages. After 1888, when the railroad came through, he added a general store. Unfortunately, Stout's hotel burned in 1892, and he never recovered financially. However, the resort was a success, and Seaview remains a popular ocean-side community.

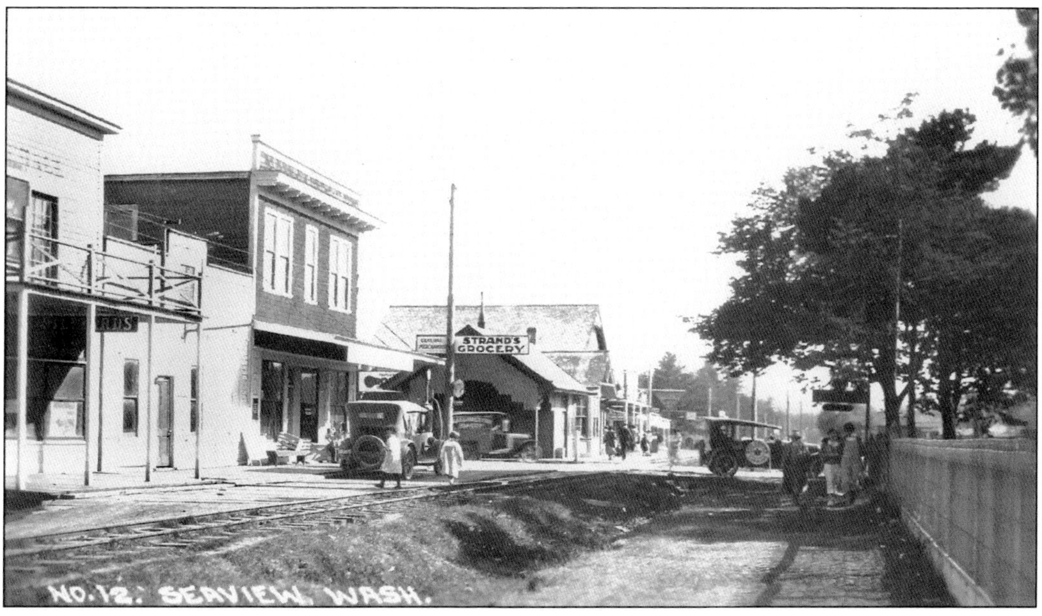

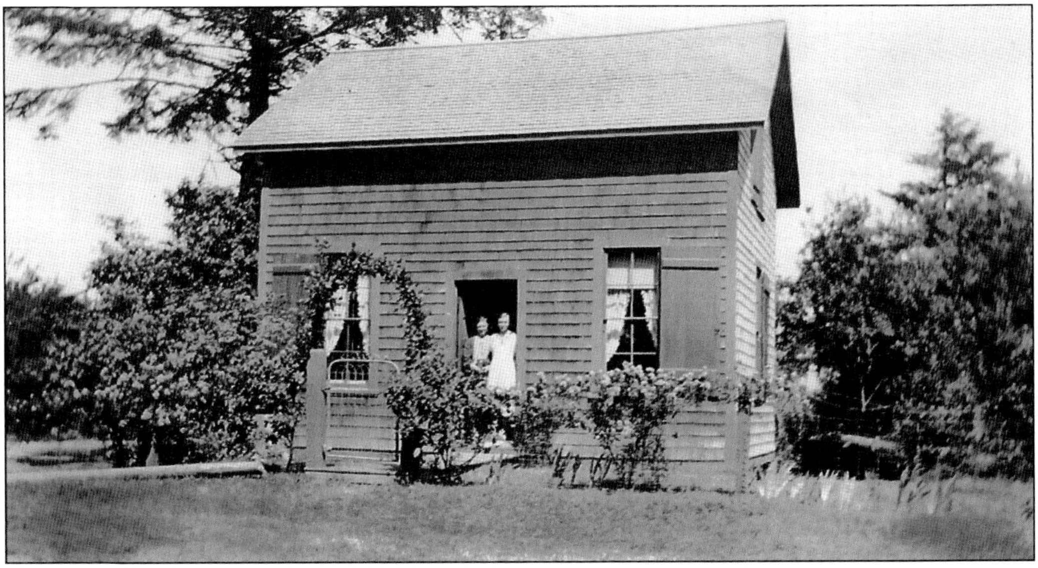

Seaview Cottages. By usual definition, a "cottage" is small, but that was not the case with many of the vacation cottages built in Seaview at the end of the 19th and beginning of the 20th centuries. The Seaview cottages were often quite grand, perhaps built with turrets, a great deal of gingerbread, or even with the addition of a carriage house. However, most were of simple frame construction and were built with only a layer or two of newspapers nailed to the wall as insulation. As new owners remodel, they can often ascertain the year their cottage was built by reading the papers.

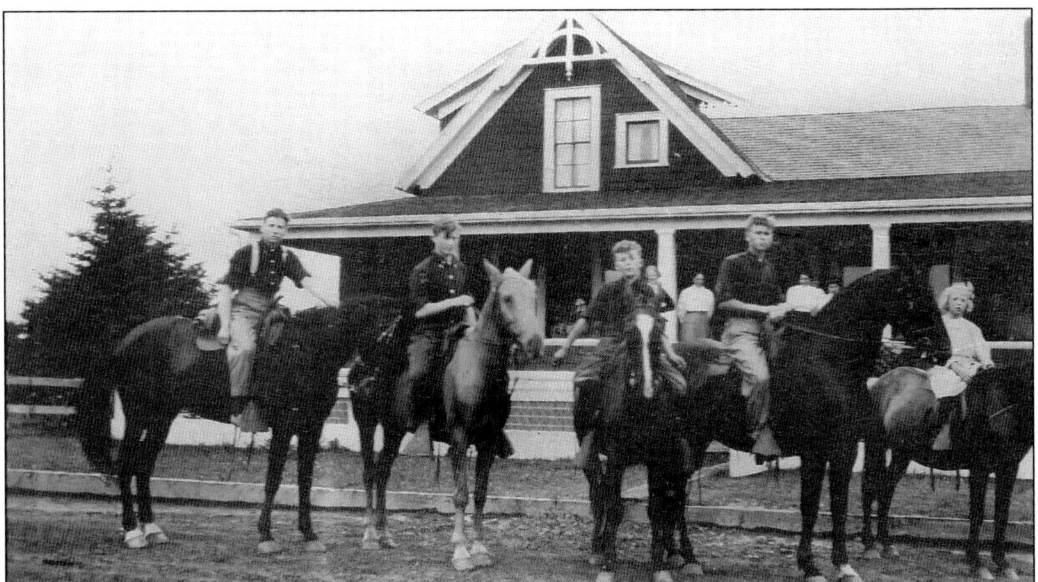

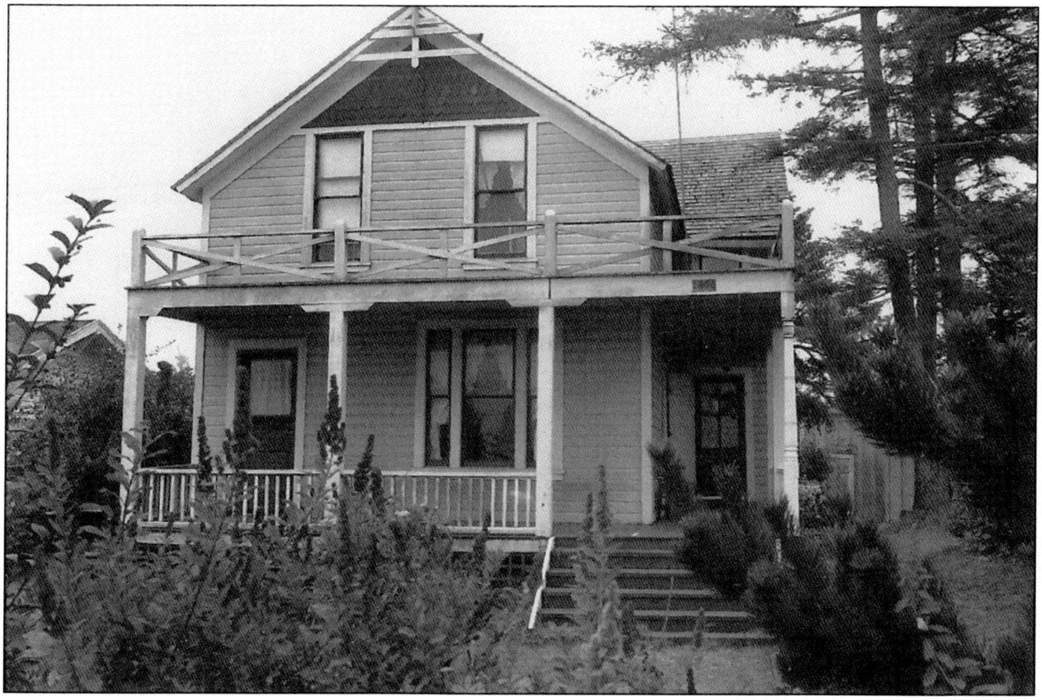

Summer Vacation. Although some summer residents brought the family cow to provide fresh milk or, perhaps, a few hens for eggs, they were dependent upon the area for many other foods. Seafood was easily obtainable, and for most, getting it was an enjoyable recreation. Produce, however, was another matter, and vacationers depended upon full-time residents to provide vegetables for the table. Martha Turner Murfin remembers that her mother had a wonderful garden: "She sold her produce to the Seaview summer people and to the local markets. . . . My brother, Bob, and some of the neighbor boys had a delivery route that went out Holman Road to the Butte, back along the railroad bed and over Boulevard and then around by the Shelburne Hotel. . . . I was allowed to go along and help. Our 'delivery truck' was a wagon pulled by our little horse, Brownie."

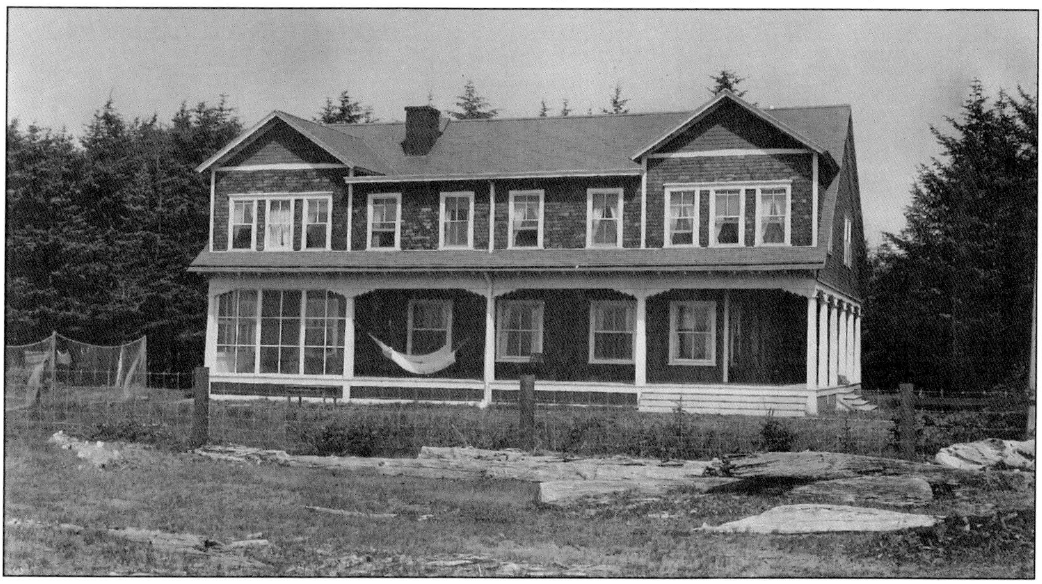

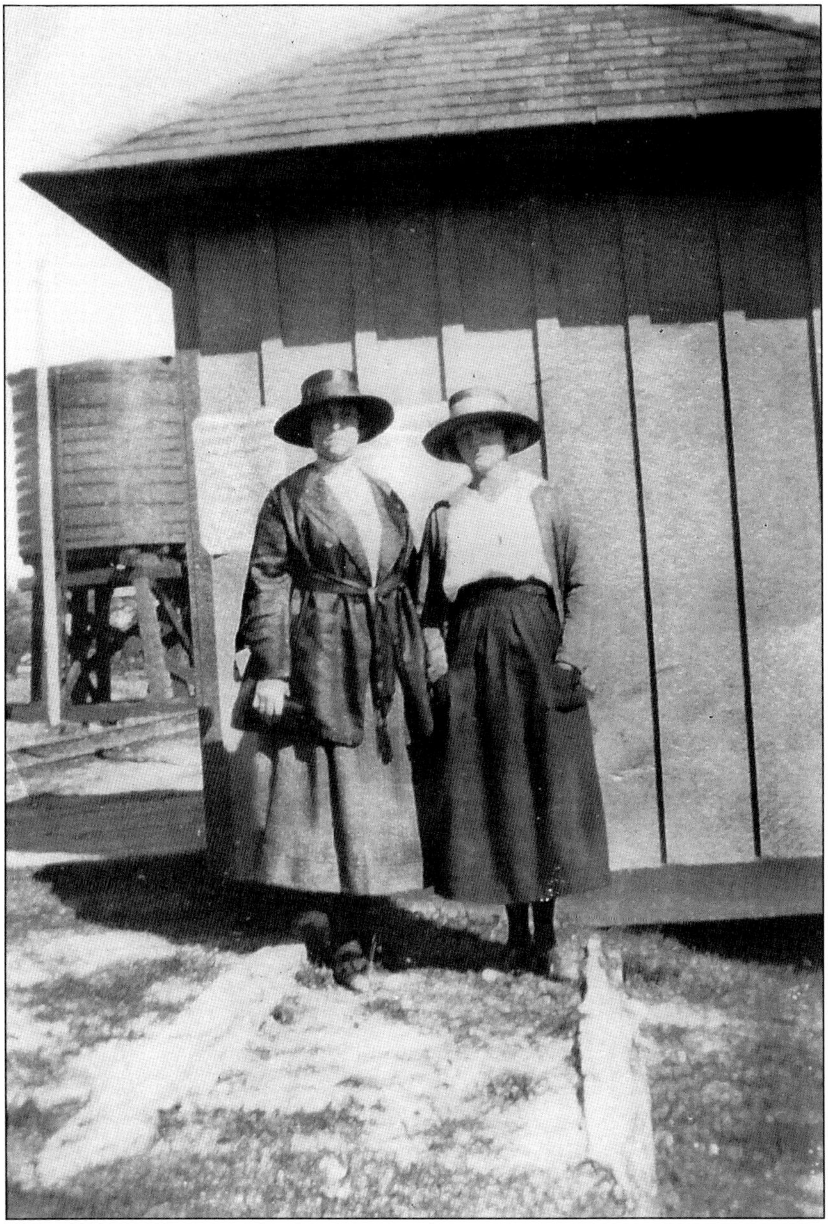

Holman Station. The station on Holman Road was a regular passenger stop during the summer months and was the location of a water tank as well. The little three-sided station served the resort subdivision just south of Seaview that had been named for James D. Holman. Pioneer Holman arrived on the North Beach Peninsula in the 1840s and built the very first hotel in the area—Holman House in Pacific City. It was a prefabricated building purchased in San Francisco for $20,000 and shipped to Pacific City at an additional cost of $8,000. In 1852, when Pacific City was found to be within the boundaries of the Cape Disappointment Military Reservation, Holman moved to his Donation Land Claim just outside the military zone. His claim included land overlooking the Pacific Ocean, Baker's Bay, and the Columbia River. In 1873, Holman subdivided his ocean property and promoted it as a Portland summer resort. The resort was known as "Holman" and also as "The Willows" because of the numerous shrub-like willow trees in the area.

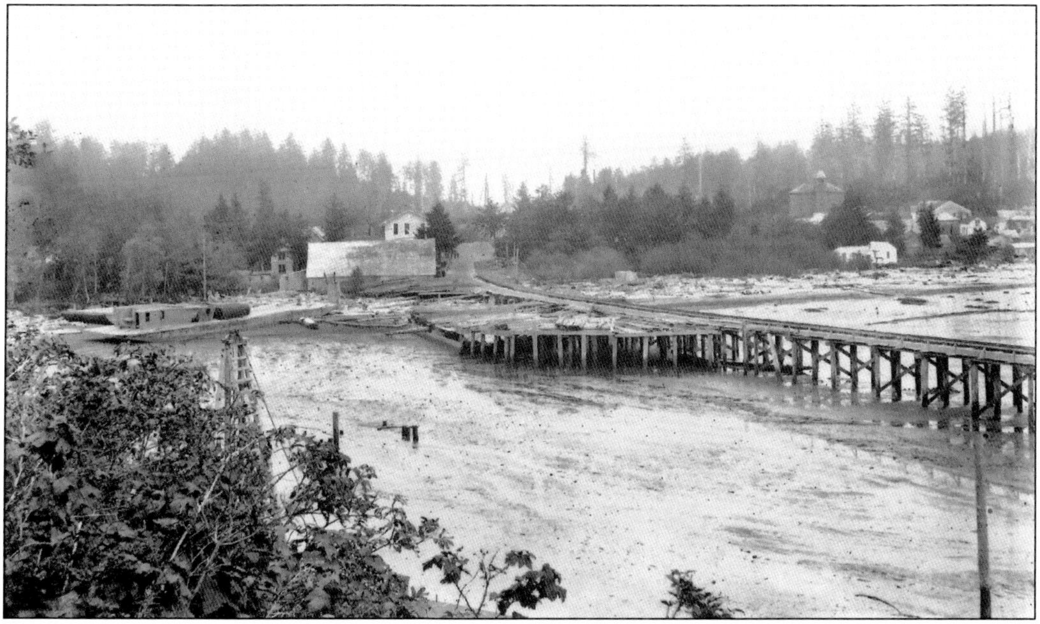

WHEALDONBURG, UNITY, AND ILWACO. Called No´skwalakuthl by the Chinook Indians, the area on Baker's Bay began to be settled by whites in the late 1840s. The quiet little fishing village was at first called "Whealdonburg" after early settler Isaac Whealdon. The soldiers at Cape Disappointment's Fort Canby called it "Unity" during the Civil War years, when there was much talk of the Union. In 1873, James D. Holman subdivided his land there and filed the plat for the town of Ilwaco, a name honoring his Native American neighbor Elowahka Jim. The name was made official by the post office department three years later, but it was not until 1890 that Ilwaco was incorporated—two years after the southern terminus of the railway had been established there. (Above, King Family Archive; below, PCHS.)

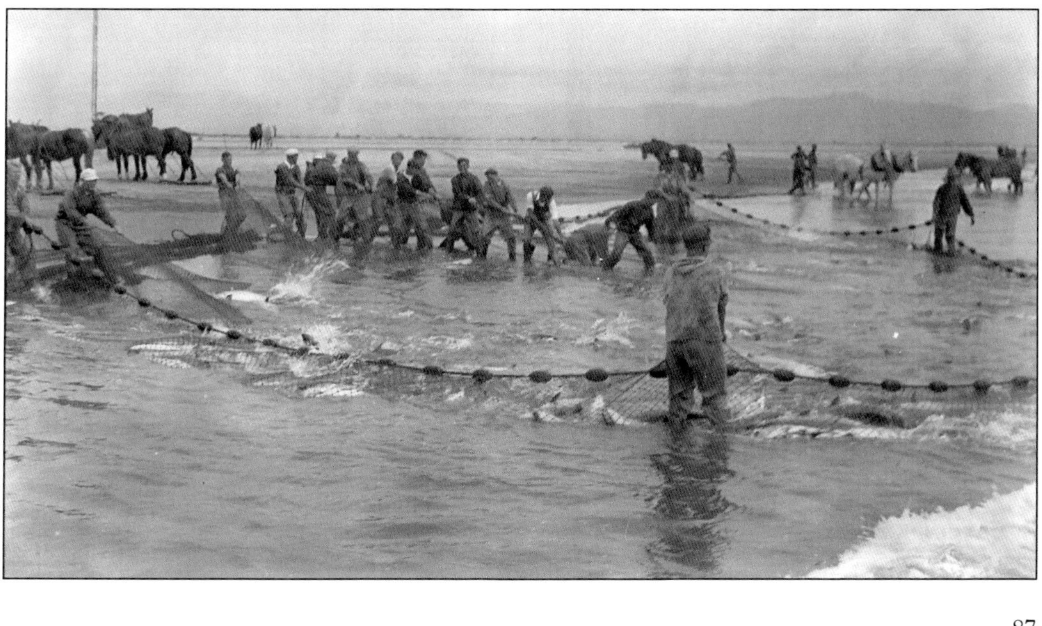

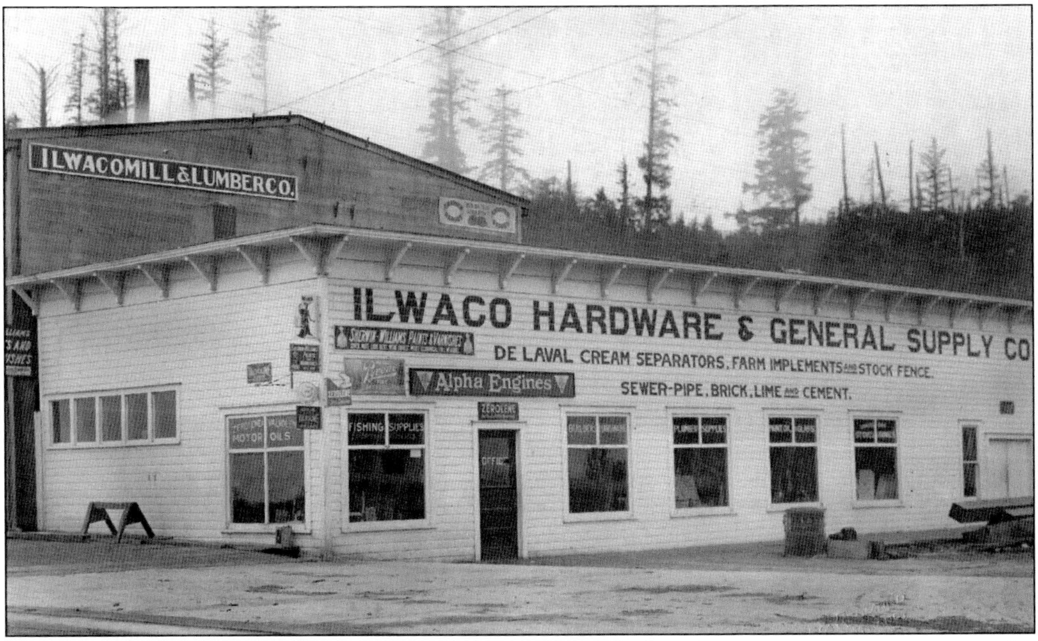

A Working Town. Though it was the first stopping-off place for most visitors coming to the North Beach Peninsula, Ilwaco was a working town rather than a resort community or tourist destination. Generally, travelers getting off the boat at the Ilwaco wharf immediately boarded the train, heading for communities to the north. The people of Ilwaco, primarily of Scandinavian or Finnish heritage, supported themselves by working for the Ilwaco Mill and Lumber Company or by salmon fishing for the canneries. At the dawn of the 20th century, the largest cannery in Ilwaco was owned by B. A. Seaborg, one of the directors of the IR&N. His cannery crew, like others on the Columbia, were mostly Chinese working on seasonal contracts as fish slimers and cutters. Only those of European descent were allowed to do the actual fishing. (Above, Charles Doupé.)

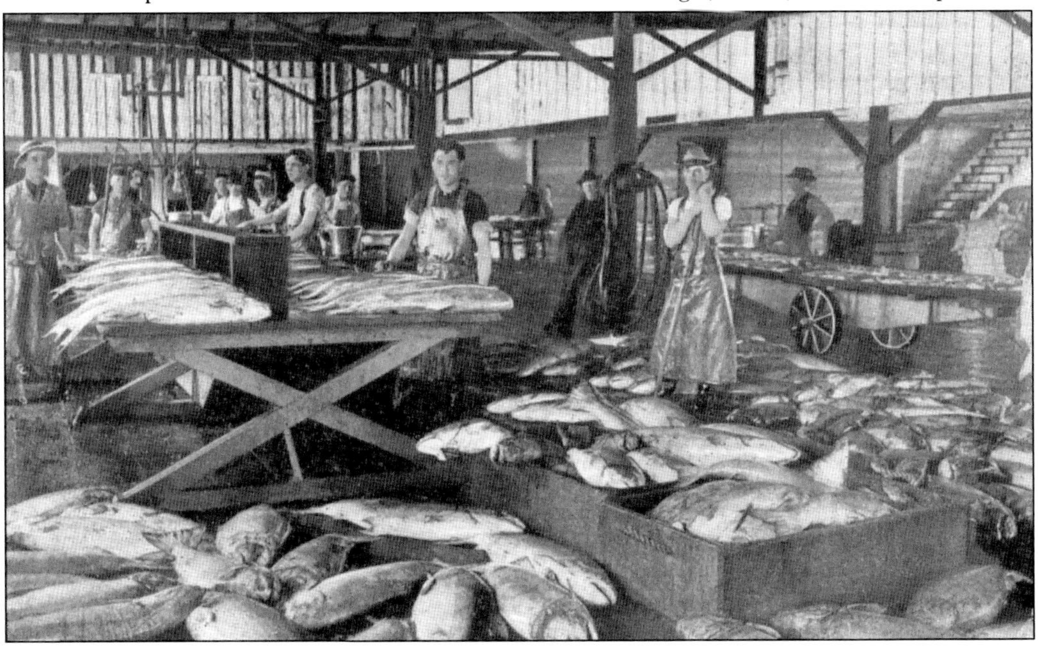

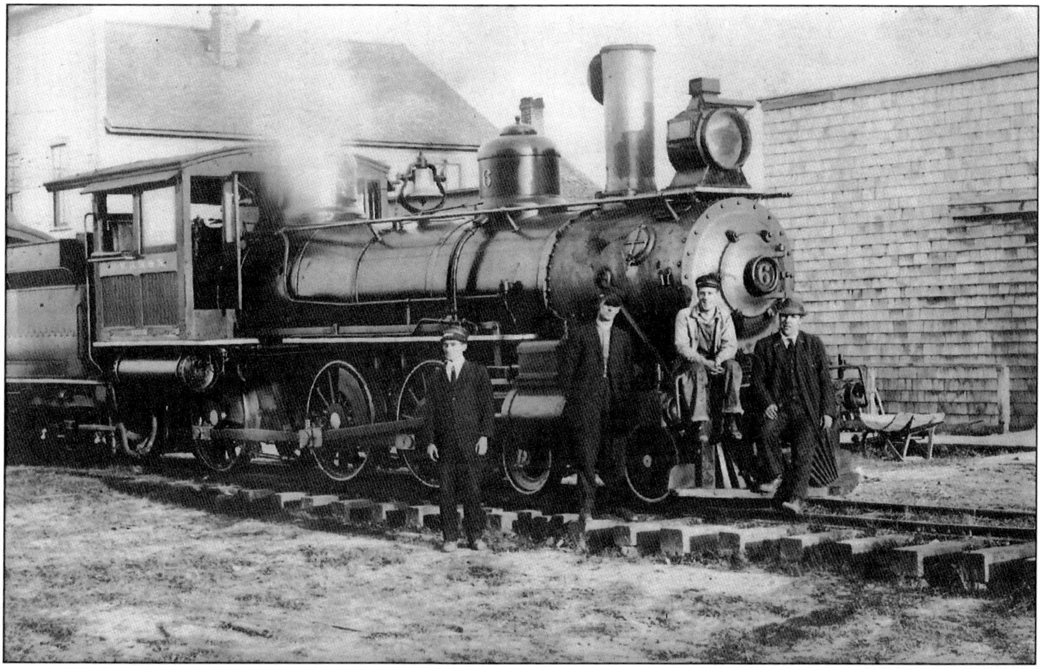

Ilwaco Versus the Railroad. Even though Ilwaco was the end of the line for freight and passengers heading south on the peninsula, it was still the OR&N Company that provided most of the connecting river transportation. The company's small steamer, the *Nahcotta*, and larger vessels such as the *T.J. Potter* met the trains and made the necessary link with destinations in Oregon and points farther south. Shortly after the city incorporated, Ilwaco challenged the right of the railroad to the continued use of the shore off First Street for its railway wharf. A court ruling found in the railroad's favor, but bad feelings between town and railroad continued for some years. (Above, Charles Mulvey; below, Charlotte Herrold Davis.)

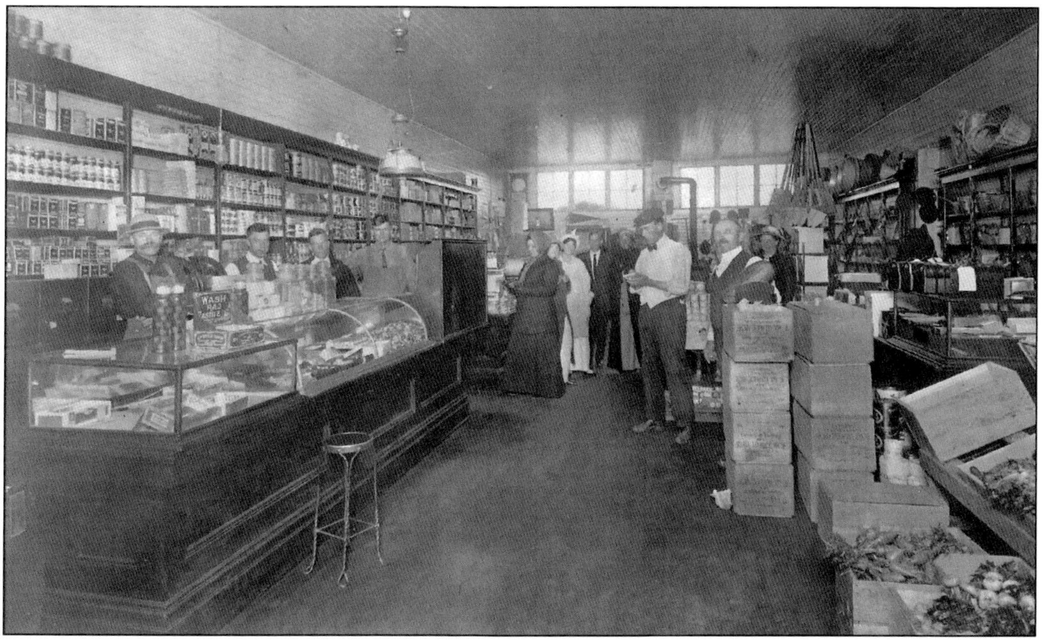

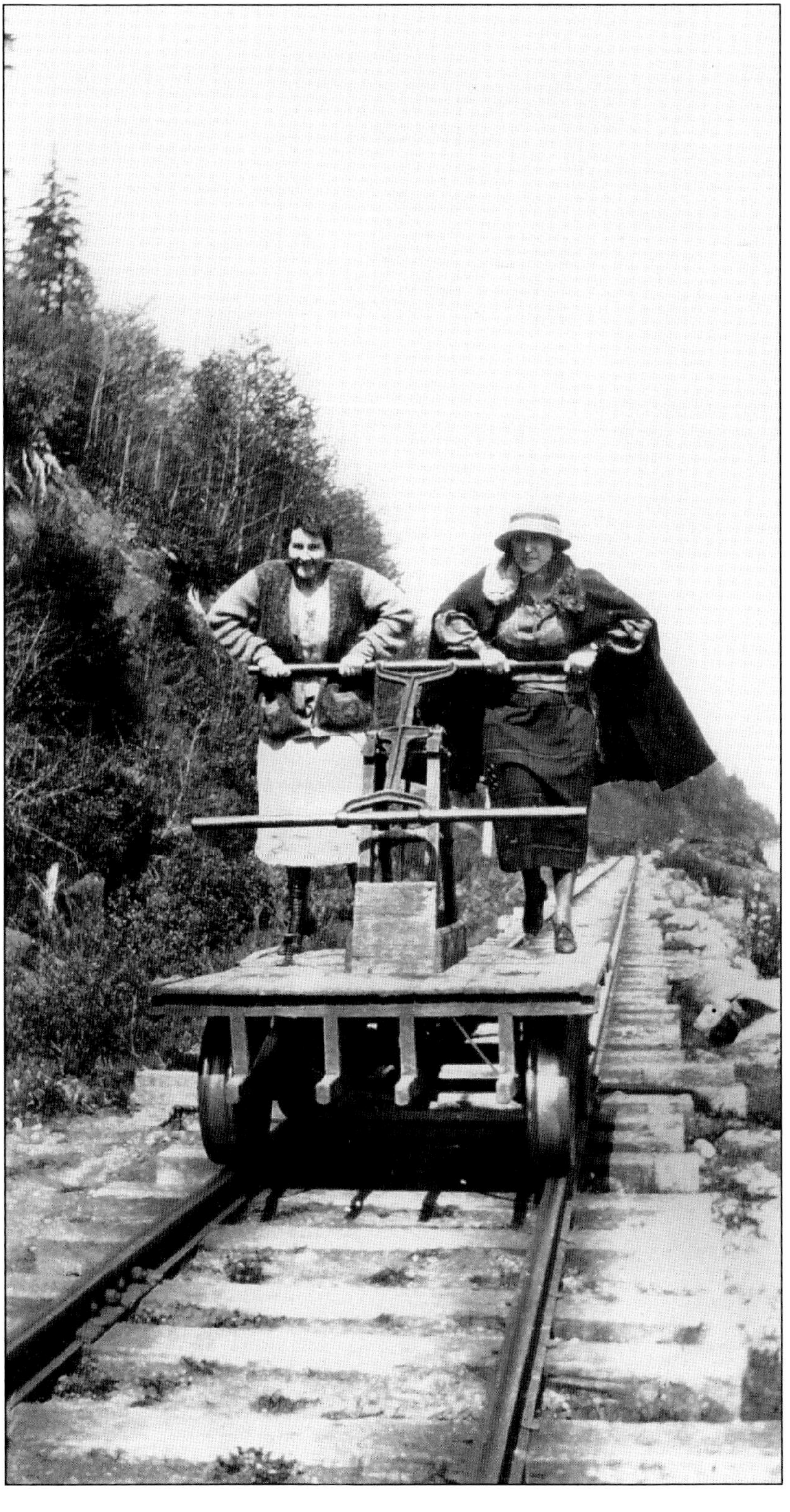

All in the Family. Year after year, the little train followed the rails from Ilwaco to Nahcotta and back again. She was a familiar sight—as much a part of the community as were the summer homes, the neighbors' livestock, or the fishing boats on bay and river. People depended upon the train to bring their mail and supplies, to take their products to market, or to help them out in an emergency. She was even the source of a playful moment now and then—perhaps a moment for display in the family photograph album. It wasn't that they took the train for granted exactly; but just as with a favorite relative who could be exasperating one moment or good for a chuckle the next, residents and visitors alike simply counted on the train being there. (Adelle Beechey.)

Five

A Regular Schedule at Last!

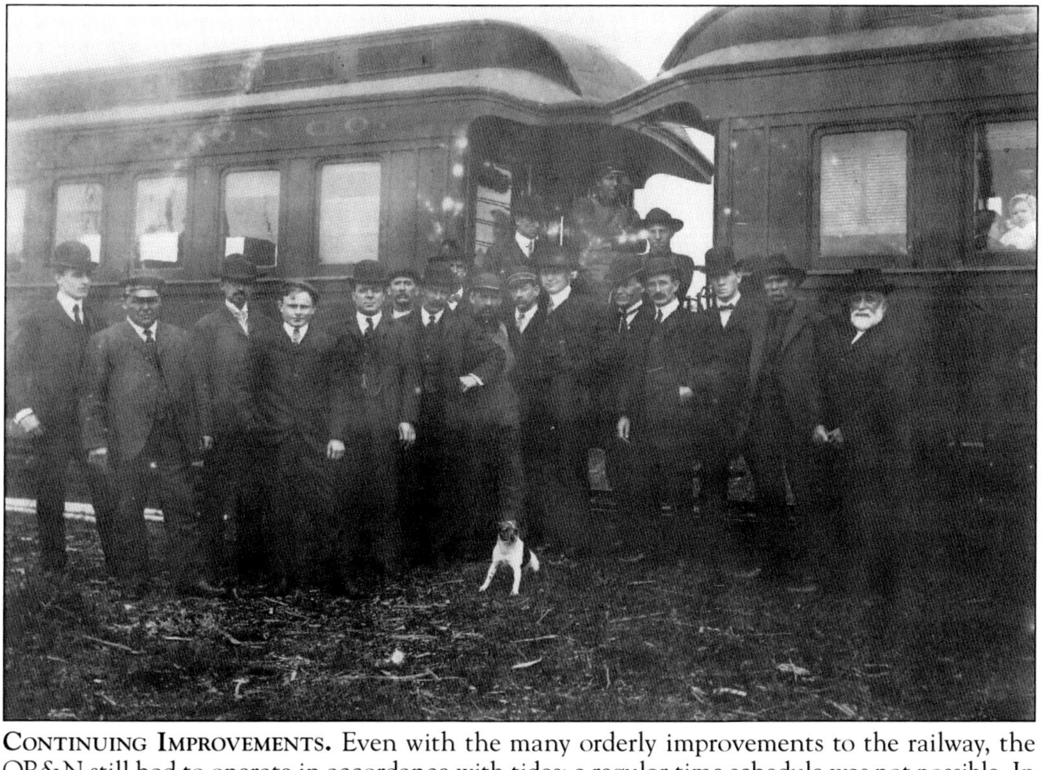

Continuing Improvements. Even with the many orderly improvements to the railway, the OR&N still had to operate in accordance with tides; a regular time schedule was not possible. In addition to that problem, the aging Ilwaco wharf needed major repairs, which the company did not consider a worthwhile investment. In the early 1900s, meetings were held to seriously explore the possibility of extending the line eastward from Ilwaco. (WSPRC.)

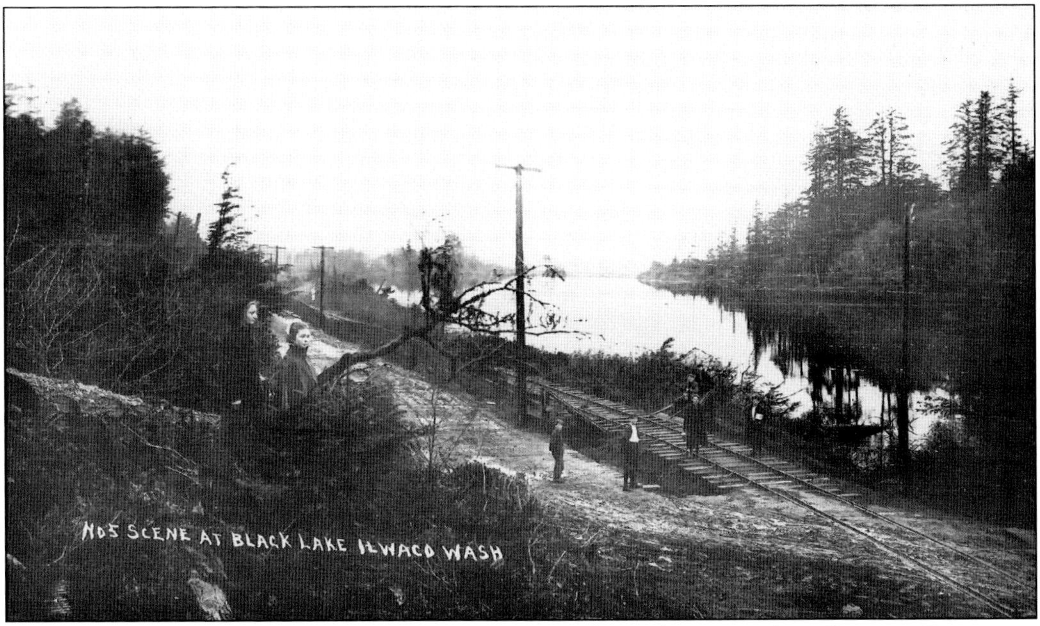

EASTWARD HO! At first, the OR&N's plan was to proceed 17 miles upriver from Ilwaco to Knappton, where it would hook up with the Columbia Valley Railroad Company's promised line along the north bank of the Columbia. By March 1907, fourteen engineers plus 400 to 500 laborers were preparing the grade. Two months later, the trestle at Black Lake was completed and tracklaying (narrow-gauge track on standard-gauge ties) began. Not long after the Ilwaco junction was finished, the OR&N learned that the proposed "North Bank" railroad had been scrapped. Construction on the Ilwaco extension came to a standstill, and when construction resumed, Cook's Station, 14 miles from Ilwaco, had been named as the revised destination. Shortly thereafter, the line refinanced and reverted to the name Ilwaco Railroad.

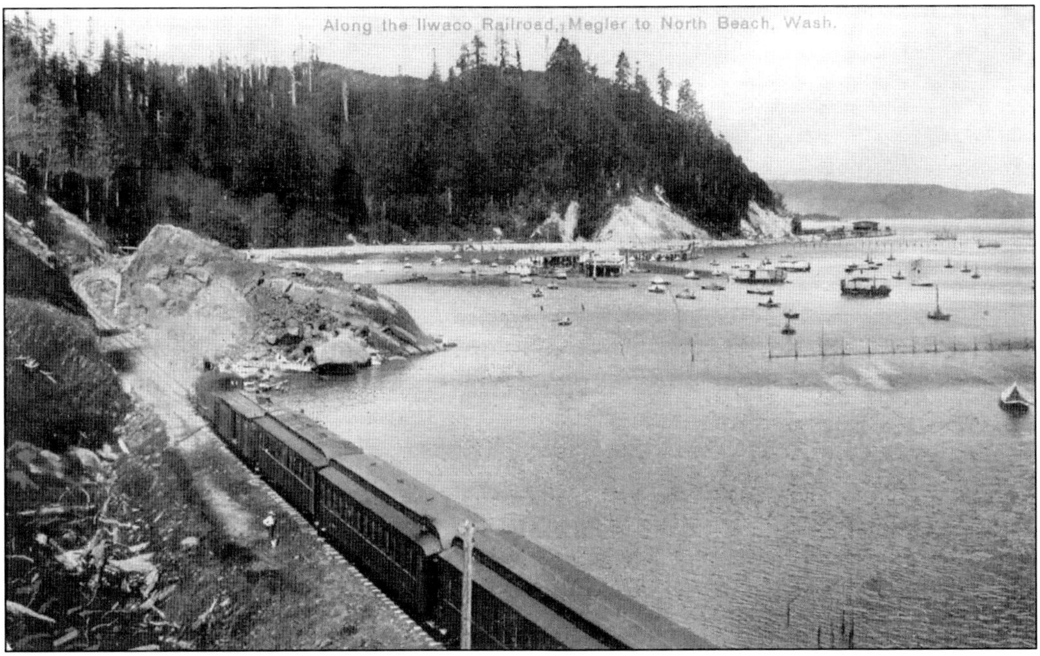

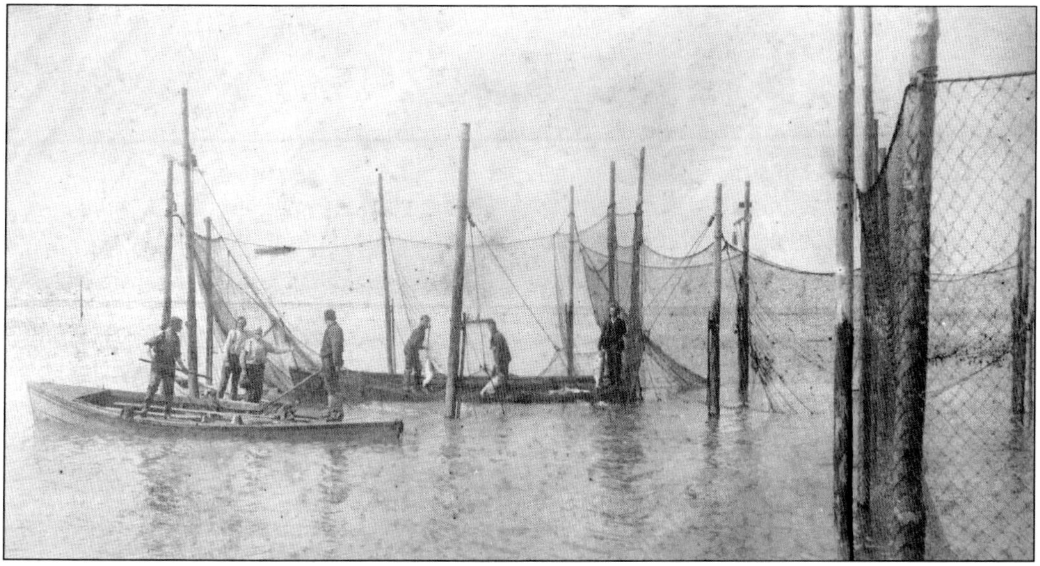

The Next Stop Upriver. The next upriver stop from Ilwaco was the fishing village of Chinook, named for the Chinook Indians who had once occupied the north shore of the lower Columbia. Its settlement began in the 1850s by fishermen, many of whom were Scandinavian sailors, but not until 1892 was a post office established there. Salmon fishing was the town's main industry, and by the 1880s, Chinook was famed throughout the United States for its salmon fishery. The turn-of-the-century census records show that salmon supported the entire population of 700. Most of the salmon supplied to the Chinook Packing Company came from fish traps placed along the river. As many as 10,000 pounds of salmon might be processed through the cannery in a single day during the spring or fall salmon run.

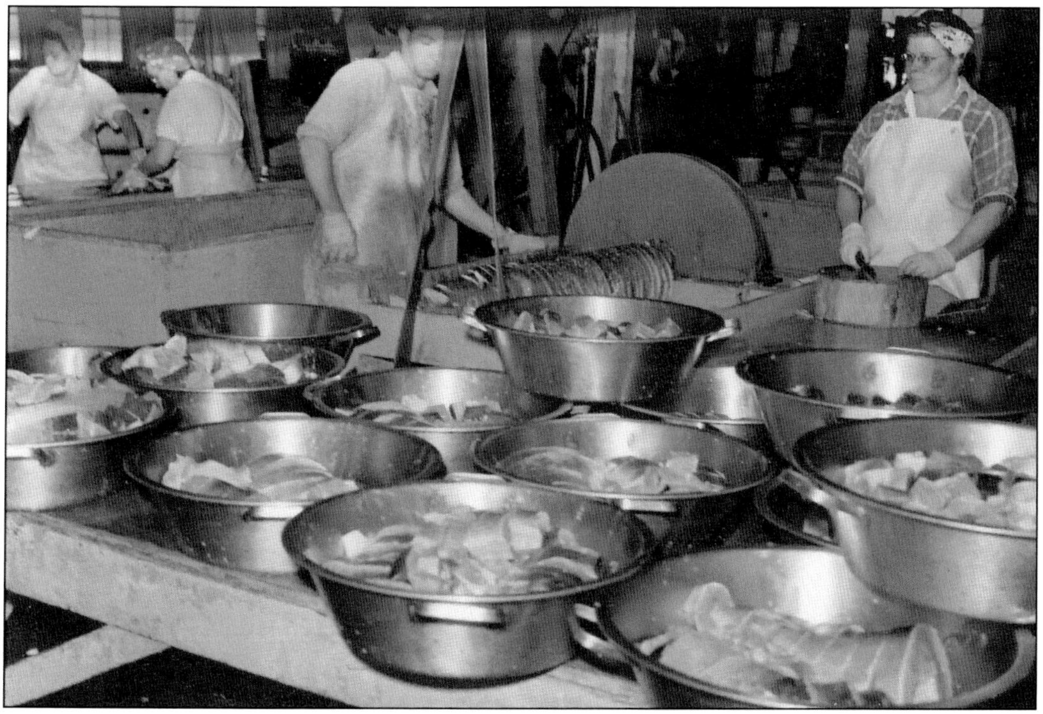

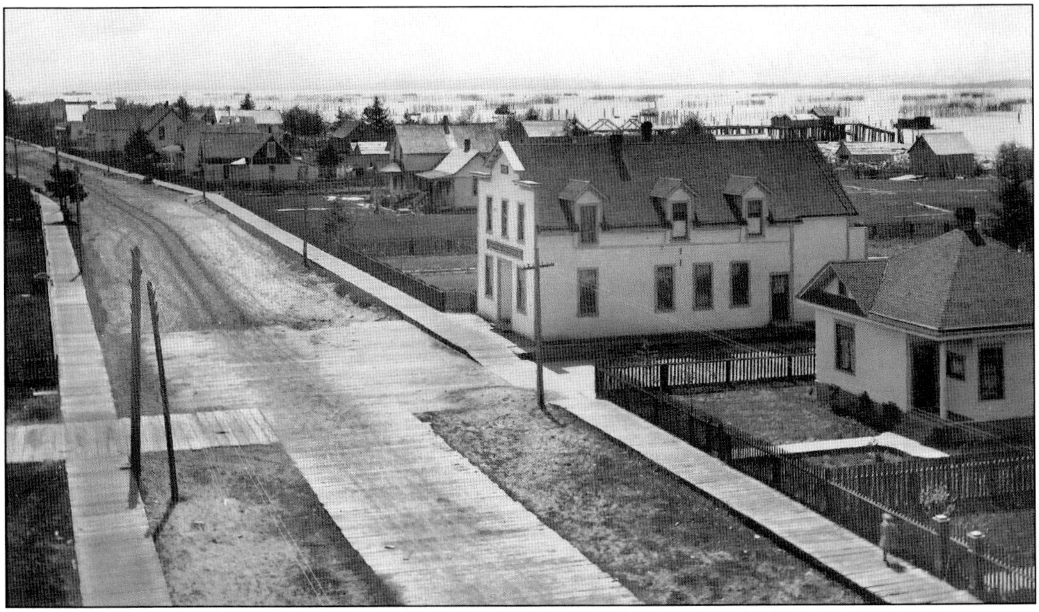

No Rails through Downtown. Unlike the main streets of Long Beach and Ilwaco, there were no railroad tracks on the main street of Chinook. The line ran one block to the north rather than through the center of town, perhaps a subtle reminder that the railway was not the primary focus of the community. In Chinook, fishing had been and remained the main occupation. It was in Chinook, too, that the first hatchery in the state of Washington was built—a community project by forward-thinking citizens. From earliest times, Chinook had looked to the river for its livelihood, and the arrival of the train did little to change that. However, the train did provide transportation to Megler for large quantities of canned salmon for trans-shipment to the east.

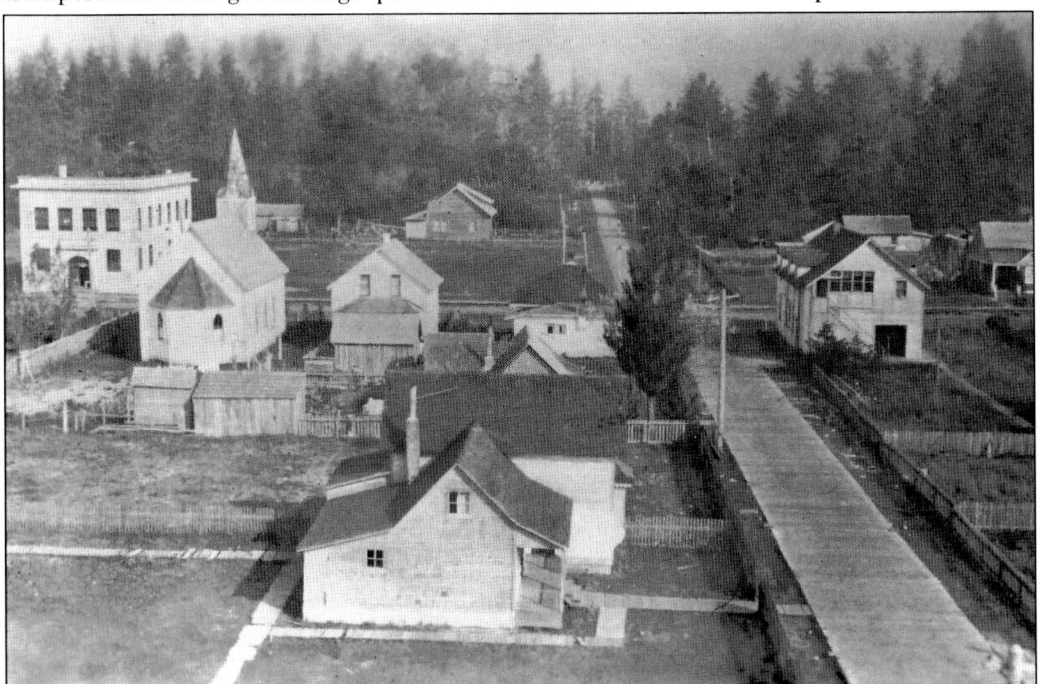

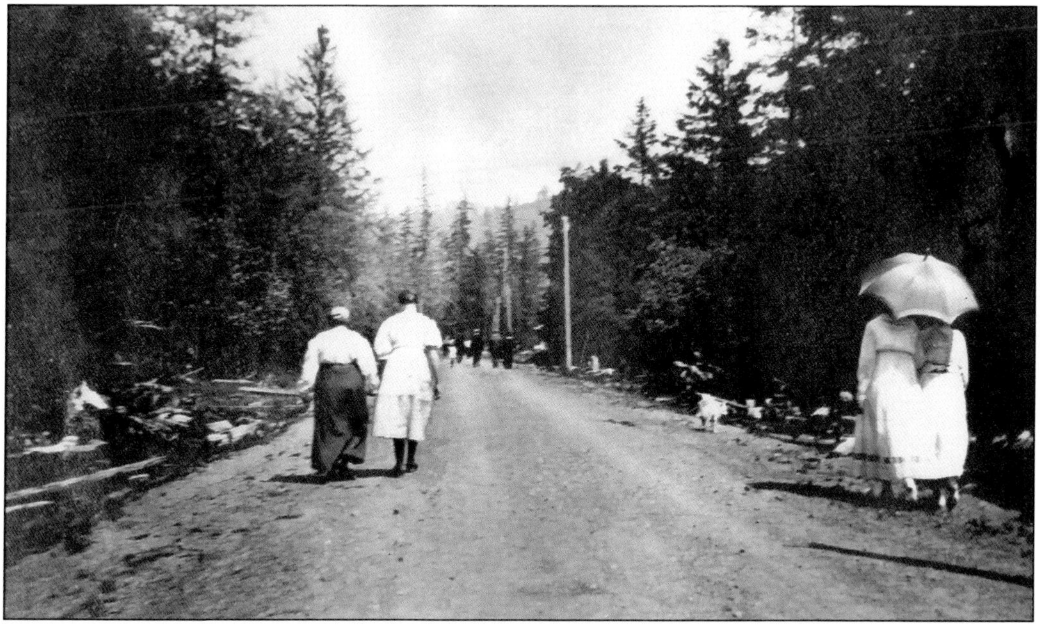

DAILY LIFE WITH THE TRAIN. Those meeting or catching the train walked to and from the depot along Railroad Avenue, the town's main cross street. Ironically, before the railroad was awarded the mail contract between Chinook and Ilwaco, Chinook's mail was taken directly to Ilwaco, where it was off-loaded and then sent back to Chinook by stage. Freight deliveries to and from the train were made by wagon or, more rarely at first, by the newfangled automobile-trucks. The train was considered a convenience when there was business to transact on the peninsula or in Astoria. Ninety-one-year-old Louise Sager Krager remembers that salesmen often arrived by train and "when the train came in, more fresh produce was available." In addition, the train brought visitors to town more often, which some thought a mixed blessing. (Above, Charlotte Herrold Davis; below, WSPRC.)

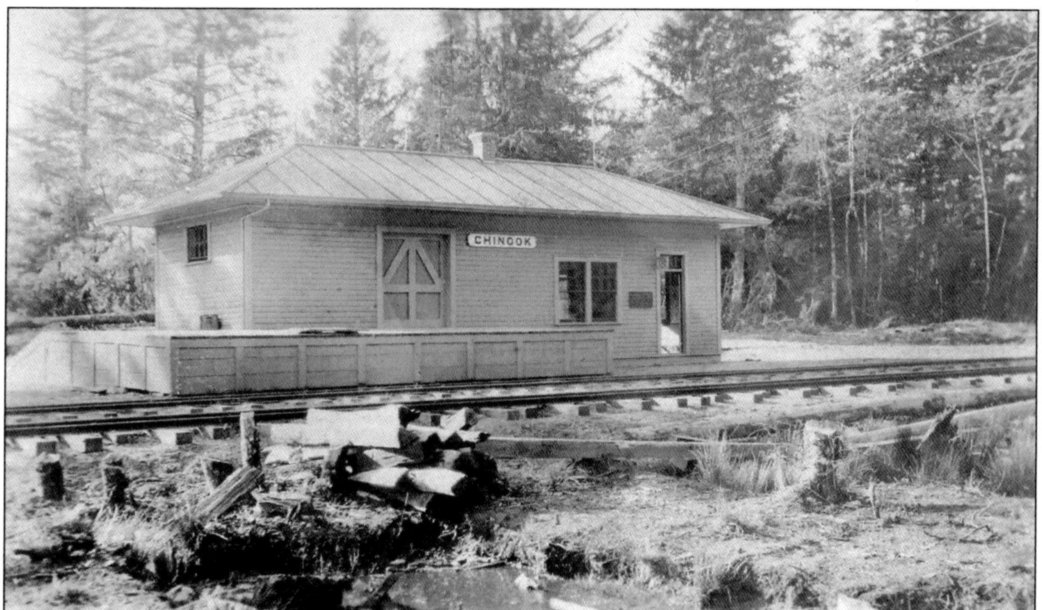

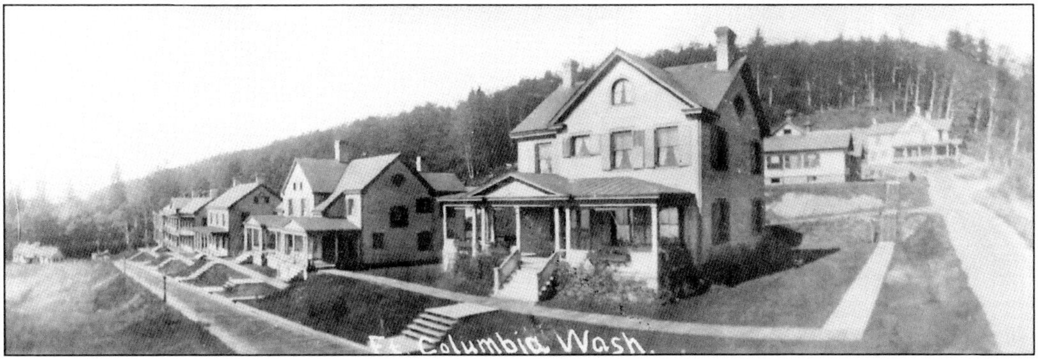

FORT COLUMBIA. Two miles beyond Chinook, sitting atop Scarborough Head, was the U.S. military installation Fort Columbia. The fort, built on land acquired by the U.S. War Department in 1867, was part of the system of forts guarding the mouth of the Columbia River. Because Loomis's 1894 permission to tunnel through Scarborough Head (and under Fort Columbia) had expired, the OR&N needed to reapply for permission from Washington, D.C.

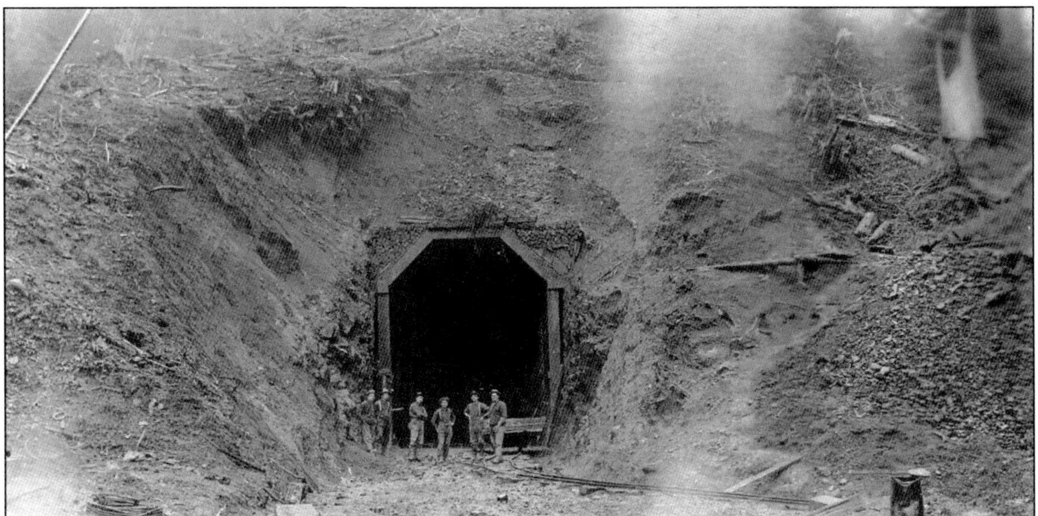

DIGGING THROUGH ROCK. The most time-consuming part of building the extension was digging the 800-foot tunnel through the basaltic rock of Scarborough Head. Camps were established at the east and west sides of the hill, and two gangs of 40 laborers each began work from either end, making the tunnel wide enough to accommodate standard gauge. Project engineers anticipated that the extension would be completed by July 11, 1907. (WSPRC.)

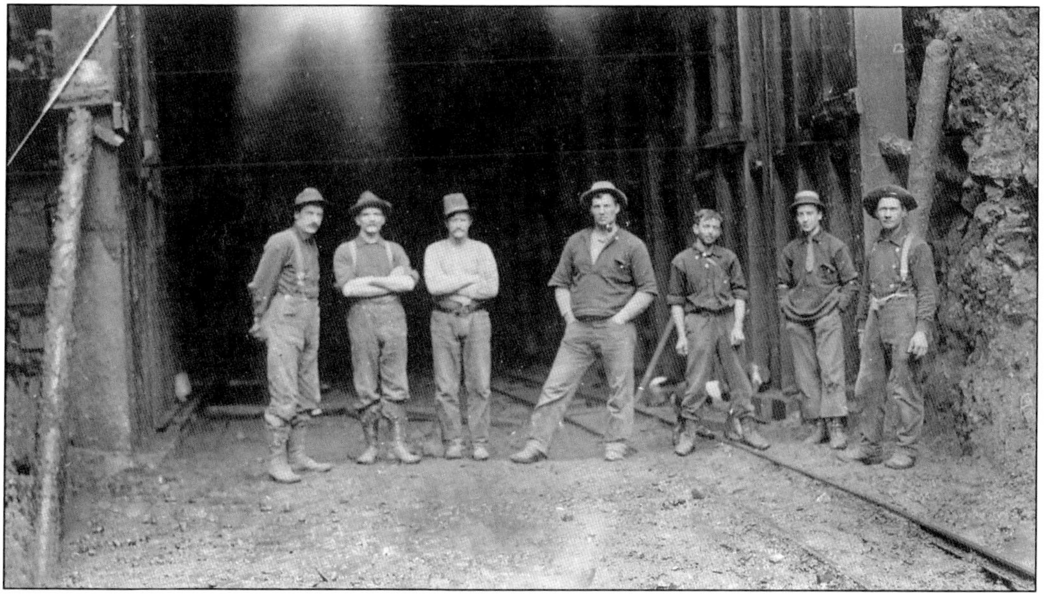

LABOR INTENSIVE. Maintaining a labor force for the project was difficult. A record high daily pay rate of $2.75 was offered, but when the first month's wages were paid, 40 men went off on a spending spree, leaving the job behind. By October 1907, the tunnel had moved forward 200 feet from each end, but 450 feet of digging remained. (WSPRC.)

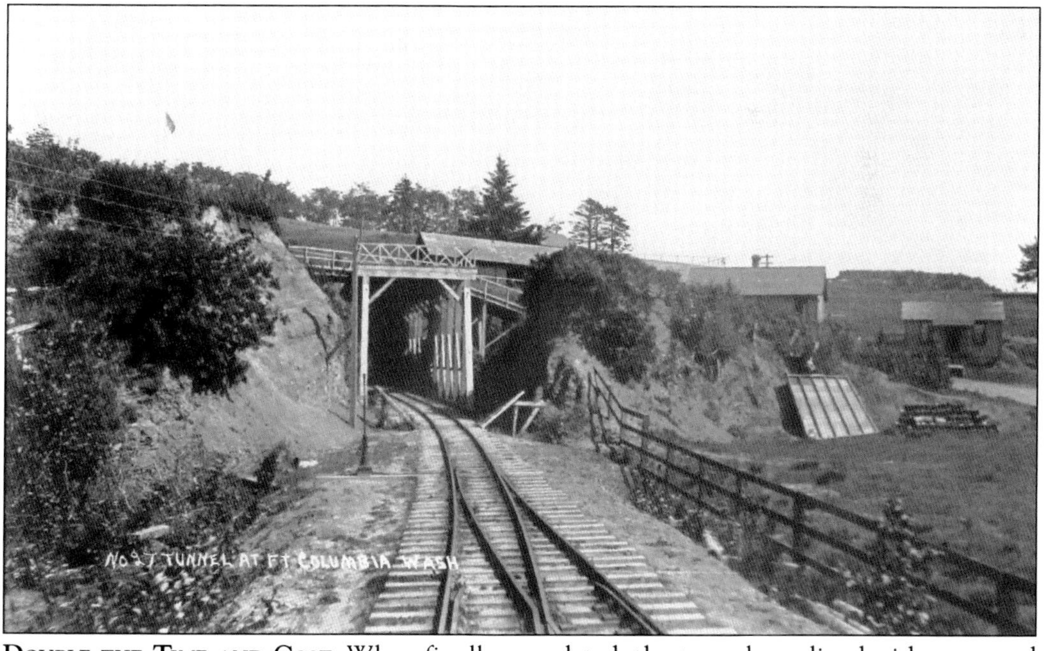

DOUBLE THE TIME AND COST. When finally completed, the tunnel was lined with untreated timbers. The construction of the tunnel and preparation of the roadbed in the rocky strata along most of the route was the heaviest work imaginable. In the end, the 13.39 miles of the extension was more time consuming than building the original rail line up the peninsula and cost almost twice as much. (WSPRC.)

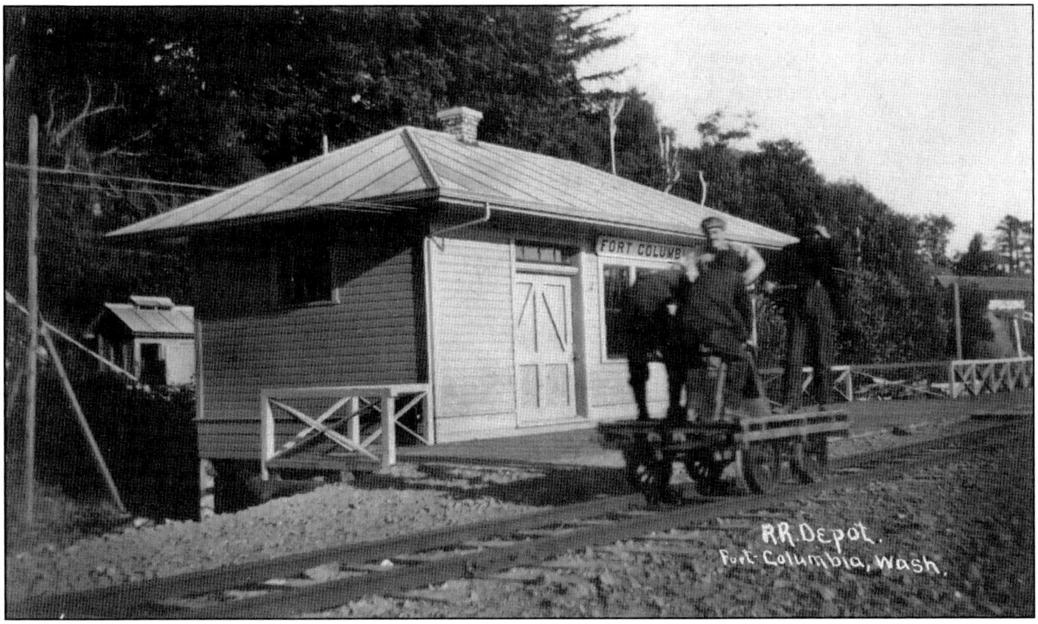

FINISHING TOUCHES. A small station was built at the west end of the tunnel, but it would not be until 1921 that the county would build a trestle road around Scarborough Head. Kay McGowan Garvin, born in 1911, remembers the drive from McGowan to Chinook School before the trestle was built: "We drove up and over Fort Columbia hill in a Model T Ford that had curtains of isinglass. Yitz Herring drove. It was a lousy road—just one lane wide with pull-outs every now and then. There wasn't much traffic, but if you did meet another vehicle, one car had to back up or down until they reached a pull-out so the other car could pass. Riding to school must have frightened me because I wrote a will—just in case. I was about six." (Above, WSPRC; below, OHS-30611.)

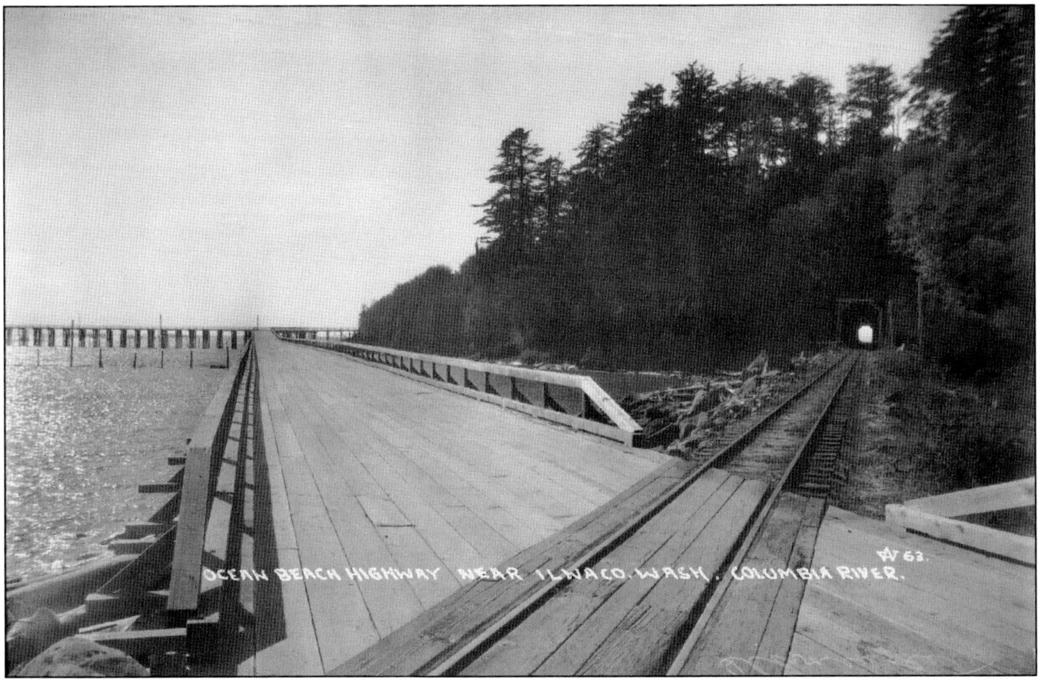

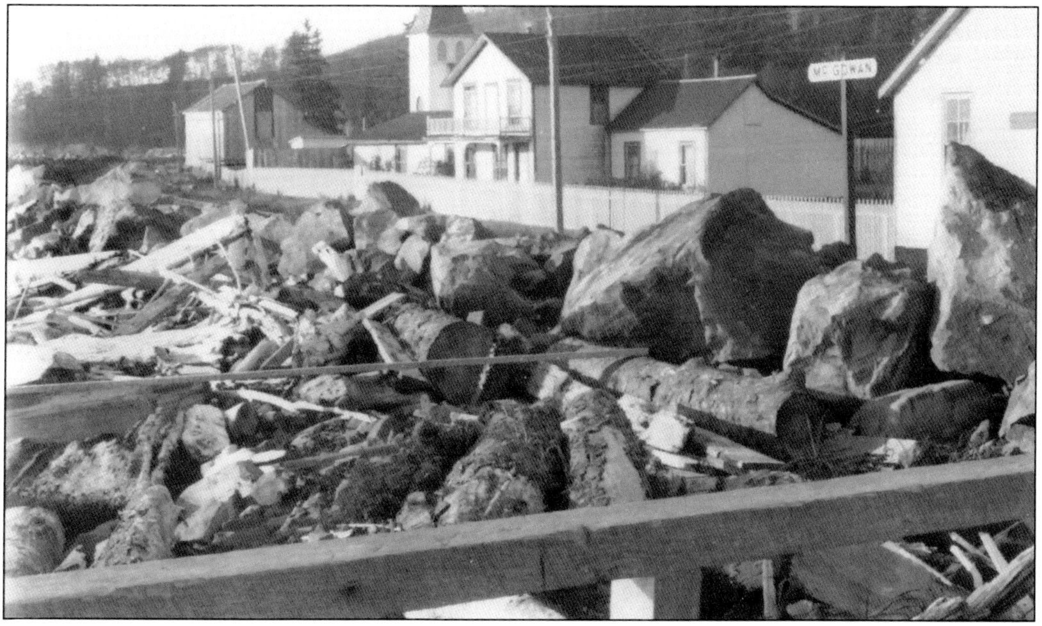

COMPANY TOWN. East of Scarborough Head, the tracks crossed a long filled area constructed of waste from the tunnel. Then came McGowan, a "company town," owned and operated by P. J. McGowan. McGowan had filed a donation land claim for the site in 1853, moving there permanently in 1884. He first engaged in salmon salting and established the earliest salmon packing company in Washington. In 1884, he took his four sons in partnership and they began canning salmon. The settlement that grew up around the company holdings included workers' houses, a post office, and a small church, which still serves as a north shore Columbia River landmark. The roadbed along the river, the most costly and most scenic of the extension, lay along a shelf blasted out of the cliff face. A siding ran along McGowan's dock. (Above, PCHS; below, CCHS.)

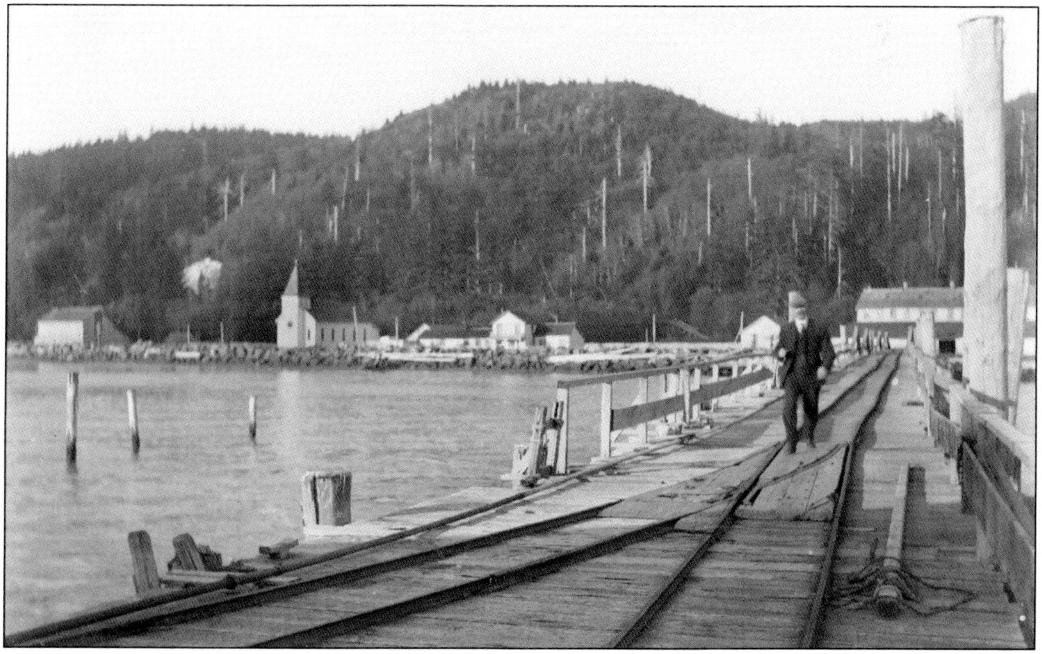

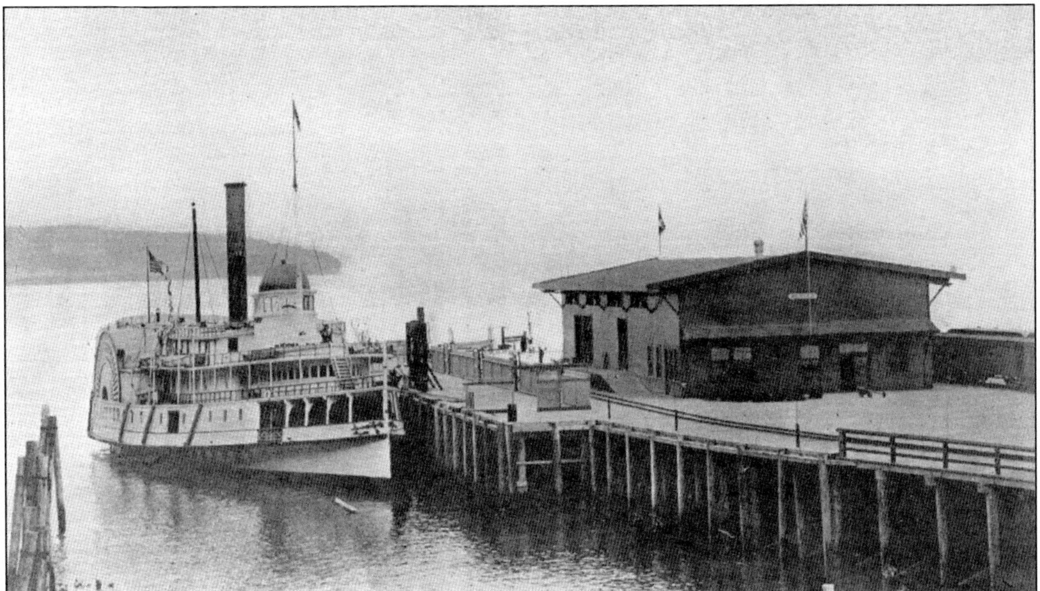

The "Potter" at Megler Wharf.

THE MEGLER TERMINAL. The new terminus at the point of land known as "Cook's Station" was named in honor of J. G. Megler. He had once owned a cannery in the area and had served almost continuously in the Washington state legislature since territorial days. The new wharf was said to be the largest on the Columbia and, lit with electric lights, was a spectacular sight at night.

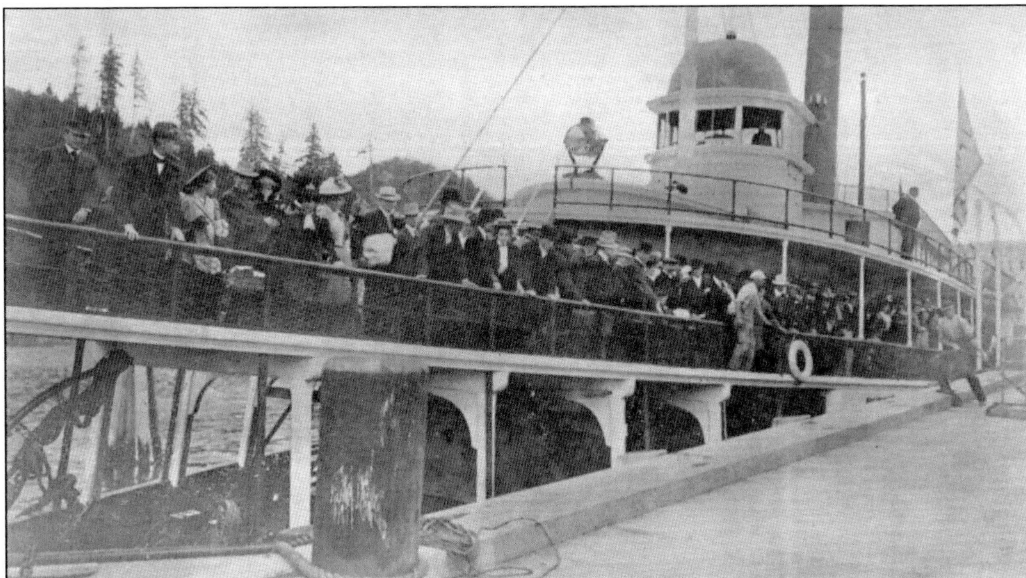

Bound for North Beach—Megler Wharf.

PASSENGER FRIENDLY. Passengers at Megler used specially designed ramps that helped speed up disembarkation from steamers, and the modern 120-by-60-foot depot made waiting convenient. Additional special touches included "name trains": the *Potter Special* left Nahcotta on summer Sundays to connect with the last OR&N steamer at Megler; the *South Bend Special* provided a passenger connection for one-day service to the beach from Puget Sound.

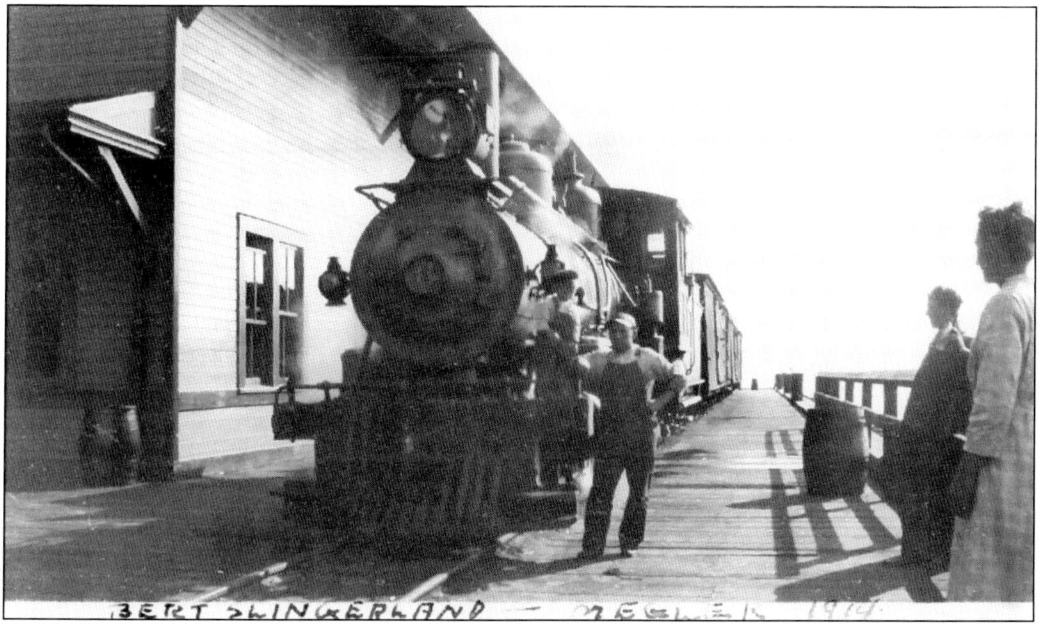

IMPROVED SERVICE. Upon completion of the new dock, service over the entire system was inaugurated on June 1, 1908. Train service improved immensely, with boats now running to meet trains instead of the other way around. The wide dock accommodated two tracks, each of which ran to the far end of the terminal facilitating both passenger and freight trains, sometimes simultaneously. Since most boats moored on the upriver side of the dock, freight could be loaded on the east side of the terminal while passengers could be disembarking from a train on the west side. Trains came straight off the wharf, passing a long siding and engine facilities before heading west toward the peninsula. The Megler-to-Nahcotta run took three hours. At last, the trains could abandon the tide schedule. (Above, Adelle Beechey.)

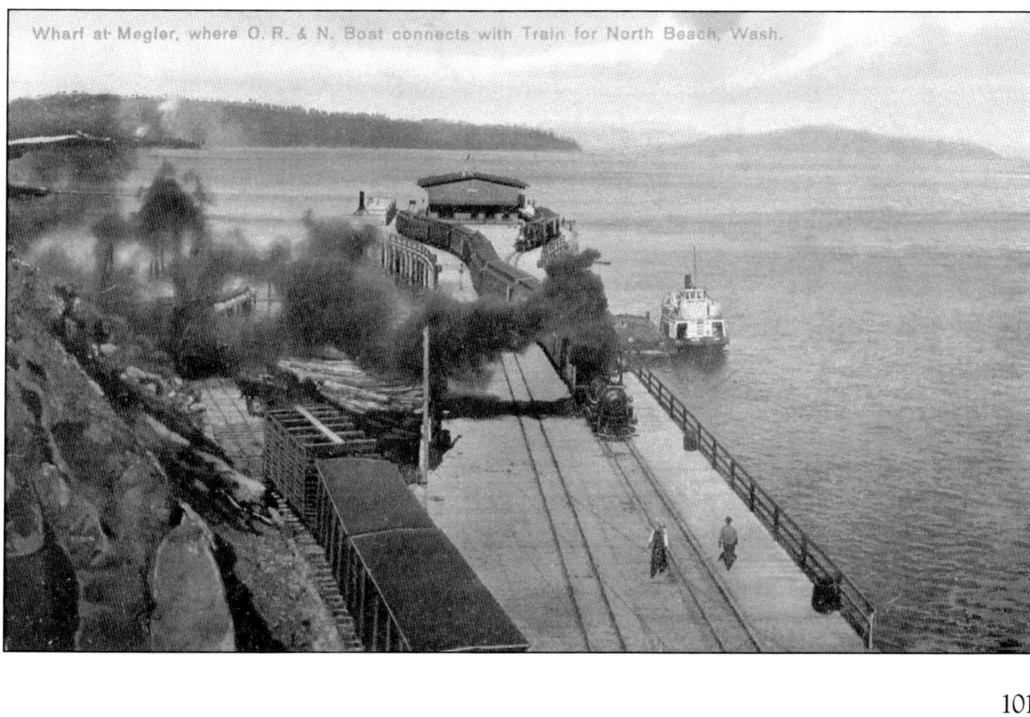

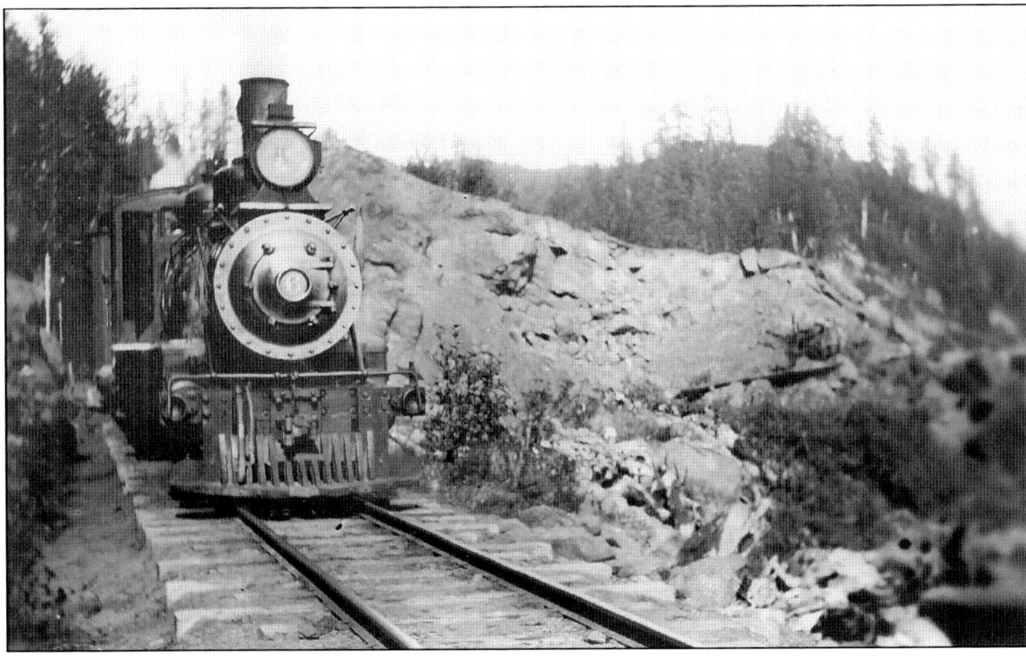

ADDITIONAL ROLLING STOCK. At the time the extension was being constructed, three new locomotives were purchased: a Baldwin 4-4-0 costing $2,645, which was given the number 5; a Baldwin 10-Wheeler costing $5,700, No. 6; and the last locomotive the line would acquire, another Baldwin 4-4-0, No. 3, costing $2,500. No. 6 was the heaviest locomotive ever to operate on the Ilwaco line and was hard on the roadbed along the sandy peninsula, particularly north of Long Beach where the rails were lighter. Nevertheless, No. 6 was put to good use on summer weekends when 600 to 700 passengers disembarked at Megler from the *T. J. Potter*. At those times, passenger cars could not accommodate everyone, so the old flatcars were permanently outfitted with benches and put into use to handle the crowds. (Below, Adelle Beechey.)

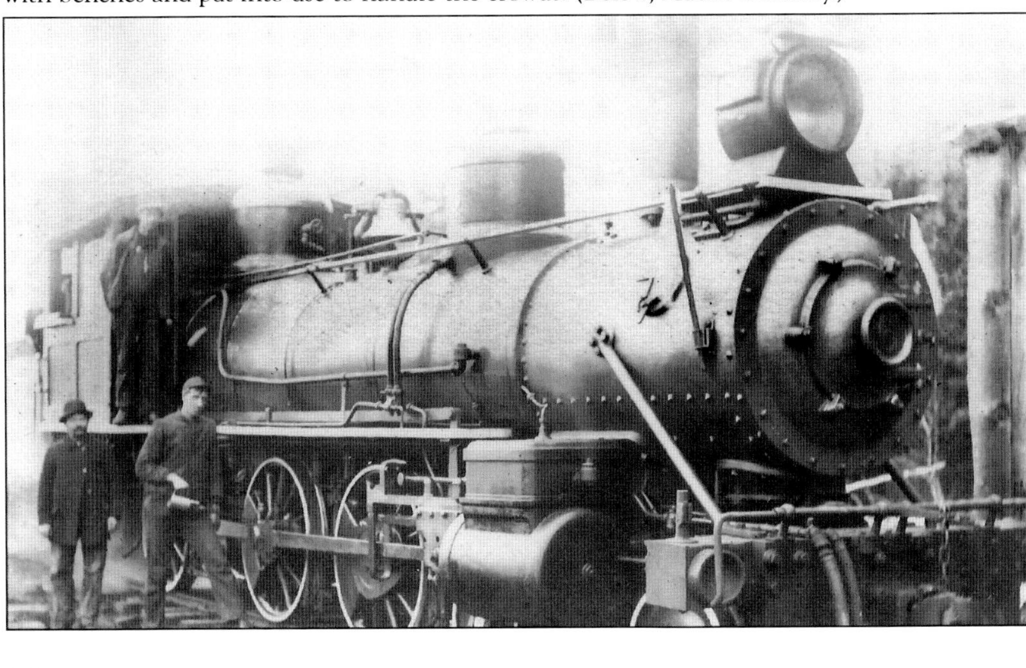

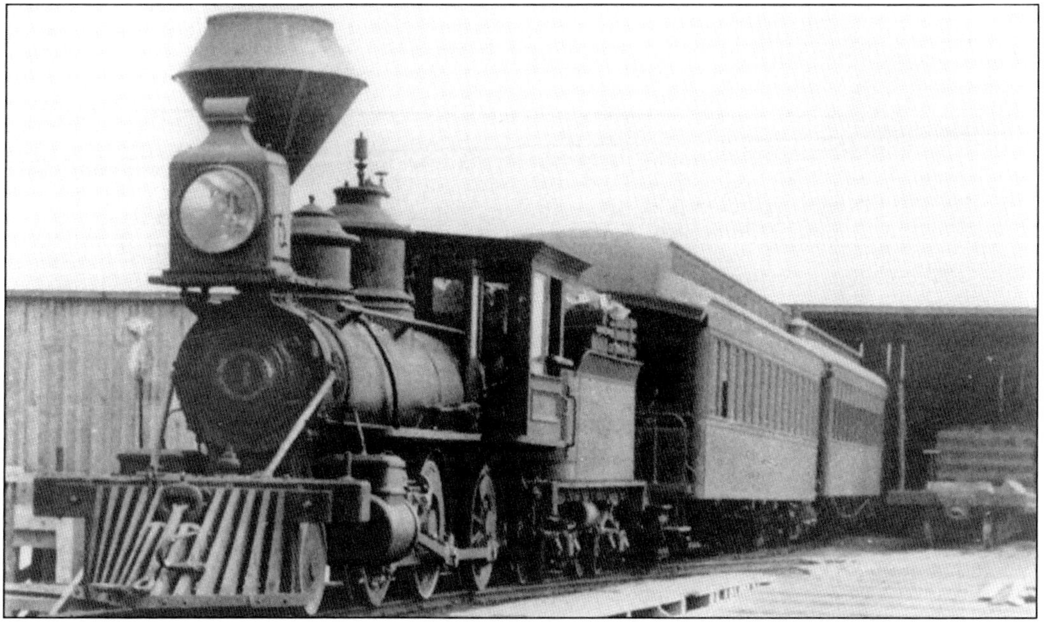

Rules and Regulations. All of the Ilwaco Railroad's locomotives were still equipped with oil or carbide headlights, which posed a continuous risk of fine. New regulations required the line to equip its engines with electric generators and lights. In 1910, the railroad presented a petition to the Washington Railroad Commission requesting that a variance be allowed. The reasons stated were that the line had no "dangerous or difficult places" and summer locomotives Nos. 5 and 6 ended their runs no later than 9:00 p.m. The commission accepted this petition, and it was not until 1915 that engines were rebuilt with turbo-generators and electric lights. (Above, PCHS; below, Charles Mulvey.)

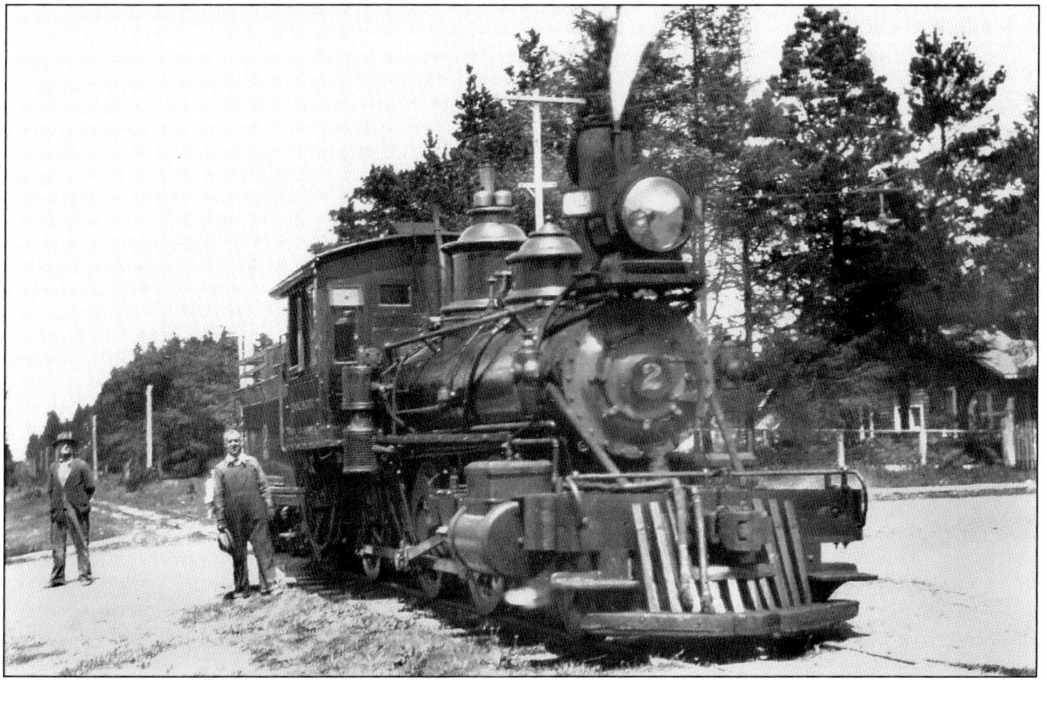

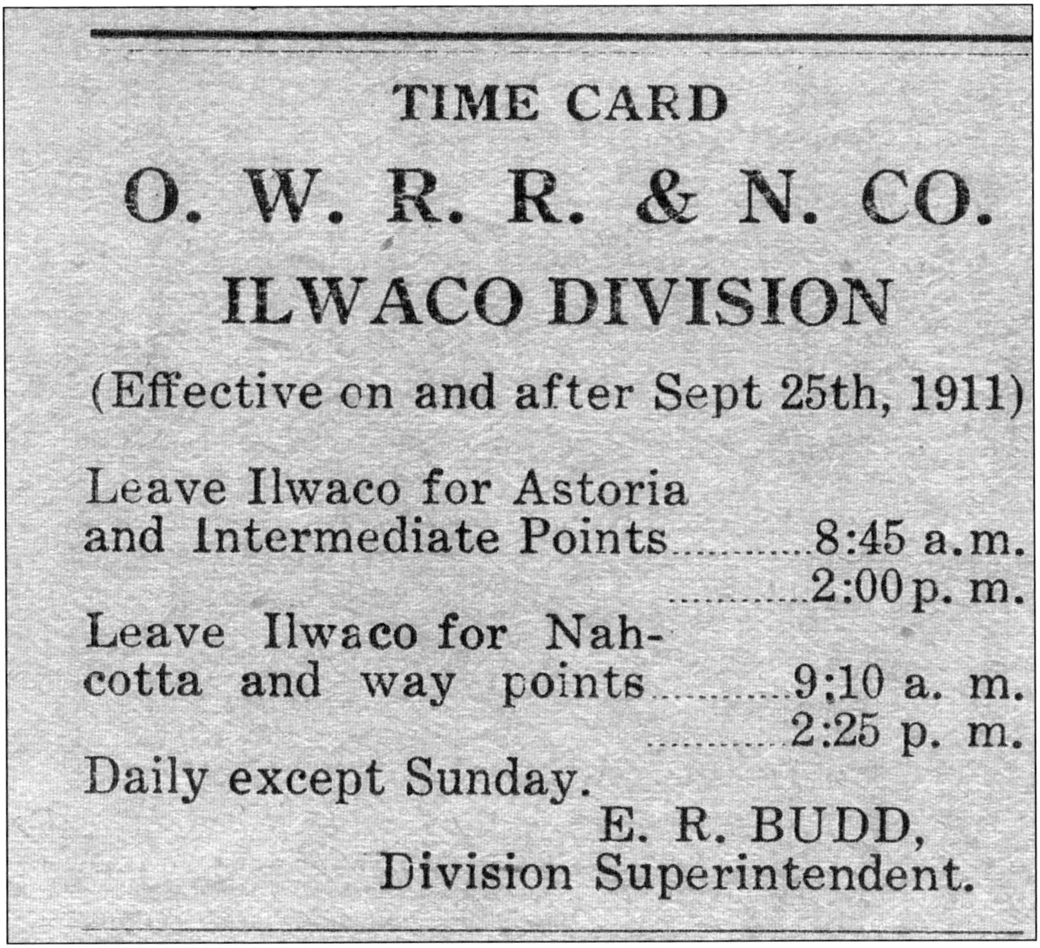

TIME CARD

O. W. R. R. & N. CO.

ILWACO DIVISION

(Effective on and after Sept 25th, 1911)

Leave Ilwaco for Astoria and Intermediate Points............8:45 a.m.
............2:00 p. m.

Leave Ilwaco for Nahcotta and way points............9:10 a. m.
............2:25 p. m.

Daily except Sunday.

E. R. BUDD,
Division Superintendent.

The O-WR&N. In December 1910, Union Pacific merged all of its subsidiaries, worth $110 million, into one corporation and formed the Oregon-Washington Railroad and Navigation Company. The North Beach Peninsula's narrow-gauge railroad was included in the O-WR&N's "Ilwaco Division" along with the Columbia River steamers upon which the railway depended. The new company streamlined its management and invested in further improvements to the line. The *T. J. Potter* was refurbished once more, the Chinook depot grounds were blacktopped, the Nahcotta dock was rebuilt, and buildings and rolling stock were repaired and spruced up. In addition, the O-WR&N printed posters, planned advertising campaigns, and became an active member of the North Beach Push Club, which had been organized that same year to promote the area. The results were rewarding. The year 1910 was considered a record season, and 1911 was even better. Four regular trains and two extras were run each way that summer, and both passenger and freight traffic doubled.

Six

THE FINAL UPS AND DOWNS

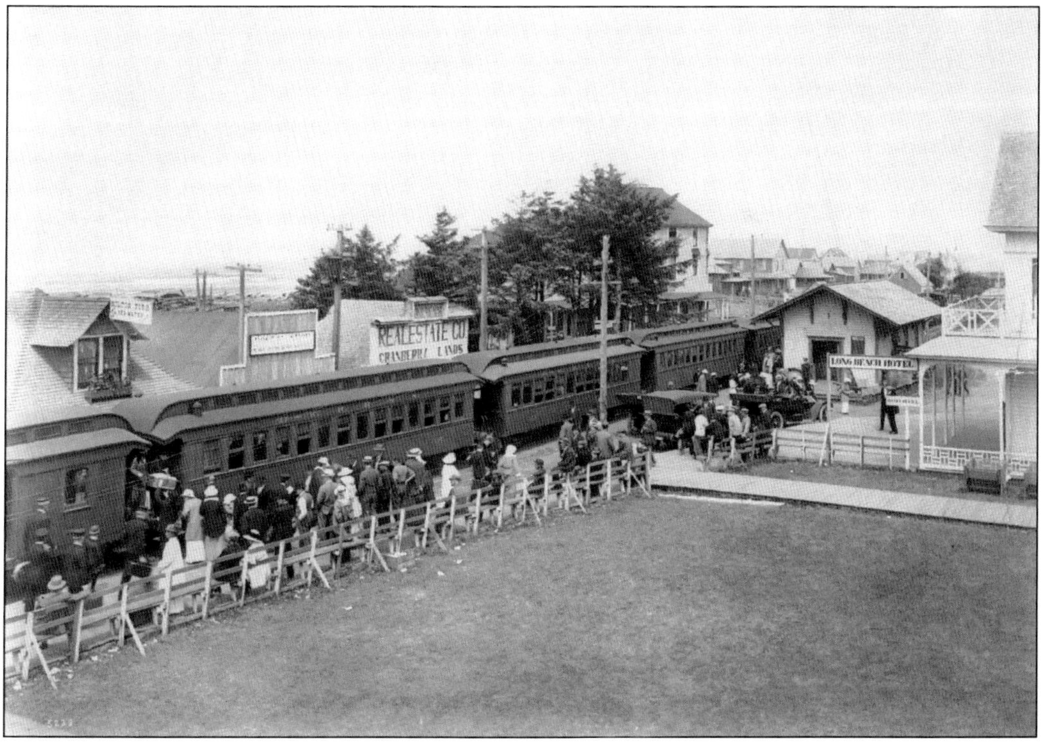

A PEAK YEAR. Passenger travel reached its zenith on the O-WR&N in 1913. Trains usually passed one another at McGowan, but, occasionally, they passed on the siding at Long Beach. When that occurred, crowds gathered to see the excitement of both trains. Stories persist on the peninsula concerning travelers headed in one direction to visit friends and being embarrassed to see their presumed hosts passing in the opposite direction. (OHS-11035.)

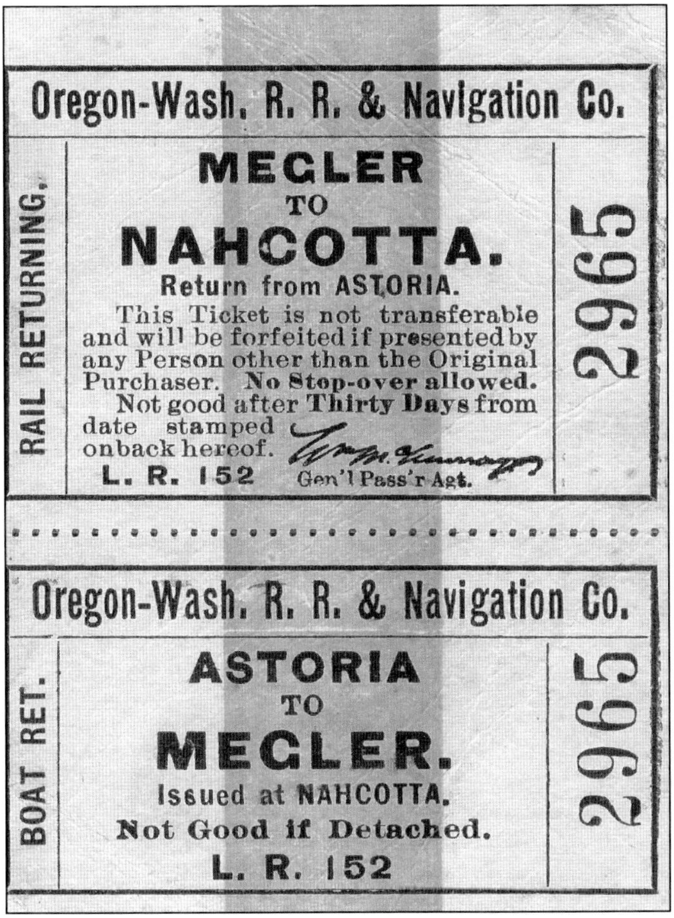

Oregon-Wash. R. R. & Navigation Co.

RAIL RETURNING.

MEGLER TO NAHCOTTA.

Return from ASTORIA.

This Ticket is not transferable and will be forfeited if presented by any Person other than the Original Purchaser. No Stop-over allowed.

Not good after Thirty Days from date stamped onback hereof.

L. R. 152 Gen'l Pass'r Agt.

2965

Oregon-Wash. R. R. & Navigation Co.

BOAT RET.

ASTORIA TO MEGLER.

Issued at NAHCOTTA.

Not Good if Detached.

L. R. 152

2965

Prosperity and Changes. The record business of 1913 was credited to a combination of factors—good weather, the closure of the Moclips resort to the north, and an aggressive advertising campaign. Passenger tickets sold during the summer season between Portland and the beach numbered 26,000, and, locally, 39,000 tickets were sold. Improvements to the line were made that year, as well. When a new, four-stall engine house was built at Nahcotta, the locomotive facilities in Ilwaco were no longer needed. The engine barn and turntable were dismantled, spur tracks laid in their place, a new depot planned, and the track was planked along the main street of town. (Above, the Les Wilson family.)

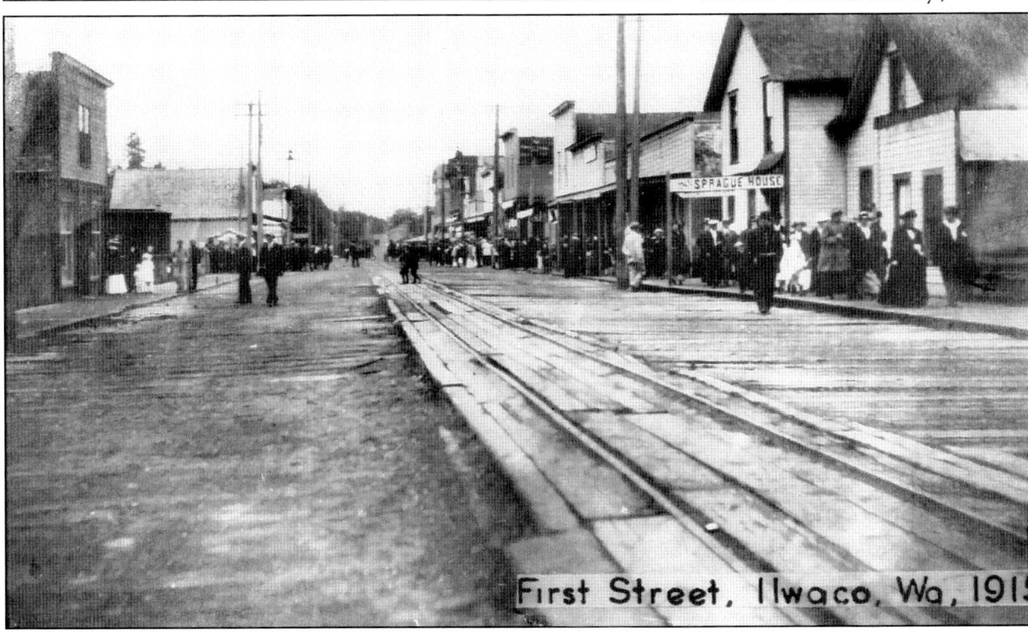

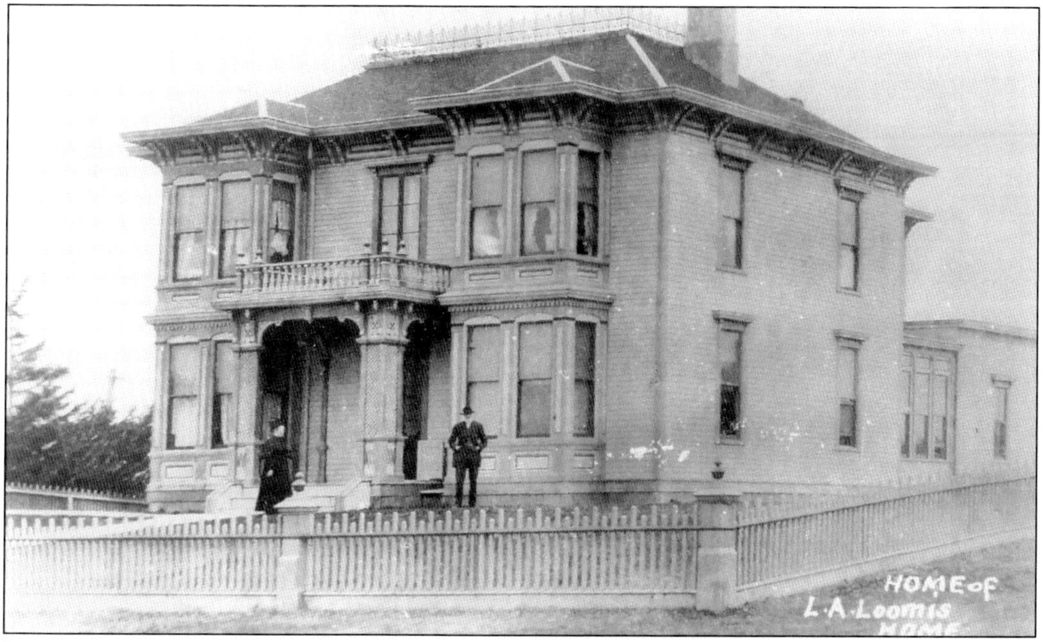

End of an Era. Lewis Alfred Loomis died on July 19, 1913. A special train draped in black carried the funeral party from the Loomis Mansion to Nahcotta. From there, the mourners went on to Oysterville, where the deceased was given a Masonic burial and laid to rest next to his wife, Louisa Glover Loomis, who had died two years previously. (Adelle Beechey.)

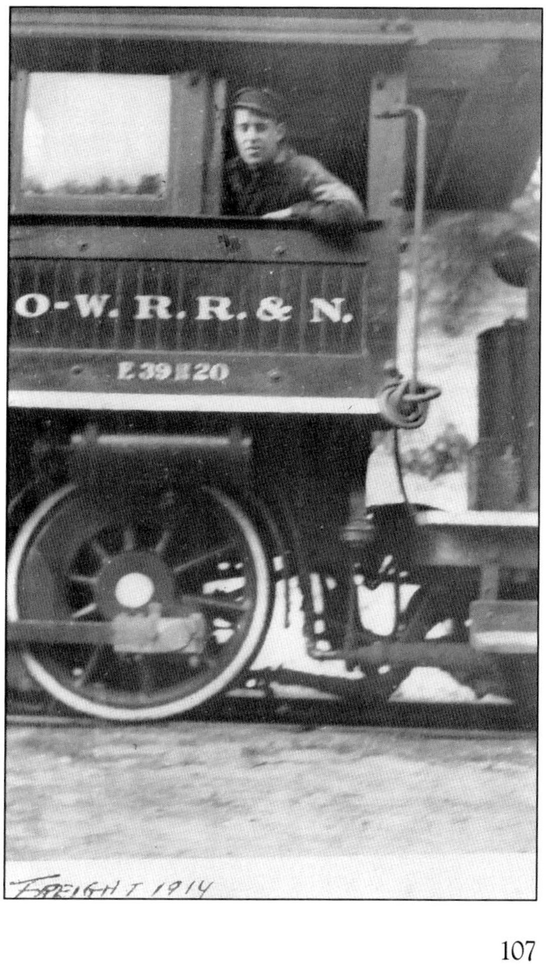

"The Peninsula Pike." Despite the new management's efforts to improve the line, local newspapers continued to poke fun at the railroad. The editor of the *Ilwaco Tribune* composed a poem, "The Peninsula Pike," which said in part: "From Megler to Holman there's 900 pains, To scourge your anatomy's function. In fact those who ride are near void of their brains, When they get down to Ilwaco Junction."

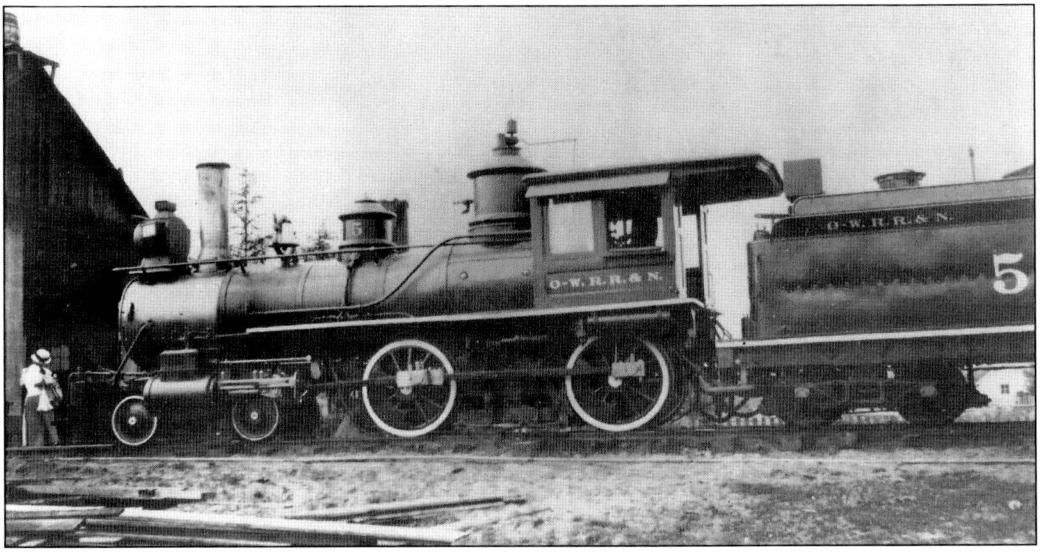

Uniformity on the Line. In 1915, O-WR&N's parent company, Union Pacific, re-lettered all rolling stock with its name and, in addition, put the initials O-WR&N at one end of each passenger car. Also, the prefix "N" was added in front of each number to indicate "Narrow Gauge." Locomotives were renumbered as well. No. 3 became N-1; No. 4 became N-2; No. 5 became N-3; and No. 6 became N-4; though later the "N" was dropped and just a single number appeared on each locomotive. So that the fuel requirements of the locomotives would be uniform, N-2 was converted to oil. A large steel tank provided storage for oil at Megler and, as the company owned no tank cars, oil for an emergency tank at Nahcotta was transferred in a tender borrowed from an idle locomotive. (Both, PCHS.)

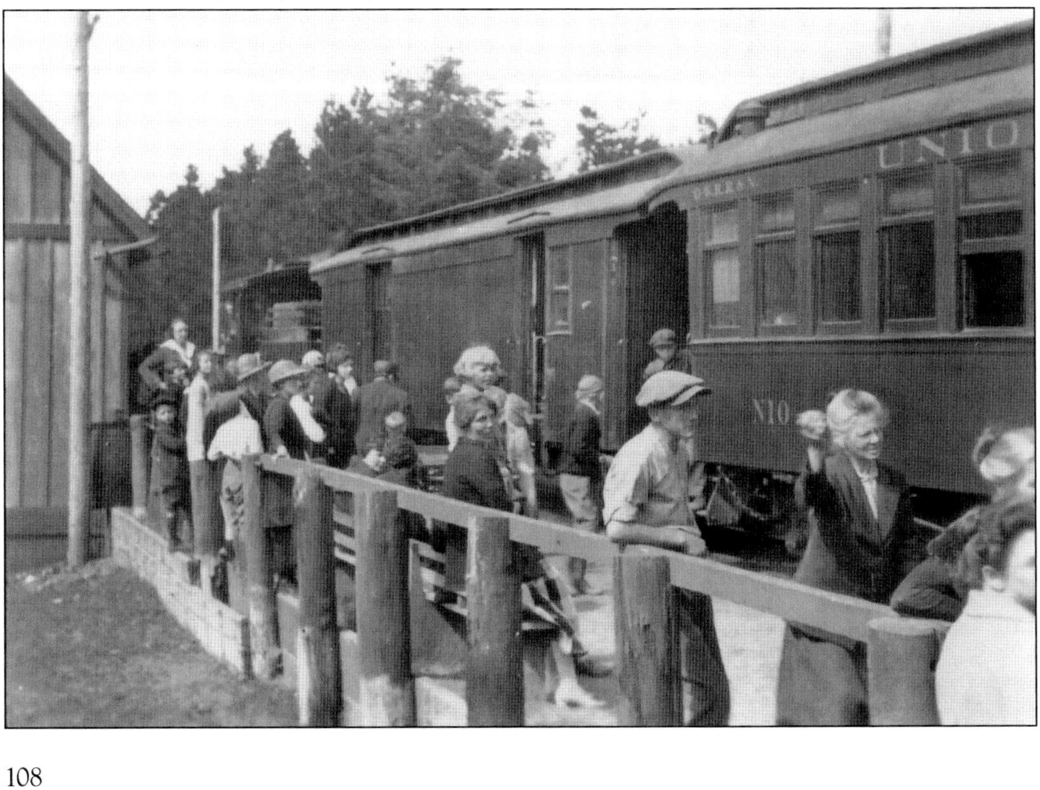

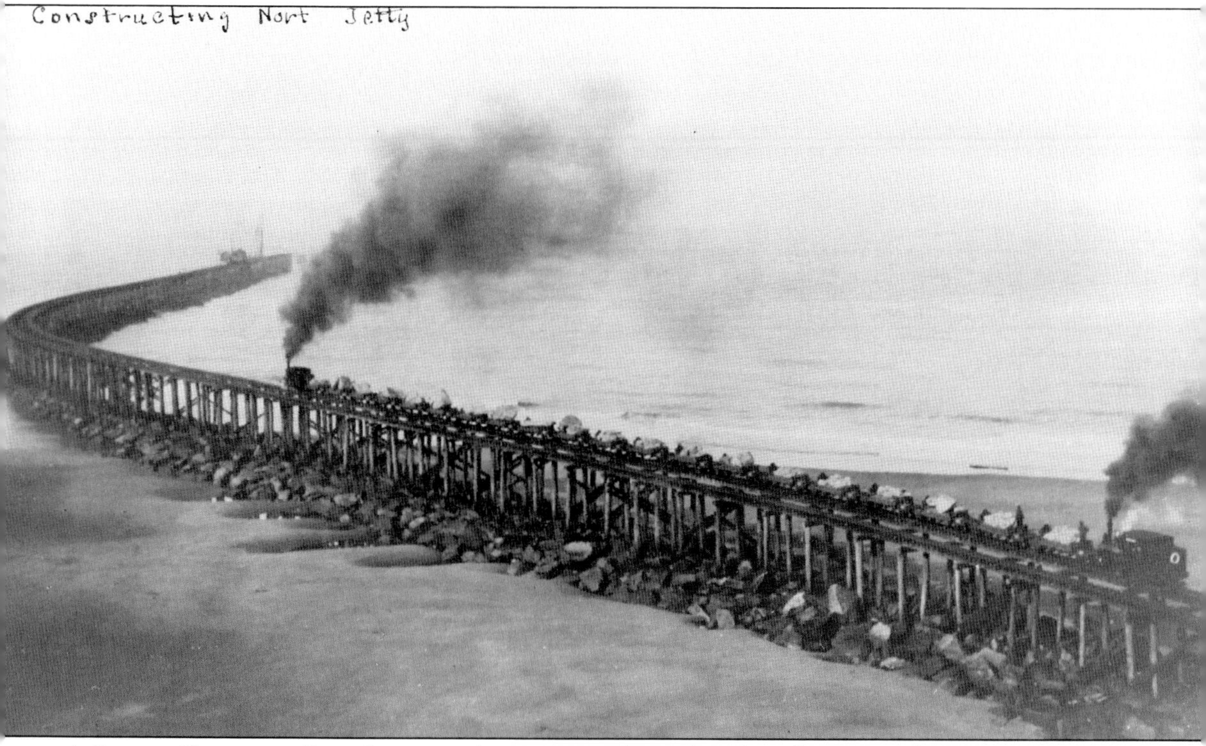

A Second Railroad. For a few years, there was another railroad on the peninsula, but it posed no threat to the O-WR&N. The second line, complete with yards, rolling stock, and a large machine shop, was dedicated specifically to the construction of the north jetty at Cape Disappointment. This was the second jetty constructed in an effort to stabilize the channel at the mouth of the Columbia River, the first having been completed on the Oregon side in 1895. In 1914, a Portland, Oregon, firm under the direction of the U.S. Corps of Army Engineers began the north jetty. During the two-year project, rock and boulders, some weighing as much as 50 tons, were barged to the jetty Rock Train, hauled by steam engine over an ever growing 2-mile-long trestle and then dumped to form the jetty. An estimated 250 construction workers were employed on the project and, as an indirect result of the construction, the O-WR&N gained incidental business transporting supplies and passengers. (PCHS.)

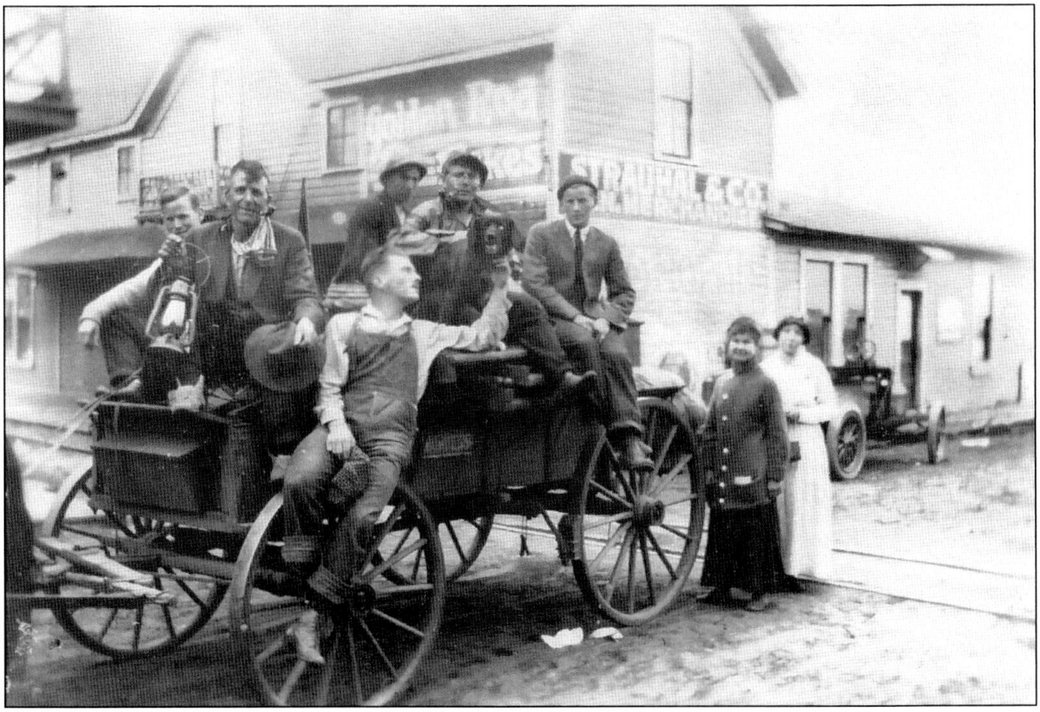

Horse-Drawn and Horseless Carriages. Although buggy rides along the beach had been popular since stagecoach times, it was not until the first upland road between Long Beach and Ocean Park was built in 1911 that motorized "buggies" began to arrive in substantial numbers. Since the North Beach Peninsula was still inaccessible by road, automobiles were transported from inland points by boat. The fare for transporting an automobile from Portland to Astoria was $80. It cost another $13 for the combined boat and train fare from Astoria to Ilwaco. It was the responsibility of the auto owner to load the car onto the railroad's flatcar at Megler and off again in Ilwaco. The railroad kindly provided the necessary planks for the transfer procedure. (Below, Sydney Stevens.)

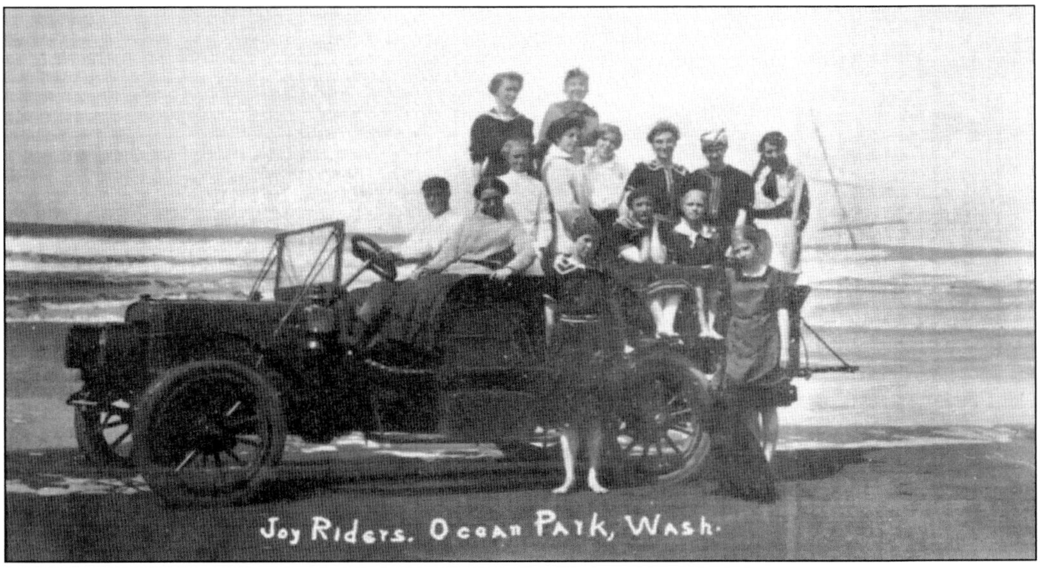

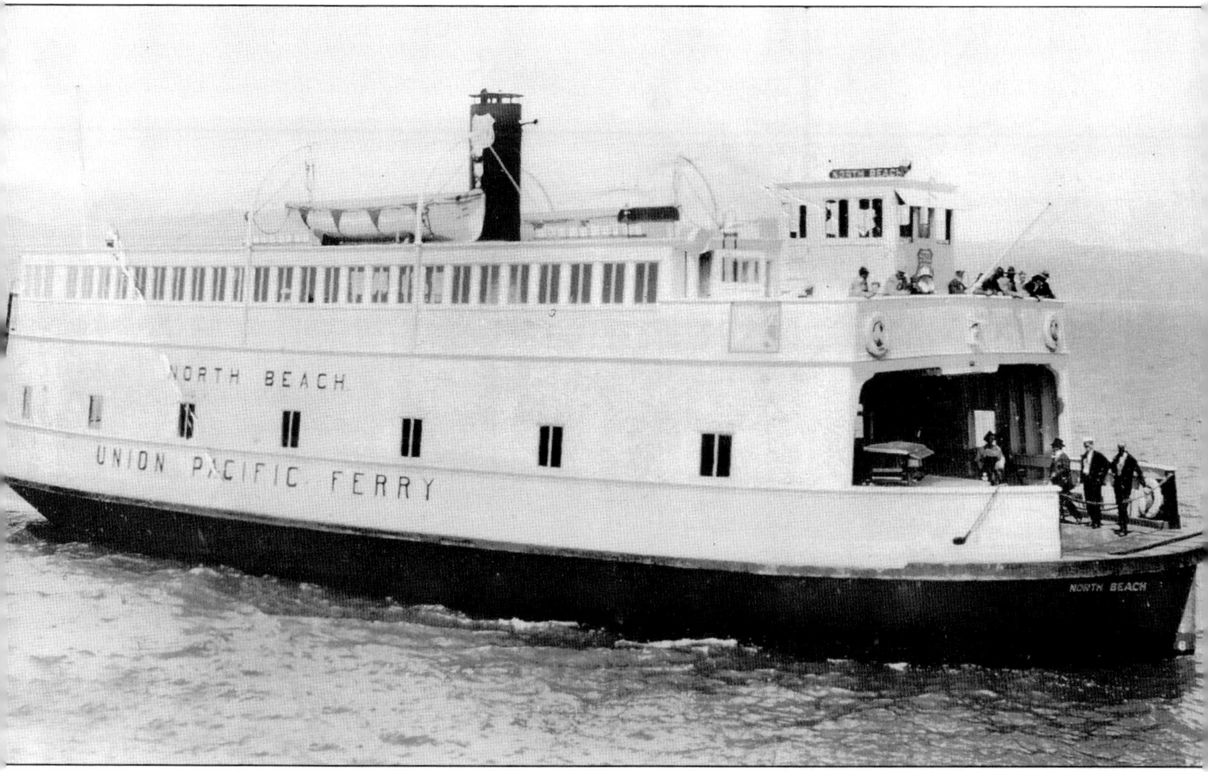

Competing for Auto Business. The first, primitive ferry between the Oregon side of the river and the dock at McGowan where the road to the peninsula began could transport eight cars. Two trips were made daily at a charge of $3.50 to $5, depending upon the automobile's weight. In 1920, Capt. Fritz Elfving began operating a large scow as a ferry. That summer, 700 cars were transported and Elfving quickly formed the Astoria-McGowan Ferry Company. In May 1921, his ferry *Tourist* was christened, using cranberry juice in deference to Prohibition. The well-built vessel had two 90-horsepower engines and a 64-foot hull divided into four watertight compartments, and it could accommodate 15 cars and 30 passengers. Seeing Elfving's success, the Union Pacific contracted for its own ferry and extended the road from McGowan to the Megler dock. Its vessel, the *North Beach*, began its run the summer of 1927. Interestingly, the ferry was of a single-ended type and used a turntable installed on the afterdeck to move automobiles once they were on the ferry—definitely a railroader's touch!

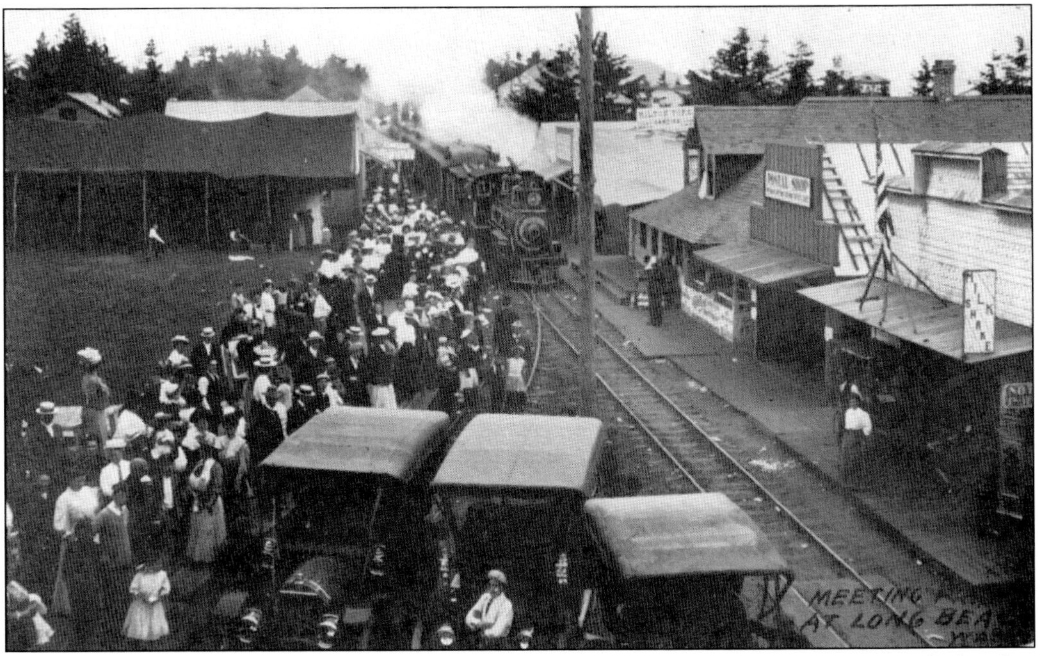

AUTOMOBILES, A FAMILIAR SIGHT. During the 1920s, automobiles became an increasingly familiar sight on the North Beach Peninsula. Soon lodgings especially designed for auto travelers began to appear, and patronage of the railroad declined as local residents and summer visitors became accustomed to the freedom of movement motor cars offered. The railroad passenger count decreased by more than 5,000 between 1924 and 1928. Nor could the railroad compete with the door-to-door service and lower rates of the North Beach Transit Company, a trucking firm that operated between Astoria and Ocean Park. Its two 4-ton trucks ran on a daily schedule, and in 1928, the company was awarded the mail contract for the peninsula. This was, perhaps, the most telling blow to the railroad, whose original reason for being had been closely linked to the mail contract.

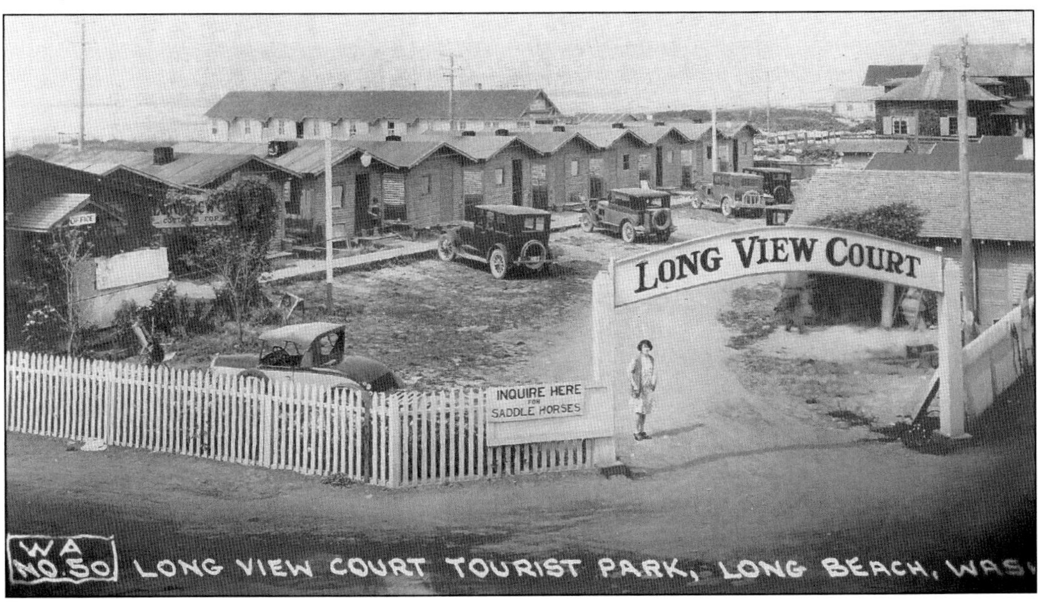

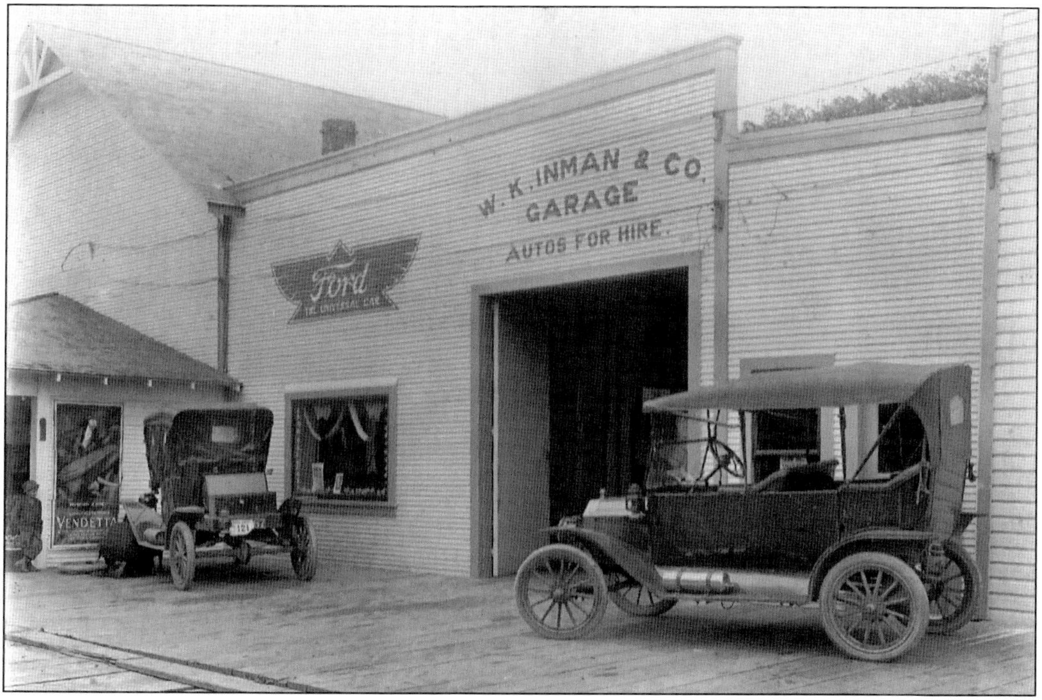

ADJUNCT AUTO BUSINESSES. With the increased use of automobiles, related businesses soon started up. Garages opened in every community from McGowan to Oysterville. Gas pumps appeared in front of grocery stores and in farmers' barnyards. Most mechanics were self-taught, learning the basics through trial and error and by tinkering with their own machines. Even the non-mechanically inclined automobile owner became adept at making minor adjustments and at changing tires. Virginia Williams Jones has vivid memories of her father repairing a flat tire: "It wasn't easy but he did it right on the spot. He actually patched the inner tube—not the tire. I can remember how he would spit on his mended patch or hold it under water to see if it leaked before he used his tire iron to put it back in the casing." (Both, PCHS.)

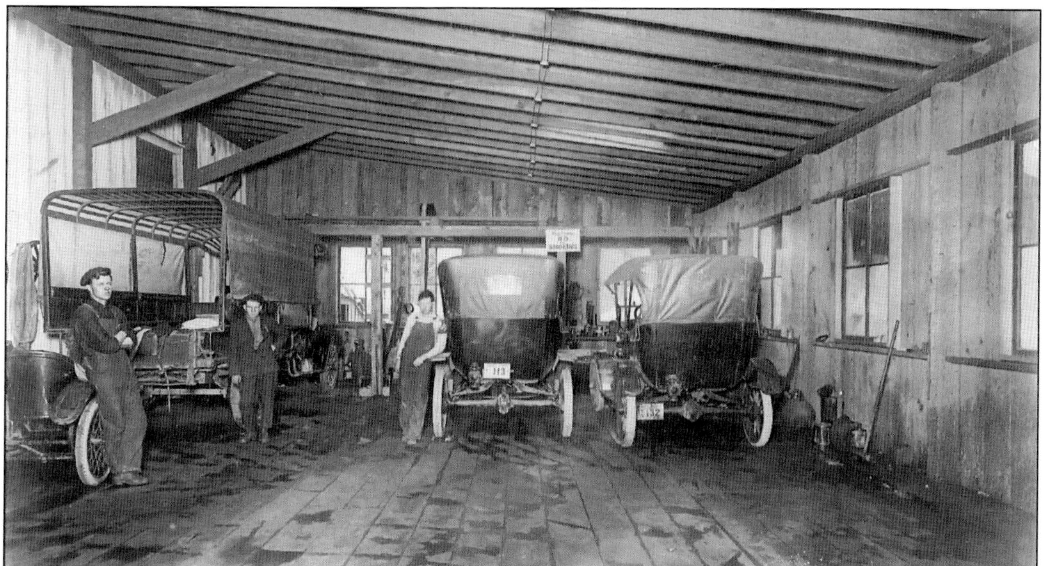

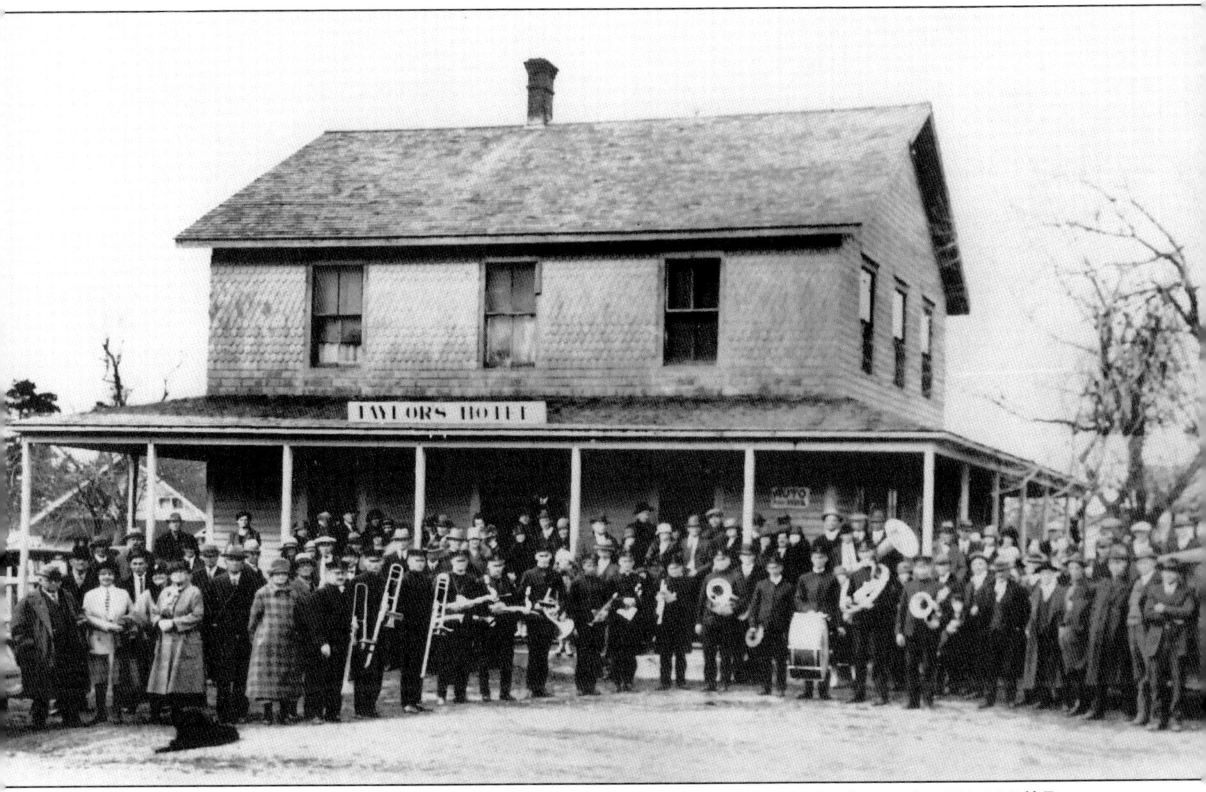

K-M Hill Boosters. Pictured above at the Taylor's Hotel in Ocean Park are the K-M Hill Boosters, who had worked tirelessly for several years toward the completion of what would eventually become Washington State Highway 4. Welcomed by a brass band, they had met to celebrate their success and to plan for the first caravan over the route. On May 29, 1925, the Willapa Harbor Pilot ran a news story, which said in part, "Tired, dusty and hungry, but very enthusiastic, the caravan of 50 or more Longview, Portland, Castle Rock, Kalama and Kelso citizens reached the North Beach resorts on Saturday afternoon, having successfully and without mishap traversed the entire distance of newly constructed road through three counties to the sea . . . the first caravan that ever went down the North Bank of the Columbia . . . the first car to cover the distance known as Ocean Beach Highway." Behind them traveled a service car that carried "in addition to the crane and other wrecking equipment, an assortment of tires, patches, and some spare parts and inner tubes."

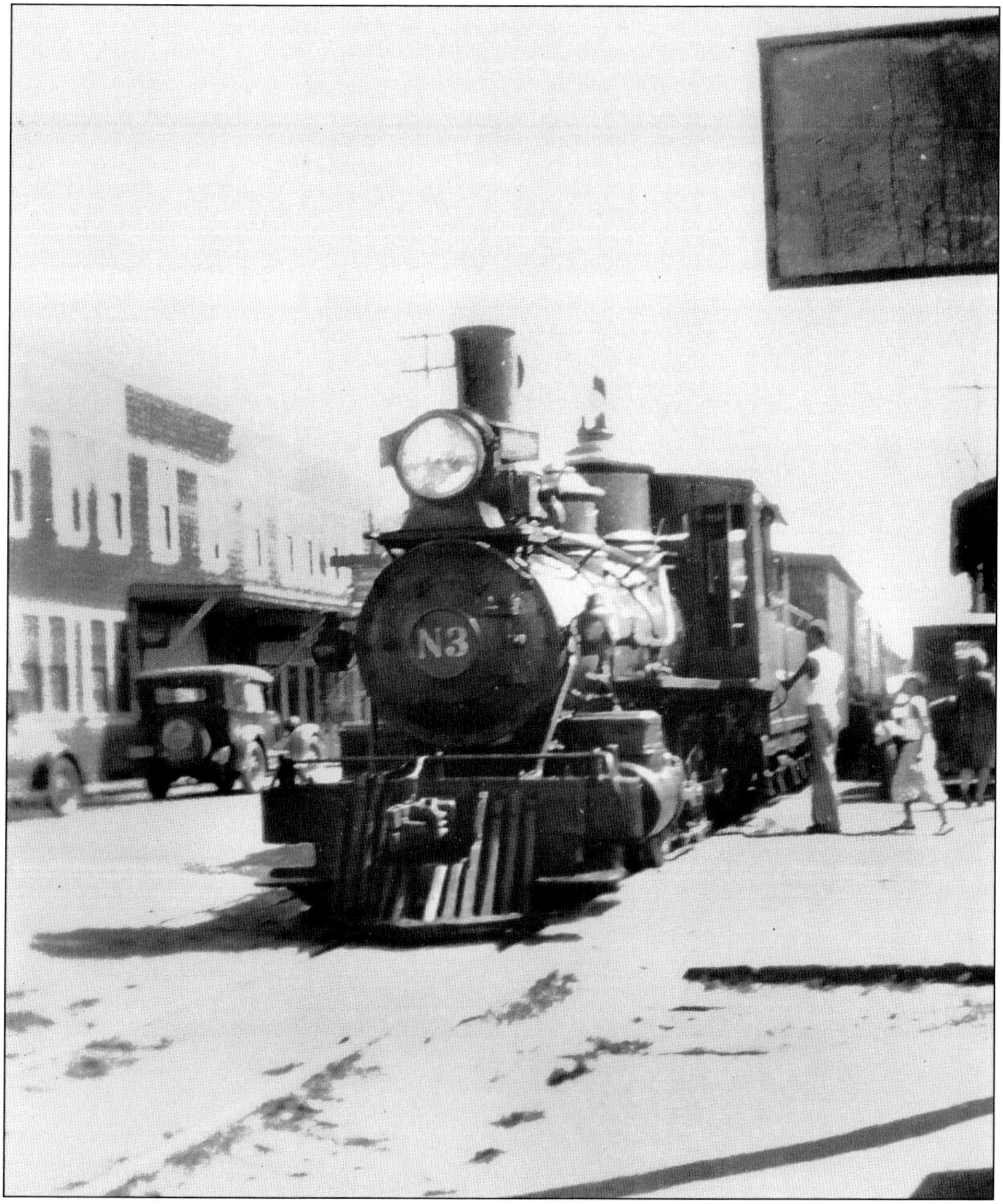

Permission to Abandon. By October 1929, the Union Pacific's continuing losses on the North Beach Peninsula prompted them to file petitions to state and federal authorities for permission to abandon the 27 miles of their Ilwaco branch. Hearings began in April, and though community and civic groups protested vociferously and cited the revenues they would lose through devaluation of property, their support came too late to save the little railroad. The matter was finally settled in the railroad's favor. On July 12, 1930, the Interstate Commerce Commission issued the certificate and Washington Public Utilities Commission granted permission allowing abandonment. Although the railroad was then free to cease their operations immediately, they chose to continue service until after the summer season was over and the transient population had left the beach. The last train was scheduled to run September 10, 1930.

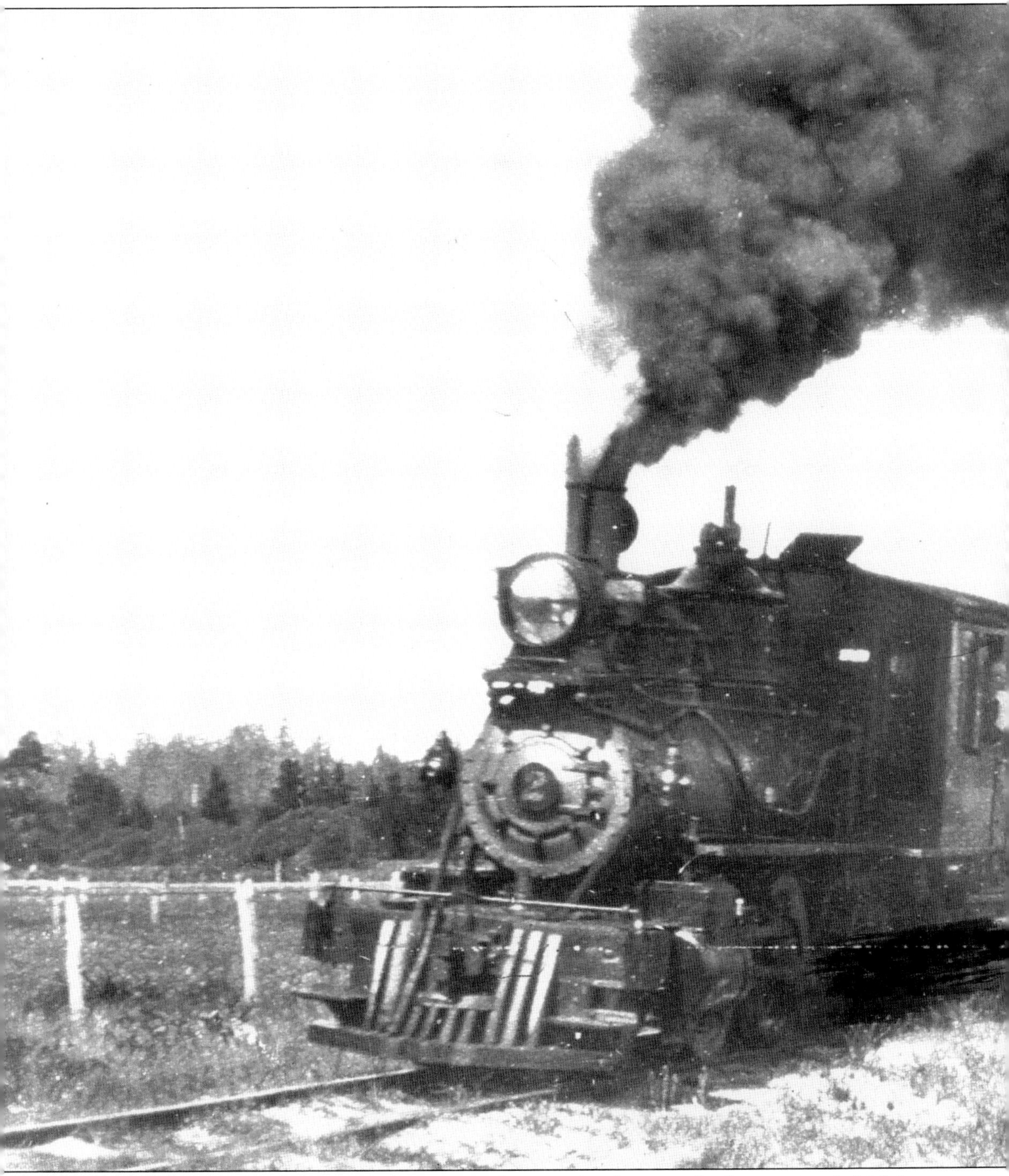

THE LAST RUN. The last train, its locomotive decorated with a wreath of mourning, left Nahcotta September 9, 1930, one day earlier than originally planned. It made its way from Nahcotta to Ilwaco and back again with Clem Morris at the throttle of locomotive No. 2, dragging a coach and the combine. Adelaide Taylor of Ocean Park, who had been on the first train in 1889, was given a seat of honor. In Ilwaco, school was dismissed early, businesses closed, and Mayor W. C.

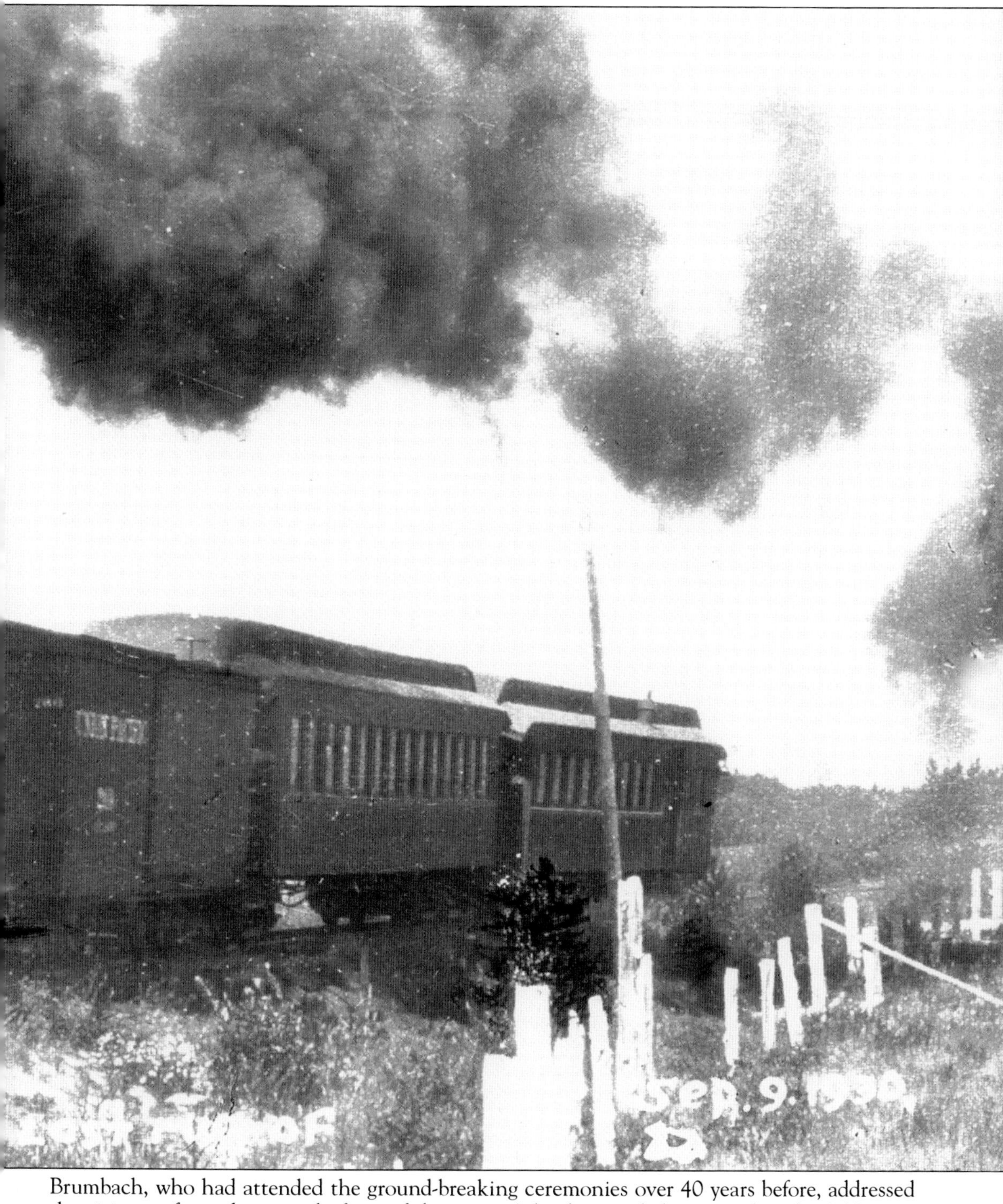

Brumbach, who had attended the ground-breaking ceremonies over 40 years before, addressed the citizenry from the rear platform of the train. A bugle sounded taps, and as the 3:30 train departed for the last time, the salute fired from the town cannon was answered with a last, long trailing whistle from the locomotive. (Adelle Beechey.)

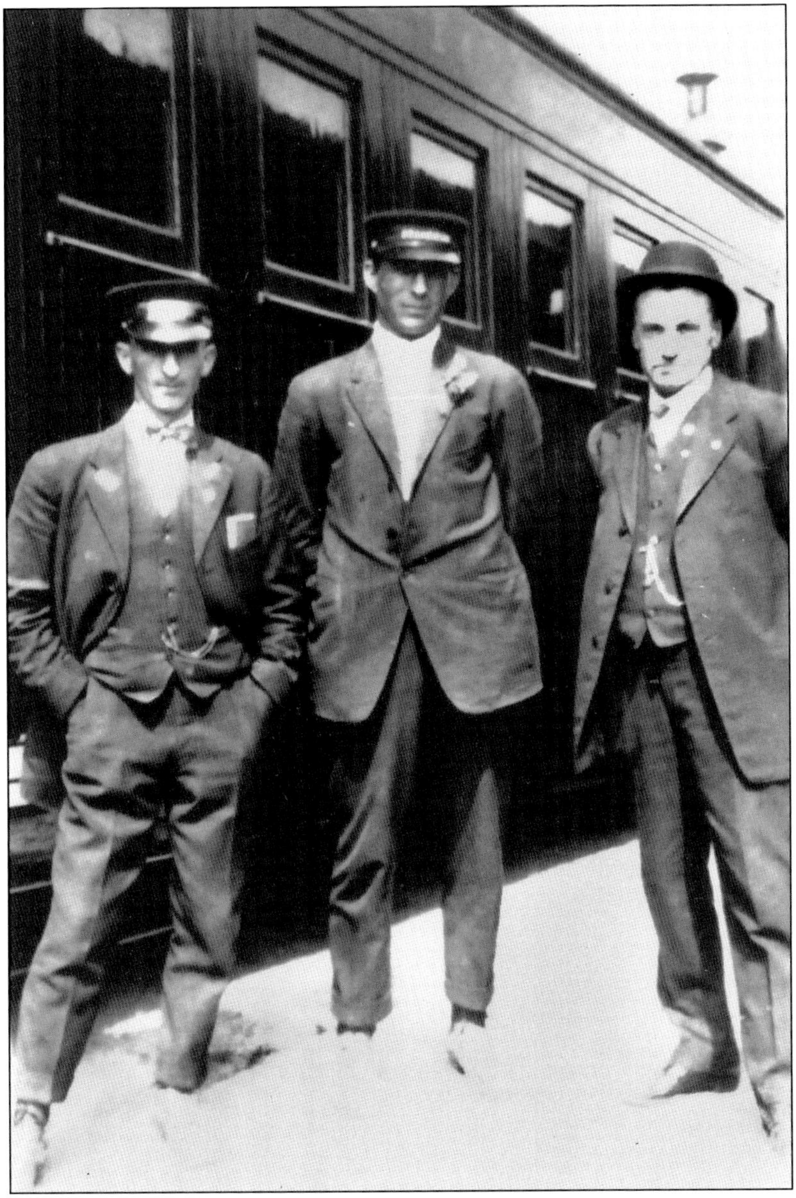

The Aftermath. Provisions were made by the Union Pacific for employees who so wished to be transferred to other parts of the UP system. A few stayed on for awhile, however, to help with the clean-up and keep watch over the railroad property until it could be sold. Although they were adversely impacted by the Great Depression and sales went slowly, the rails (except those in Ilwaco and Long Beach, where they had been cemented into the streets), rolling stock, and equipment were eventually sold to a Portland, Oregon, salvage concern. Several coaches were sold for $50 apiece to private individuals who transformed them into homes or, in one case, a diner. The Washington State Highway Department acquired title to most of the old right-of-way and soon built a modern highway over it, widening and reinforcing the tunnel under Fort Columbia for vehicle traffic. Station grounds, depots, and other property continued to be sold for years. Nowadays, few remnants of the railroad remain except in private collections and at the Columbia Pacific Heritage Museum in Ilwaco. (Matt Winters.)

Seven

Gone but Not Forgotten

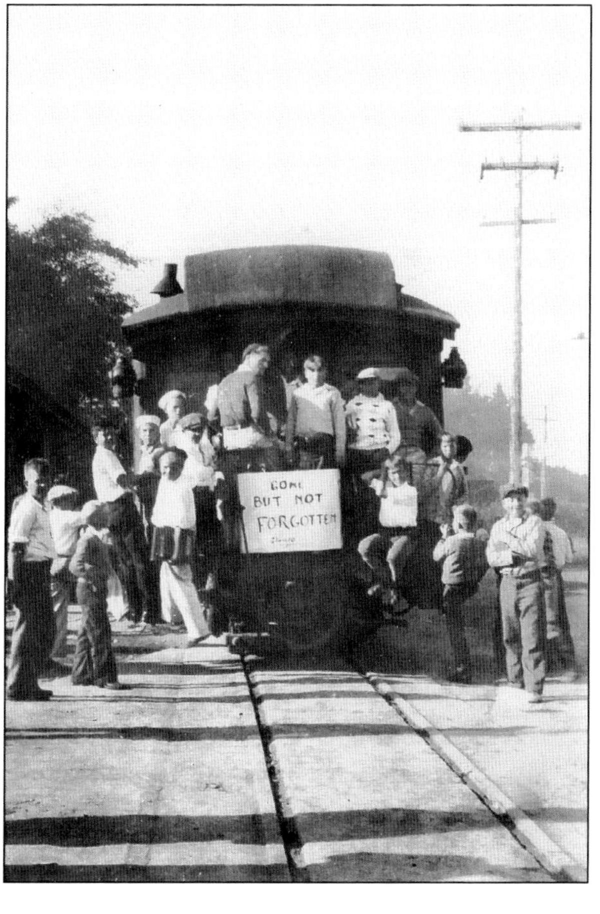

"Gone but Not Forgotten." As it turned out, the sign placed on the back of the train for its last run was, indeed, prophetic. For almost 80 years, residents of the peninsula have continued to talk about the Ilwaco Railroad and to lament its passing. Many long for its return, even though they know the little narrow-gauge train is a part of a past that cannot be recaptured.

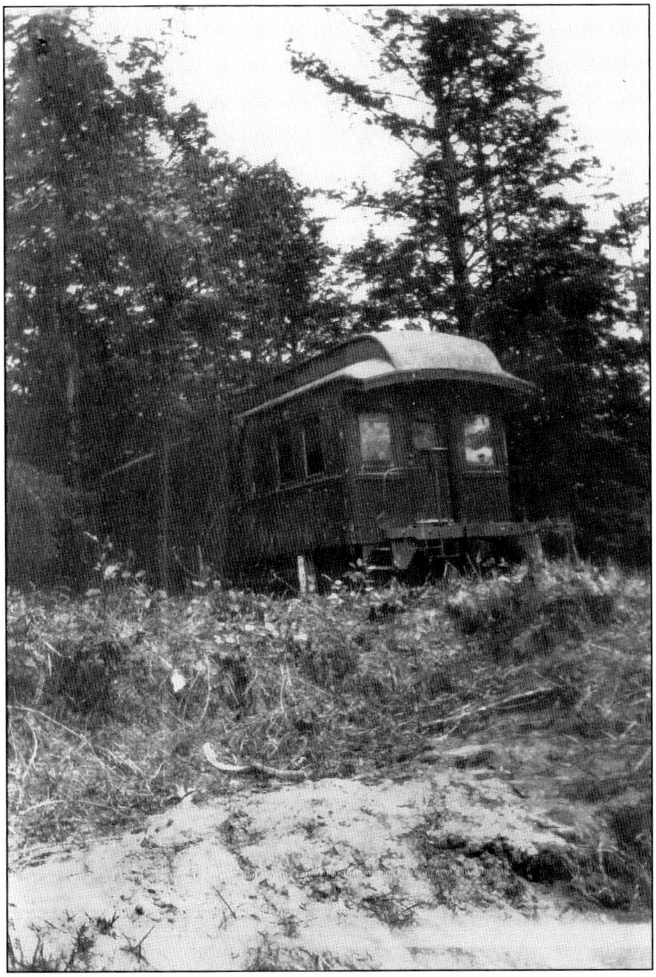

Coaches in the Community. For the next half century, railroad coaches could be seen here and there on the peninsula. Though they had been privately purchased and converted to other uses, now stationary with their tracks long since removed, the little cars were a ready reminder of the narrow-gauge railroad of an earlier generation. In recent years, the Columbia Pacific Heritage Museum has had the good fortune to acquire the passenger coach *Nahcotta*, originally purchased by the IR&N from the Pullman Company. It is one of the oldest surviving examples of the Pullman Company works, which opened in Chicago in 1883. Although it has been renovated by the previous owner, much of the structural material and some of the interior, including the hanging lamps, appear to be original. It is the CPHM's largest artifact. (Below, PCHS.)

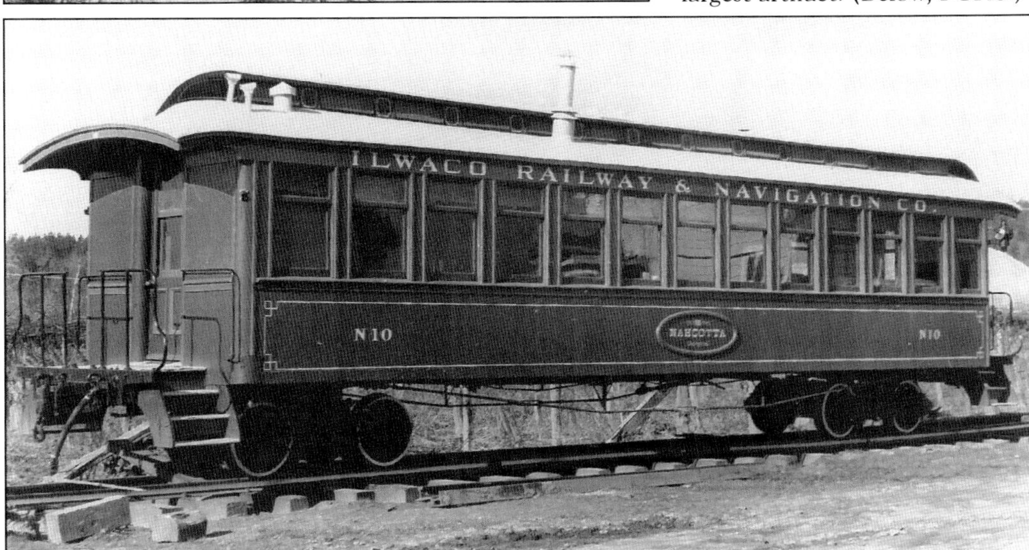

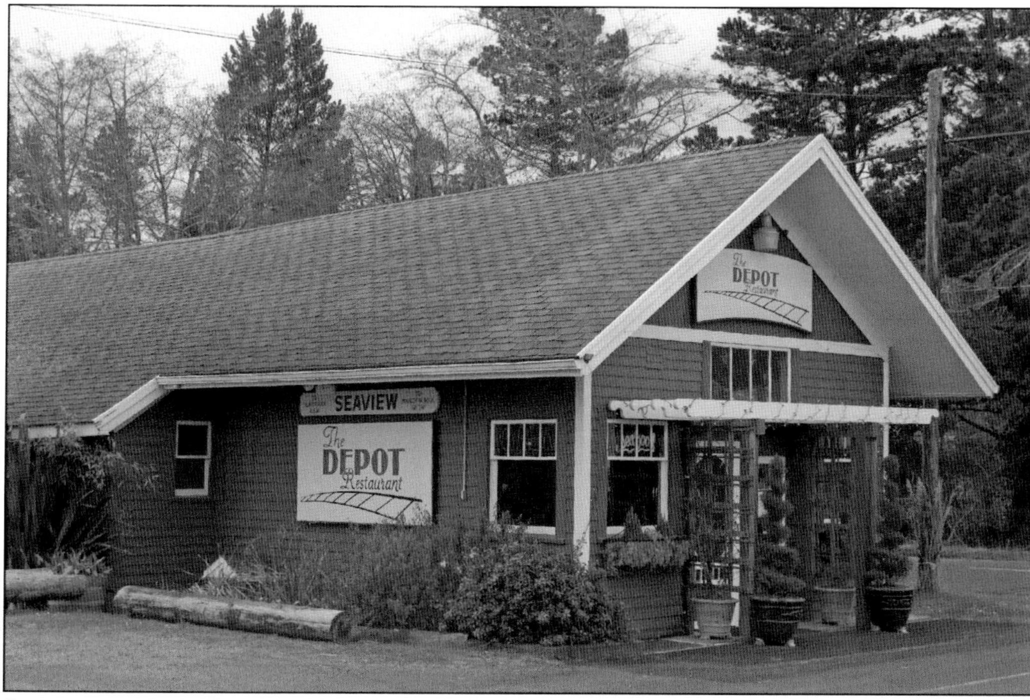

STRUCTURES LEFT BEHIND. Depots and other buildings were left behind and eventually found other uses or were dismantled. Some became homes; some were used as storage facilities for other businesses; another became a gas station. The most familiar to recent generations of peninsula residents is the Chinook Depot, pictured above. And the recent acquisition of the Ilwaco Freight Depot by Columbia Pacific Heritage Museum ensures that it will be preserved for future generations. For the time being, it remains in an altered condition and is being used as exhibition space, but there is a strong desire by the community to see it, as well as the *Nahcotta* passenger coach, restored to "as it was" when in use by the IR&N.

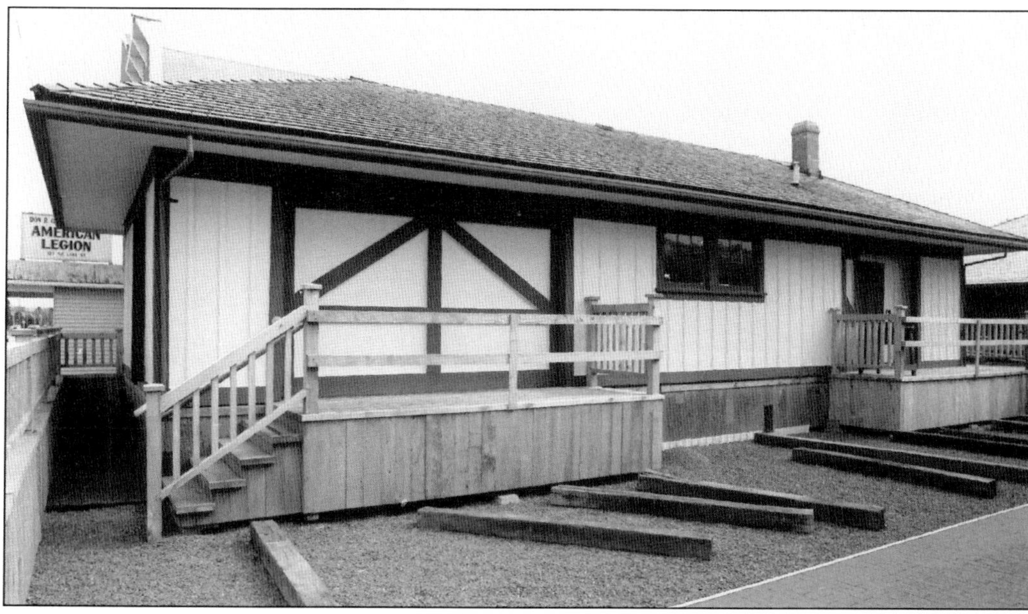

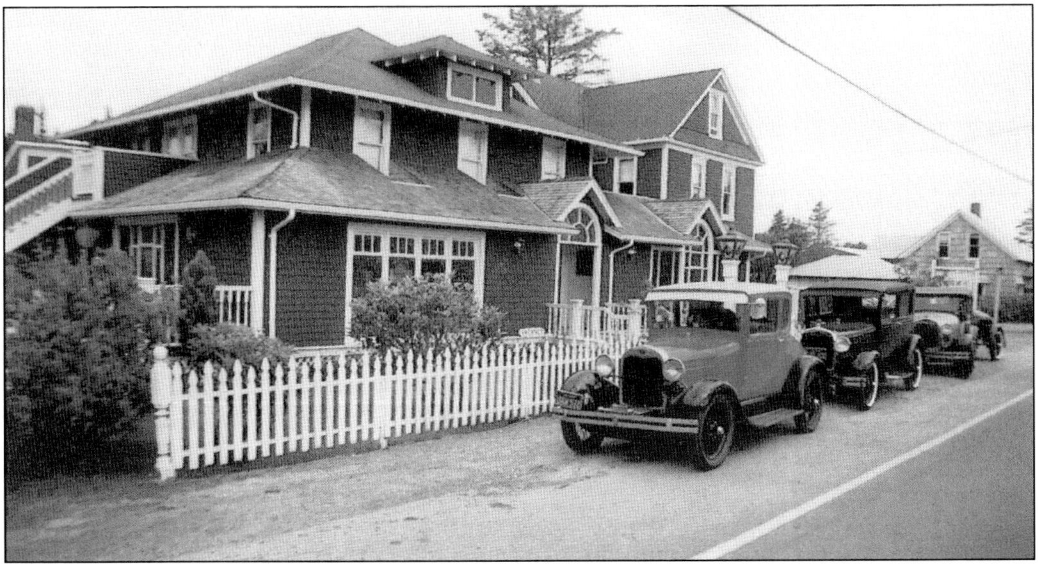

TOURIST DESTINATION. Though visitors began coming to the North Beach Peninsula even before Loomis entered the stagecoach business, it was the railroad that popularized "the beach" and established it firmly as a tourist destination. Hotels and, these days, bed-and-breakfast inns and motels, still abound on the peninsula. Of the two old remaining hotels—Taylor's in Ocean Park and the Shelburne (above with vintage cars) in Seaview—only the Shelburne remains in the overnight accommodation business. Long Beach continues as the primary tourist destination with its unspoiled sandy beach, its numerous curio and souvenir shops, and its many restaurants featuring local seafood. These days, festivals and celebrations entice visitors from afar and a modern highway system makes the journey easy. Summertime visits in the days of the train have evolved into a year-round tourism industry.

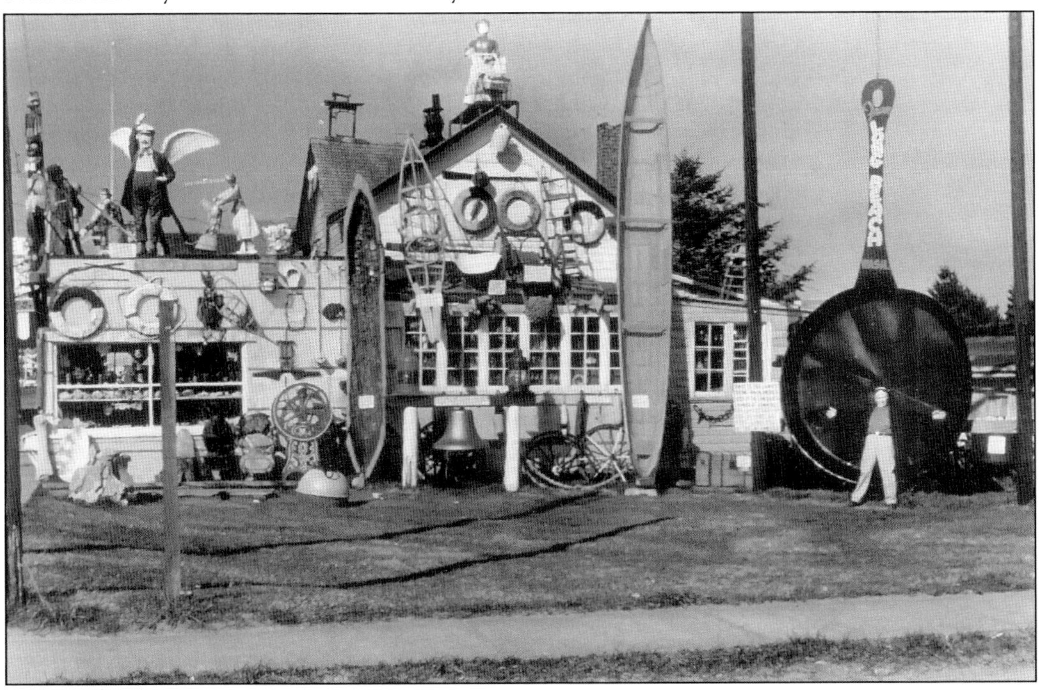

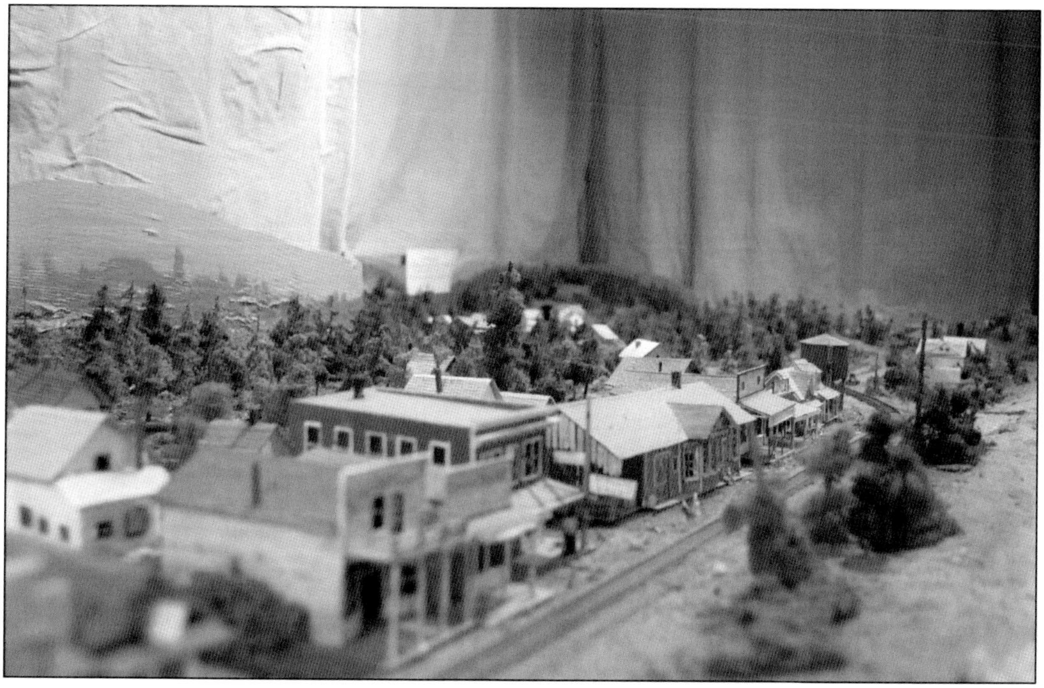

Celebrating the Past. The North Beach Peninsula's narrow-gauge railway is remembered and honored in many ways. One of the first permanent exhibits to go on display at the Ilwaco Heritage Museum (now the Columbia Pacific Heritage Museum) was the 50-foot N-scale operating diorama of the IR&N, complete with villages from Ilwaco to Oysterville. The quirky little train has been commemorated in books and articles, depicted by artists, and its image used as the postage cancellation for a variety of centennial events on the peninsula. The annual "Clamshell Railroad Days," sponsored by CPHM and the Peninsula Model Railroad Club during the third weekend of July gives the community and its visitors an opportunity to celebrate the IR&N with exhibits, displays, and informational talks and tours.

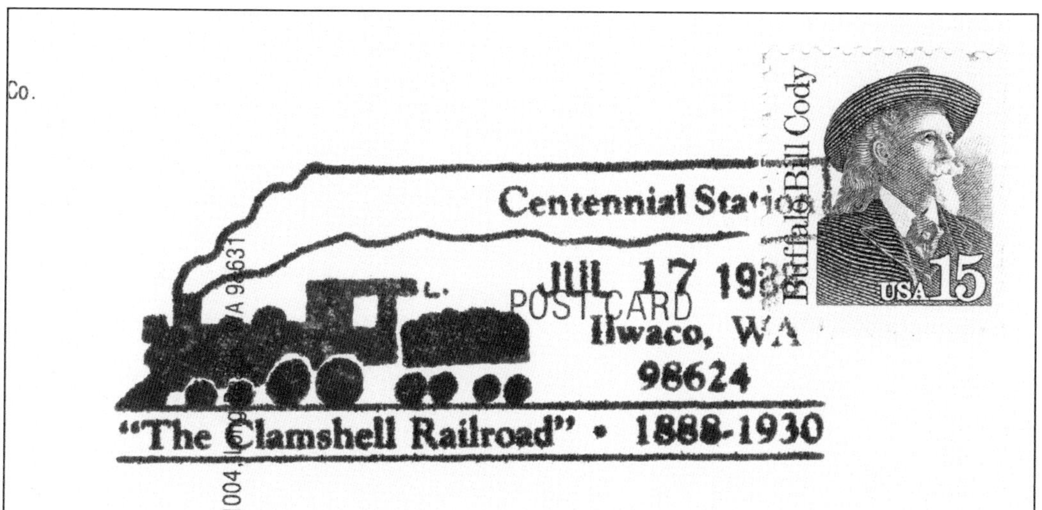

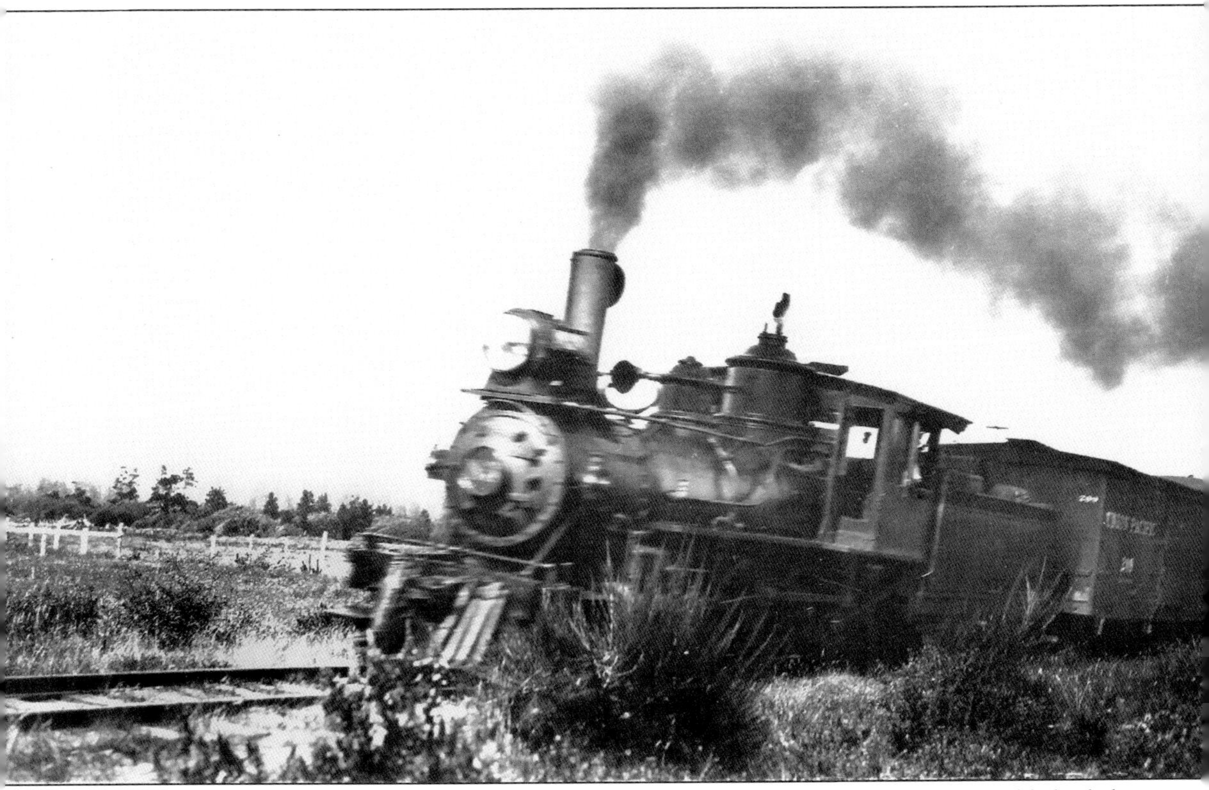

Continuing Legacy. In great measure, it was the narrow-gauge railroad that established the character of the North Beach Peninsula and of the communities that grew along its route. Today Chinook, Ilwaco, and Nahcotta retain their focus as fishing and oystering communities. The cottages and tree-lined streets of Seaview and Ocean Park underscore their residential character, and Ocean Park continues to develop as the commercial center of the peninsula's north end. Long Beach has expanded as the focal point of tourism in southwestern Washington, catering to the tens of thousands of visitors who arrive each year from inland metropolitan centers. Over the years, Long Beach has become a year-round destination of such magnitude that the entire peninsula is now known as the "Long Beach Peninsula," though the official name remains "North Beach Peninsula." Even Oysterville, now a National Historic District "where time stood still," reflects, inversely, the influence of the train that never arrived. For peninsula residents, the train remains a symbol of their own hardworking and independent spirit. Its memory is a treasured legacy. (Charles Mulvey.)

Bibliography

Chinook Observer, various issues 1910–1992. Chinook and Long Beach, WA.

Feagans, Raymond J. *The Railroad that Ran by the Tide*. Berkeley, CA: Howell-North Books, 1972.

Jessett, Thomas E. "*Clamshell Railroad*." Ilwaco, WA: Murfin Publishing Company, 1967.

Lloyd, Nancy. *Observing Our Peninsula's Past, Volume One*. Long Beach, WA: *Chinook Observer*, 2001.

McDonald, Lucile. "The Clamshell Railroad." *Coast Country*. Portland, OR: Binfords and Mort, Publishers, 1966, pp. 98–104.

Shaw, Frederic, Clement Fisher Jr., and George H. Harlan. "Clamshell Railroad." *Oil Lamps and Iron Ponies: A Chronicle of the Narrow Gauges*. San Francisco, CA: Bay Books Limited, 1940, pp. 112–137.

Stevens, Sydney. *P is for Papa Train: The A-B-Cs of the Long Beach Peninsula's Narrow Gauge Railroad, 1889–1930*. Oysterville, WA: Mrs. Stevens' ABCs, 2000.

"Terminals Improved." *Pacific Journal*. Chinook, WA. November 10, 1905.

The Sou'wester. Volume X, Nos. 1, 2, and 4, 1975; Volume XVIII, No. 3, 1983. South Bend, WA: Pacific County Historical Society.

Turner, Frank. "From Auld Lang Syne." *Ilwaco Tribune*, 1952–1958 issues. Ilwaco, WA.

Webber, Bert. "Anton's Other Railroad." *Swivel-Chair Logger*. Fairfield, WA: Ye Galleon Press, 1976, pp. 174–175.

Williams, L. R. *Our Pacific County*. Raymond, WA: *Raymond Herald*, 1930.

Wolf, Edward C. *A Tidewater Place*. Long Beach, WA: The Willapa Alliance, 1993.

INDEX

About the Columbia Pacific Heritage Museum

The Columbia Pacific Heritage Museum had its beginnings in 1983 as the Ilwaco Heritage Museum. It grew from the deep conviction by a group of community-minded citizens that an institution that honored the past could breathe new life into the present town of Ilwaco and could, perhaps, imbue it with vitality for the future. Noreen Robinson, Junior Marsh, Wayne O'Neil, Les Peterson, Emery Neale, Charles Doupé, and Patricia Aslin Erikson were not museum professionals, but they had energy and determination and knew how to get things done. They met over coffee each morning at Red's Café in Ilwaco and enthusiastically developed their plan.

Their first step was to enlist the help of the City of Ilwaco, asking for the soon-to-be-abandoned Telephone Utilities Building on Lake Street. Creating an office in one corner of that building, they then formed a nonprofit corporation called the Ilwaco Heritage Foundation. Ultimately, Noreen took charge of the fledgling foundation, developing the Ilwaco Heritage Museum. She applied for grants, established a corps of volunteers, and appealed to professionals in the field for suggestions and guidance, and piece-by-piece the museum took shape. Gradually, the foundation and the museum grew.

Twenty-four years later, in November 2007, with an active membership of 350 people and an annual visitor count of more than 11,000, the museum officially changed its name to the Columbia Pacific Heritage Museum to better reflect its original mission of serving the entire region. Today the museum has 4,550 square feet of permanent exhibition space, 1,600 square feet of temporary exhibition space, and another 12,000 square feet that can be used for special events such as the Clamshell Railroad Days, cosponsored each July with the Peninsula Model Railroad Club.

Estimates put the museum's archive of two-dimensional items at 15,000 and the collection of three-dimensional objects at 8,500. The staff now includes two part-time museum professionals plus a cadre of eight regular volunteers and an additional dozen on-call volunteers. Most importantly, the Columbia Pacific Heritage Museum has become a community fixture—a repository and resource for the area's treasured heritage.

Columbia Pacific Heritage Museum
115 Southeast Lake Street
PO Box 153
Ilwaco, WA 98624-0153
(360) 642-3446
www.columbiapacificheritagemuseum.org

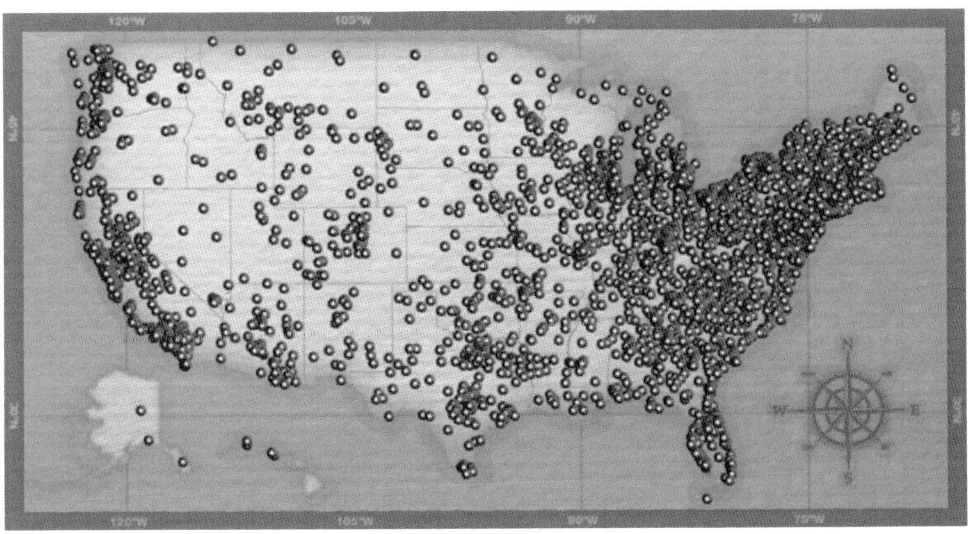